INTERURBAN

The Tiger Woods
Phenomenon

S0-BQU-919

The Tiger Woods Phenomenon

Essays on the Cultural Impact of Golf's Fallible Superman

Edited by Donna J. Barbie

McFarland & Company, Inc., Publishers
Jefferson, North Carolina, and London

Library of Congress Cataloguing-in-Publication Data

The Tiger Woods phenomenon : essays on the cultural impact of
    golf's fallible superman / edited by Donna J. Barbie.
        p.   cm.
    Includes bibliographical references and index.

    ISBN 978-0-7864-6494-4
    softcover : acid free paper ∞

    1. Woods, Tiger.   2. Golfers — United States.
    3. Golf— Social aspects.
    GV964.W66T55 2012
    796.352092 — dc23
    [B]   2012015178

British Library cataloguing data are available

Front cover: Tiger Woods lines up his putt on the ninth green
of the Pebble Beach Golf Links during the third round of
the Pebble Beach National Pro-Am golf tournament in
Pebble Beach, California, Saturday, February 11, 2012
(AP Photo/Marcio Jose Sanchez)

Manufactured in the United States of America

McFarland & Company, Inc., Publishers
  Box 611, Jefferson, North Carolina 28640
  www.mcfarlandpub.com

To my colleagues,
especially those who went on this roller coaster ride with me
even though I hate roller coasters

Table of Contents

Introduction

Donna J. Barbie

Mine was a golfing family.[1] We talked it and watched it. We sat around the television Sundays, eating Fritos, and each of us "picked" our "guy." Dad rooted for Arnie Palmer, my brother Dana was a Jack Nicklaus fan, and I was enchanted by Gary Player's accent and black attire. Mom was the referee, although her services were seldom required. This was golf, after all. Prodded by my father and inspired by the Palmer, Nicklaus, and Player trio, Dana took up golf. Even in junior high, he was big, clumsy, and rather dorky. People teased him — a lot. Somewhat surprisingly, my brother was a natural golfer, remarkably good and graceful from the start. In high school, Dana not only lettered in golf, but he was also the team captain for a time. The "studs" scoffed. Although golf might be a "game," it certainly was *not* a "sport." Dana was *not* an athlete. Despite his gifts with a club, Dana's accomplishments earned him little respect at Bismarck High, that is, until he became a heavy-weight wrestler. In this role, Dana's size was as asset, and nearly all of his opponents were clumsy, too. Finally viewed as an athlete, he became a member of the "jock" club. Glowing with approval, Dana displayed his wrestling letter on his jacket, but no more proudly than the first he earned in golf.

Of course, Tiger Woods changed everything. Golf became a sport, and golfers were deemed athletes. Most important, the sport and the players were suddenly cool. Posting a response to Jamie Samuelsen's golf blog, DaleYp sums up the charismatic Woods best: "Fee-nommm." Clearly expressing amazement and enthusiastic appreciation, DaleYp nonetheless claims that the Tiger phenomenon is a thing of the past. Of course, he is referring to Woods the golfer, the superstar who struggled with his game during the 2009–11 seasons. Indeed, a great many people have debated whether Woods will ever dominate or captivate the way he once did, even after his win at the Chevron

1

World Challenge in December 2011. Despite differing opinions on his future prospects in the sport, everyone agrees that Tiger has been a superman golfer.

Tiger Woods is not simply a phenomenal player; he is also an everyman who has recently displayed all-too-human foibles and weaknesses. Because Woods' game, life, and story comprise so many dimensions, he provides scholars from various disciplines with manifold opportunities for fruitful analysis. Of the eleven professors who have contributed to this collection, only two or three play golf, and at least six hardly know the difference between a tee and a green. Lack of playing experience or in-depth knowledge about the sport does not impede them from making significant contributions, however, because they are familiar with Tiger Woods, clear testament to his status as a cultural icon. Their disciplines and interests — gender studies, semiotics, new media, divinity studies, physiology — all intersect with Tiger Woods' story in important ways. In some sense, their lack of *particular* interest in Tiger positions them very well. In essence, Woods serves as a lens that reveals much more than one person's life story.

This collection is thus organized into two segments. The first presents essays that focus on Tiger's superman game and how he has affected, and been affected by, the golfing world. The second includes essays that examine everyman Tiger, illustrating how his life reflects significant and oftentimes contentious issues within American culture and the world.

Tiger, the superman golfer, has been the focus of unprecedented media commentary long before his car accident and subsequent scandal. Hundreds of articles appear in newspapers and on the Internet within hours of his doing quite literally anything on the course. Stories recite his records and make predictions about his next win. They analyze his swing, his grip, his footwear. They speculate, especially of late, about his ability to surpass Nicklaus' record of eighteen major championships. They report when he signs autographs and when he does not. They discuss whether he should play more or play less and whether he should have been selected for the Presidents Cup. As sports columnist Dave Hackenberg asserts, "Woods has been the biggest story in golf." Unlike DaleYp, however, Hackenberg does not believe that Woods' superman golf has ended. Unapologetic about persistent media coverage, Hackenberg asks, "Isn't his climb back as compelling as his time at the top of the mountain and his tumble from the summit? We don't know how the story will end, so we can't stop telling it." As essays on superman Tiger illustrate, the golf aspects of Woods' story continue to inform and fascinate.

Works examining the superman golfer cannot begin to capture the full significance of the Tiger Woods phenomenon, however. Unlike many other talented athletes, Woods has transcended his sport, becoming a cultural icon in short order. Although Tiger's iconic status originally arose from his superman game, meanings enveloping his being have never been restricted to his work on the golf course. He is an individual who, like everyone, has been shaped by his upbringing and his culture. Although the everyman Tiger tried mightily to cordon off his "regular" life, those efforts ultimately proved futile. Suddenly, the everyman was exposed. Actually, the everyman was overexposed as the media published every possible aspect of his all-too-human problems and weaknesses. Vice president of the Poynter Institute Roy Peter Clark argues that celebrity scandals provide writers a unique opportunity to interrogate a story to discover "its higher implications." Unfortunately, most stories concerning the Woods scandal did nothing to interrogate even one "higher implication." These commentators failed to present the "social, political, or cultural significance" of the story. Because of this unexplored potential, the everyman Tiger is, in some ways, even more compelling than the superman. As essays on everyman Tiger illustrate, Woods' life intersects with issues that have long been debated in modern culture, reflecting problems that ordinary people wrestle with every day.

Superman Tiger

A significant element of the superman golfer is his supposed "advantage" on the course. Commentators and spectators have known that something extraordinary propelled Tiger, and a recent study verifies that he has indeed enjoyed an advantage. According to *Scientific American* writer Christopher Intagliata, economist Jennifer Brown conducted a ten-year study of PGA events, revealing that Tiger's presence at a tournament resulted in other players scoring "almost a full stroke worse than they otherwise would have." Controlling for variables like weather, course difficulty, and crowd distractions, Brown concludes that the "Tiger factor" arose from opponents' "panic." Although Brown's study does not explore what caused that panic, John Lamothe's "Creating a Competitive Advantage: The Power of Physicality, Psychology and Spiritual Discourse" considers three specific advantages that Tiger Woods profited from during the height of his dominance on the tour. Superstar athletes are often perceived as being born to greatness, with competitive dominance attributed to natural ability, incredible genetics, or just plain "gifts." Such terms mask the carefully honed physical and psychological advantages that elite athletes cultivate and exploit throughout their playing careers. More so than most superstars, Woods epitomizes an athlete who has been painstakingly created, both through his own efforts and the efforts of those around him. From a very early age, he was engineered to be a professional golfer, and his overwhelming success stands as testament to those labors. Since late 2009, however, Woods has suffered through the worst "slump" of his career. In addition to examining the advantages that he once enjoyed, Lamothe addresses whether Woods might regain the dominance that previously defined his career.

Another aspect of the superman Tiger story is the branding that "sold" him to the golf world and to millions of people who never picked up a club or watched the game. Charles Pierce, author of "The Man. Amen," argues that Tiger was shrewdly marketed "almost from the time he could walk." Earl Woods' mission to create a legendary golfer, as well as a powerful brand, nonetheless came at a cost. "Branding: At What Price?" by Michael V. Perez examines the inception and development of Brand Tiger as Earl groomed Tiger for greatness. Tiger's brand was unprecedented not only because Woods' fame preceded his move into professional ranks, but also because his first marketers endeavored to establish a global brand from the start. Perez also analyzes commercial advertisements and one "maverick" music video — all helping to define and crystallize the brand. Although these productions sometimes offer glimpses of Woods as a regular dude, they primarily market him as a nearly flawless superhero who performed extraordinary feats on the course. The brand fell into disarray, however, when the values that Woods had supposedly embodied were exposed as a carefully crafted façade. After a relatively lengthy period in marketing purgatory, Brand Tiger seems to be resurgent with continued sponsorships from Nike and EA, as well as new contracts from lesser known companies. Although Tiger can no longer stand as the near-perfect superhero, it remains to be seen if campaigns marketing a down-to-earth Tiger will also exact a price.

Tiger Woods has made an almost obscene fortune by winning tournaments and serving as a "faceman," but his successes have also revolutionized the economics of golf. As Joe Gisondi chronicles in "Showing Us the Money," no golfer has had a more significant impact on golf's bottom line than Tiger Woods, something not fully appreciated until after Tiger hobbled off Torrey Pines and out of sight for most of the season. Television ratings plummeted, and attendance plunged at PGA events. Until 2008, few people fully understood how much Woods had elevated golf's profile and funding since joining the PGA in 1996. Television ratings soared, network contracts skyrocketed to nearly $1 billion, galleries swelled dramatically, sponsorship money poured in at a record pace, and prize money for PGA events more than quadrupled. Tiger helped create golfing millionaires by the dozens, thanks to dramatically increased purses and endorsement deals. Tiger has been an economic superstar.

Without question, extraordinary athletic talent, marketing, and money are intrinsically interconnected in American professional sports, but another ingredient actually holds the "center," sports fans. My essay "Faithful Fandom" explores Tiger Woods' public popularity and the phenomenon of Tiger fandom. Of myriad golfers who have excelled in the sport over the past century, only two American players have attracted phenomenal numbers of fans, Arnold Palmer and Tiger Woods. No one came close to matching Arnie's Army until Tiger Woods arrived, and since then, he has been the darling of the golf world. This contribution offers written commentaries, as well as on-course observations, to illustrate the magnitude and avidity of Woods' fanbase. Tiger's win at the Chevron World Challenge attests to his fans' attachment. Hordes followed him throughout the week, cheering him on, hoping for victory. As Woods surveyed his final putt, on-air broadcasters declared that the crowd obviously wanted Tiger to win. *New York Times* reporter Karen Crouse asserts that the fans were "stressed out," and one admitted that he was so nervous he was shaking. Fans that experience that level of emotion do not just disappear.

Not all golf aficionados have adored Tiger, and some have even downright disliked him, even before the scandal. Many attribute their antipathy to Woods' tendency toward ungentlemanly behaviors on the course. In "Celebrations and Conniptions in the 'Gentleman's' Game" I offer an analysis of Tiger Woods' behaviors on the course prior to and since the infidelity scandal. Beginning with discussion of golf's gentlemanly code of conduct, this essay verifies that Woods has never entirely adhered to those conventions. Unlike the majority of professional golfers, Woods has displayed intoxicating celebrations and unrestrained fits of pique. The golf world has typically overlooked Tiger's bad-boy tantrums, probably because of his great success on the course, but after the scandal, those conniptions were no longer an occasional "minor" unpleasantness. Suddenly, bad behavior seemed to define the fallen man. In February 2010, Tiger pledged during his televised apology to become more "respectful" of the game. That pledge raises some important questions that I address and analyze. Although a single tournament cannot be perceived as predictive, Tiger's behavior at the 2011 Chevron indicates that he has ameliorated some negative displays. His game was not perfect, yet he showed far less exasperation, and he threw no clubs. On the other hand, the victory celebration was as exuberant as ever. Crouse claimed that his trademark fist pump was so vigorous that "it was a wonder he did not wrench his arm out of its socket." ESPN analyst Gene Wojciechowski asserts that it was an expression "of exultation, of relief, of validation." Although he does not decry that celebration, Wojciechowski worries that Woods might revert to "Badass Mode" on the course. Only time will tell if Tiger can celebrate without also spawning conniptions.

A bit of club-tossing and even Tiger's much reported off-course bad behaviors seem to pale in comparison to the highly publicized sexual molestations that were allegedly committed by a Pennsylvania State football coach and Syracuse University basketball coach. These cases are indeed significantly different, particularly in terms of criminal culpability. But the situations are nonetheless linked by a disturbing reality. Many people involved in sports believe that their celebrity protects them from exposure and sanction. Sarah D. Fogle's "Ego, Entitlement and Egregious Behavior" examines how a sense of entitlement has become prevalent in American society and is shaping the behavior of young people and adults alike. Some critics see the trend as an epidemic and trace it to parenting styles that teach children they are so special that they do not have to face negative consequences. In particular, young men who reach the professional ranks often are conditioned to believe they are beyond society's rules and norms. It is no surprise that extraordinarily talented young athletes are likely to expand their sense of entitlement as a result of a high salary, media coverage, and lucrative corporate endorsements, not to mention the adulation of fans. Fogle also offers examples of "entitled" athletes, including Tiger Woods. Tiger himself claimed in his televised apology that a sense of entitlement led him to think he was above it all. As Woods' biographer Steve Helling argues, "Each win, each endorsement, each interview was a carefully selected brick that formed a wall around Tiger, insulating him from the harsh realities of the outside world. Tiger Woods had created a fortress of privilege for himself. For years, everyone thought it was impenetrable" (233). Golf writer John Feinstein speculates that "if more people in golf had stood up to Tiger and his people early, maybe things wouldn't have turned out the way they did" but later asserts that scenario would be unlikely because "No one tells Tiger Woods what to do" (98, 101).

Everyman Tiger

Although Tiger has certainly been viewed as a superman golfer, his recent "slump" has prompted some commentators to declare that he may have joined the ranks of the good, but no longer great, professional golfers. Others disagree. They await Tiger's next string of exhilarating wins. Even if Woods makes that charge, people now realize (if they had not always known) that Tiger is not really superhuman. He is human, a flawed everyman who is subjected to the same cultural expectations as "ordinary" people. Ironically, as both superman and everyman, Tiger is caught in a difficult double-bind. Because of his iconic status, Woods' adherence to the rules (or lack thereof) is always on public display. As a result, when Tiger misses the mark, and he has done so quite spectacularly, his fame robs him of the typical everyman's anonymity. Such is the price of celebrity.

Tiger, like everyone else, bears markers of race and ethnicity. Because he is a person of color and because he excels in a sport that has been tainted by racism, Woods' ethnicity has been an important factor in his life and his emergence as a player. As Tim Rosaforte reports, young Tiger automatically fell suspect when a bunch of jerks hit balls into neighboring homes for "kicks." Course managers automatically accused Woods because he was the only "black" kid in sight (37). In "Reluctantly Playing the Race Game" Linda H. Straubel and I examine how Tiger's dominance in golf has not insulated him from America's preoccupation with race. Although Tiger's father offered stories of racial discrimination and harassment, Tiger has tried to avoid dealing with race. Rather, he has stressed his aspiration to be the best golfer ever, without racial qualifier. As a result of such declarations, many perceive that Tiger has "disidentified" himself as black and repudiated any obligations to the African American community. Despite Tiger's efforts to distance himself from racial matters, he has never been able to avoid becoming entangled in highly-pub-licized racial controversies. As chronicled in this chapter, such firestorms indi-cate that Tiger Woods has never been able to dodge the race "game" and likely never will.

Everyone has a body, and Tiger's has sometimes failed him. He experi-enced a significant knee problem even before he turned pro, and as he has aged, that knee and other physical ailments have had a tremendous impact on his game and his life. Focused on human physiology, Jonathan French's "Painful Pleasures" illuminates how a precision golf swing results from the complex coordination of neurons and muscles. Relying heavily on the sense of sight, players train the cerebellum, the little brain, to establish muscle memory that results in smooth, finely tuned, coordinated movement. Earnest professionals, such as Tiger Woods, practice intensely to achieve a reliable swing, and the reward of repetition is exactitude. However, the price is often the inflammation and pain of tendonitis and bursitis. Because the body some-times cannot repair itself quickly, if at all, people often turn to anti-inflam-matory medications to reduce swelling and pain. Tiger Woods has long suffered from repetitive stress injuries, and evidence indicates that his medical advisors prescribed anti-inflammatory drugs and sleep medications to help him recover from injuries. However, such drugs can result in physical and psychological dependence, as well as producing a profound sense of well-being and euphoria. Some testimony indicates that Woods also used prescrip-tion drugs to enhance sexual activity, and many commentators have reported that he was treated for sexual addiction. Because all of these behaviors are connected to the brain's reward system, this essay describes how medications dilute pain, help people to forget stress, and enable them to feel joy.

Although Tiger might sometimes wish to jettison his celebrity to enjoy the anonymity of regular citizens, escape has not been possible. When he had a relatively minor car accident, for example, a local Florida news station immediately reported that he was in serious condition, fighting for his life. Even though he was quickly released from the hospital, the coverage only increased. According to Robert Lusetich, author of *Unplayable*, Team Tiger floundered without a credible crisis-management plan, and he argues that Tiger was "no longer dealing with the domesticated animals of the golf press" but was "mauled every day by the wild animals of the tabloids, who'd stop at nothing" (xvi). The media circus that ensued surprised even the most cynical critics. Steve Master's "Responsible Adults in the Toy Department" explores the nature of that coverage, noting how sports writers — historically among the least respected reporters in the newsroom — acquitted themselves more professionally than the vast majority of colleagues. Master begins by establishing the magnitude and voyeuristic nature of the media frenzy. Not only did the breadth of coverage — at a time of war and widespread economic suffering — reflect poorly on the values prioritized in newsrooms, but traditional ethical boundaries and journalistic sourcing standards buckled under the tidal wave of sensationalism. Given that Tiger is a professional athlete, one might assume sports writers were most responsible for the breakdown in journalistic standards. This was not the case; in fact, the sports pages and broadcasts often offered refuge from tabloid-style reporting. Despite competitive pressures, most reported on the scandal in ways relevant to their beats and true to the professional standards so often discarded by others in the newsroom.

Everyone makes mistakes. As the world is now aware, Tiger Woods has indeed committed some whoppers. Just like anyone who hopes to make amends for his transgressions, Tiger apologized to those he hurt. Unlike most other people, however, Tiger was more or less forced to apologize publicly not only because his lapses had been so widely publicized, but also because the list of victims was long. University of Missouri doctoral student Rebecca Dierking reports that many celebrities employ a "semantic slide" to avoid fully accepting responsibility for wrongdoing. She concludes, however, that Tiger apologized "unequivocally." Focused on Tiger's televised apology, "Public Apology and Acts of Contrition" by James G. Shoopman analyzes the now common public ritual of confession and repentance. Shoopman begins by reviewing the growing body of scholarship on the nature of apology, its risks and benefits, as well as the motives for performing acts of contrition. Offenders offer apologies when they are intrinsically or extrinsically motivated to restore a damaged relationship despite the pain and risks of apology. This act causes an offender to endure shame and to relinquish power to the offended or victimized person. Scholars of apology identify six characteristics of an effective apology, and this chapter tests Tiger's televised apology against those six criteria, by discussing the probable reasons that various portions of the carefully scripted apology were included and emphasized, ultimately rendering a provisional judgment on whether this final apology can be accepted as truthful, sincere, and voluntary.

As *Gentleman's Quarterly* writer Charles Pierce claims, the young Tiger drew women's attention and admiration. Homing in on one of Tiger's early admirers, Pierce describes her attire, a "frilly lace top" and "a pair of tiger-striped stretch pants that fit as though they were decals," claiming that this "preposterous" woman certainly was not "Mary Magdalene come back to life." Pierce thus joins the female objectification club. In "Par for the Course: The 'Bimbo Tally,'" Libbie Searcy criticizes mainstream media's portrayals of the women with whom Tiger had affairs. Some of these women were involved in the sex industry, making them easy media targets, and all of them received criticism for their involvement with a married man. Although negative portrayals of these women are unsurprising and, to some degree, understandable, close examination of media coverage reveals what *should* be surprising and inexcusable: the media's reductive objectification and categorization of the women. The media criticized Tiger as well but also tended to portray him as a victim of "temptresses," of women who, apparently, do not deserve the kind of individualization and analysis afforded to the adulterous Tiger. This essay serves not as a defense of the women who became sexually involved with Tiger but as an analysis of sexist media coverage that helps to shape public perception of *all* women, of powerful men, and of sexuality in general. Ultimately, media coverage of the scandal reveals a great deal about — and reinforces — a patriarchal culture's perceptions of gender and sexuality.

Although some have resisted using electronic communication, many people throughout the world, as evidenced by the Arab Spring and Occupy Wall Street movements, have embraced the revolution. Tiger Woods has joined that club. Since his fall from grace, Woods has found a practical forum to tell his side of the many reported stories: social media. He has indeed learned how to "Tweet Your Troubles Away," and whether he turns to Twitter, Facebook, or his website (TigerWoods.com), he ingratiates himself to still-faithful fans who follow his posts. In this essay, Lynnette Porter and I discuss Woods' trouble gaining sympathy or winning new fans when he talks in person to the press, whereas his well-managed messages illustrate the softer side of Tiger's personality when he explains his actions, apologizes for bad behavior, or even promotes products. To supplement the study of Tiger's use of social media, the chapter's authors also surveyed Woods' fans online. An analysis of Woods' use of social media to ameliorate more negative press reports, combined with insights provided by Woods' fans, illustrates the perils and perks of managing one of sports' most ardent fandoms.

As all of these essays verify, Tiger Woods is an amazing phenomenon — simultaneously a superman and an everyman. After finishing a single stroke behind Tiger at the Chevron, Zach Johnson declared, "We all at one point thought he was Superman" (qtd. in Crouse). Johnson's use of the past tense is noteworthy. Tiger *has* been a superman golfer, but everyone now knows he does not, and never has, hovered above mere mortals. He continues, of course, to be a cultural icon, but he is also an everyman who walks the earth, celebrating triumphs and enduring travails, just like everyone else.

Notes

1. A variation of this opening paragraph appeared in *Horsehide, Pigskin, Oval Tracks, and Apple Pie: Essays on Sports and American Culture*, © 2006, James A. Vlasich, ed., and has been reprinted by permission of McFarland, Jefferson NC 28640. www.mcfarlandpub.com.

Works Cited

Clark, Roy Peter. "When Scandals Strike Celebrities Like Tiger Woods, Try Practicing 'Collateral Journalism.'" Poytner. 18 Feb. 2010. Web. 30 Mar. 2011.

Crouse, Karen. "After Two-Year Drought, Woods Wins with Flourish." *New York Times*. 4 Dec. 2011. Web. 5 Dec. 2011.

Dierking, Rebecca. "Semantics of Irresponsibility." *ETC: A Review of General Semantics* 67.1 (2010): 105+. *Literature Resources from Gale*. Web. 18 Oct. 2010.

Feinstein, John. "No One Tells Tiger Woods What to Do." *Golf Digest*. Jan. 2012. 96–103. Print.

_____. "Not Fine by Us." *The Golf Channel*. 15 Feb. 2011. Web. 17 Feb. 2011.

Hackenberg, Dave. "Woods' Story Is What It Is, for Better or Worse." *Toledo Blade*. 20 Apr. 2011. Web. 24 Apr. 2011.

Helling, Steve. *Tiger: The Real Story*. Cambridge, MA: Da Capo Press, 2010. Print.

Intagliata, Christopher. "Tiger Woods Made Other Golfers Worse." *Scientific American*. 8 Dec. 2011. Web. 8 Dec. 2011.

Lusetich, Robert. *Unplayable: An Inside Account of Tiger's Most Tumultuous Season*. New York: Atria Books, 2010. Print.

Pierce, Charles. "The Man. Amen." *Gentleman's Quarterly*. Apr. 1997. Web. 12 Apr. 2010.

Rosaforte, Tim. *Raising the Bar: The Championship Years of Tiger Woods*. New York: St. Martin's, 2000. Print.

Samuelsen, Jamie. "Why Is Tiger Woods So Much More Compelling Than Rory McIlroy?" *Detroit Free Press*. 20 June 2011. Web. 22 June 2011.

Wojciechowski, Gene. "Tiger Woods' Victory a Mental Major." ESPN. 8 Dec. 2011. Web. 8 Dec. 2011.

PART I: SUPERMAN TIGER

Creating a Competitive Advantage: The Power of Physicality, Psychology and Spiritual Discourse

John Lamothe

In his 1996 *Washington Post* article about Tiger Woods, James K. Glassman begins by making the statement "You don't have to like golf to love Tiger Woods. His swing is a triumph of poetry over physics, sending drives 350 yards down the fairway. And, like the very best golfers — Jones, Hogan, Nicklaus — he converts passion and concentration into a kind of spirituality" (45). Glassman's assertions encapsulate two central themes that permeated most discussions of Woods during his rise to dominance. The first one revolves around the assertion that Woods' athletic abilities and performance on the golf course (i.e., driving the ball 350 yards down the fairway) transcend the game he is playing, resulting in a dramatic change to the game itself. The second theme stems from the first, but it extends Woods' transcendence beyond golf to encompass his very essence, characterizing his abilities as supernatural or divine in some way.

The first part of that equation — changing golf in a multitude of ways — is a claim so obvious and easily substantiated that it borders on ridiculousness to even question that reality. In fact, more than a few sports writers and commentators have argued that Tiger has affected golf more than any other person in the game's history. Is this surprising? Prize money, viewership, winning percentages, endorsements, scoring averages, records set, and so forth, make it difficult to mount a counterargument to such claims. He has been, in the most literal sense, a game changer. Even with all of this evidence, however, it is still astounding that an individual player's ability to hit long drives and sink difficult putts could have such a monumental impact on a game that has been played for hundreds of years. During the height of his success, there was rampant speculation (and slight panic) that Tiger's abilities to hit long drives and to score so low would make current golf courses around the world obsolete. They simply would not be difficult or long enough to handle his skill level. In hindsight, that speculation was premature, but the fact that it was even considered is just one of many testaments to the impact Tiger has had on golf.

An interesting concept arises in the final line of Glassman's opening statement as he notes that Woods "converts passion and concentration into a kind of spirituality." In this phrase, Glassman embraces a peculiar discourse, one that intertwines with "transcendence" but also moves in a distinctly different direction. The new discourse espouses athletic ability but also implies that such athletic prowess rises to something of the divine. Essentially, the spiritual language expands beyond the physical, characterizing Tiger's abilities (and by extension, Woods himself) as something that is not attainable by human effort alone. The phrase would not stand out if Glassman were the only one making such bold comparisons, but commentators employed supernatural and spiritual terms ubiquitously to describe Woods during his dominance.

Such use is a bit shocking and more than a little fascinating, especially in hindsight after the sex scandal. In a 1997 *Sporting News* article discussing Tiger's record-setting victory at Augusta, Dave Kindred echoes this spiritual discourse when he says, "He hit shots so far, so straight, so high and with such majesty as to leave mere mortals believing they should apologize for their miserable efforts in his supernatural company" (84). Of course, sports writers and commentators have a penchant for drama and hyperbole, and the game of golf itself has a history of being discussed in spiritual terms (Karp), but even that understanding does not explain the predominance of spiritual language to describe Woods. Articles with titles such as "The Chosen One" and "The Man. Amen." dominated the press during the height of his success. Even Woods' competition used such language to describe him, as when player Tom Watson stated that Tiger's abilities were "supernatural" (Lipsyte 183). And if the media fueled this fire, Woods' fans danced around the flames. In a 1998 article for *Salon* magazine, Erin Aubry Kaplan swoons over Woods and mentions a trip she and a couple of girlfriends took to watch him play in a tournament. "None of us had ever been to such an event before, but we were willing to do anything (which wound up including changing a flat tire and enduring snubs by tournament officials) for a glimpse of the Man" (132). Kaplan's devotion to Tiger "the Man," as opposed to Tiger the golfer or even the game itself, characterizes a large segment of Woods' fanbase. It is rare for an athlete, even a superstar, to draw support from the ranks of those who could not care less about the sport, and for those same fans to demonstrate a near-religious fervor and devotion, as Woods' fans do, is rarer still. But most athletes were not reared by Earl Woods, who intensified the spiritual discourse surrounding his son, essentially proclaiming him humanity's savior.

During the height of Tiger's dominance, these two themes — that his athletic skill somehow transcends the game he is playing and that his abilities are superhuman or divine in some way — merged, creating what many referred to as "the cult of Tiger." The main tenets of the faith were that Woods' athletic performances bordered on the miraculous and that his dominance on a golf course was in some way inspired by God. Everyone around him, including fans, reporters, his family members, his management team, and perhaps even Tiger himself, "drank the Kool-Aid." They had internalized the spiritual discourse and allowed it to shape their perceptions.

It is not rare for athletic superstars to be raised to the level of "superhuman" in society's eyes. With Tiger, this type of language made up a significantly larger portion of his socially constructed persona; however, elite athletes like Michael Jordan, Muhammad Ali, Babe Ruth, and even Secretariat were often described in terms that bordered on the divine. Their athletic skills were characterized as "God-given talent," or "miraculous," or "awe-inspiring." The tenor of such discourses implies a predestination of sorts, as if these elite athletes would have excelled, no matter the circumstances.

It probably should not be surprising that people have resorted to such language. Throughout history, humans have often declared things that are otherwise astounding, breathtaking, or unimaginable as examples of the supernatural. Imagine early humans witnessing a solar eclipse for the first time. It would not be surprising to hear it attributed to the hand of God. Although science has come a long way since then, it still has not completely explained exceptional human performance. According to sociologist Dr. Earl Smith, "We have few answers as to why, in a group of similarly situated athletes who possess good skills, great athletic talent, a strong work ethic, and high levels of motivation, some go on to excel above and beyond others who remain well regarded as athletes but do not become superstars" (174). So when Michael Jordan dunks as if defying gravity, or Muhammad Ali appears to glide across the ring as if on ice, or Tiger Woods slams a drive as if it is rocket propelled, the easiest explanation for their excellence is that it is beyond earthly capabilities.

What these explanations mask, however, are the many factors that contribute to an elite athlete's success. These proclamations work as a trump card, glossing over the difficult-to-explain by placing it in the realm of the unexplainable. When people leap to the God-given talent explanation, they leave unexamined and unconsidered all the carefully crafted physical and psychological advantages that the player honed every time he or she competed. In his prime, Tiger Woods had specific advantages every time he stepped onto the course, advantages that played significant roles in his dominance and that he may or may not continue to enjoy today, not the least of which may be the very discourses that surrounded him during the height of his success.

Since the sex scandal broke in 2009, few commentators have chosen to use the same supernatural/spiritual discourse to describe Woods. Partly due to his tainted reputation and partly due to his struggles on the course, Tiger appears to have lost a lot of the mystical aura that surrounded him earlier in his career. Many are asking whether Tiger will ever get it back, but the question that should be asked first is what exactly *it* is? Various writers have attempted to describe it as "his mojo," or "his edge," or "his swing," but these are just secular versions of the same trump-card explanation. Only by carefully considering several competitive advantages — both physical and psychological — that Woods enjoyed during his dominance can anyone hope to understand what it might take for him to return to elite status once again.

Physical Elitism

If in the early 1990s ESPN had conducted a survey of general sports fans that asked participants to list the 100 greatest athletes of the day, safe money would bet that not a single golfer would have made the list. In fact, many probably would have balked at the very notion that golfers could be considered athletes, instead putting them on the same level as bowlers or fisherman — skilled, but not athletic (Berlinicke and Gomen). Even as Tiger was making a name for himself as an amateur, golf was thought by most, including professional players, to be primarily a mental game that required very little physicality. Many elite and successful players of the day were far from paradigms of health and fitness.

According to golfer Nick Price, "Jack [Nicklaus] caught golf with its pants down when he came out. We've seen the same with Tiger" (Boswell 145). Although Price is talking about more than just Tiger's fitness, it is clear that golf was unprepared for the physical training that Woods applied to the game. For much of his early career, his dogged training constituted a significant competitive advantage every time he stepped onto the course. Woods himself considered fitness such an important advantage that his diet and training regimen remained a closely guarded secret until as late as 2007. Little things can set a professional player apart from the others, the best of the best, and physical fitness is far from a *little* thing. Sports science has known for decades and quantified the specific effects that physical fatigue has on performance. Factors such as muscle memory, focus, vision, execution, clarity of thought, and so forth are all dramatically affected by both cardiovascular and muscular fatigue. Although this is common knowledge in the sports community, most golfers did not embrace the kind of physical training that was commonplace in other sports (perhaps because golf has been viewed as a primarily mental game). The advantage this gave Woods cannot be overstated. He was like a track star competing against casual runners — hardly a level playing field.

In 2007 several articles outlined Tiger's physical training routine (Johnson), and his workouts parallel the specialized, intense, several-hours-a-day training of most top athletes. The main difference was that this type of muscular and cardiovascular training was practically unheard of in golf. In fact, a common myth in the golfing community was that spending too much time in the weight room and adding too much muscle would negatively affect a player's swing. Woods obliterated that myth, and the golfing community *did* take notice, but not until he enjoyed years of having a physical advantage over the competition.

Along with his physical training, Woods' "physical" approach to this "mental" game contributed to his success. Humanism, with its I-Think-Therefore-I-Am perspective on human existence, has shaped every aspect of Western culture for over 300 years, and golf is no exception. Because, according to humanistic thought, the mind is in control of the body, psychologists, instructors, and even the athletes themselves have applauded the use of "visualization" as a means for the mind to actively control the body during complex movements. Perhaps one of Earl Woods' most significant contributions to his son's success was imparting a more synergistic relationship between the mind and body instead of the top-down approach of the mind controlling the body. During his time with the Green Berets, Earl had learned about the power of the subconscious and to trust in "feeling," and he taught Tiger to use those bodily feelings on the golf course. As one writer puts it when describing Tiger's ability to make unconventional shots,

> When he [Tiger] needs to remember a phone number, he doesn't search his memory or a little black book; he picks up a phone and watches what number his fingers go to. When he needs a 120-yard shot to go under an oak branch and over a pond, he doesn't visualize the shot, as most golfers would. He looks at the flag and pulls everything from the hole back, back, back ... not back into his mind's eye, but into his hands and forearms and hips, so they'll do it by feel. Explain how he made that preposterous shot? He can't. Better you interview his knuckles and metacarpals [G. Smith].

When asked directly about this approach, Tiger has said, "My body knows how to play golf. I've trained it to do that. It's just a matter of keeping my conscious mind out of it" (de Jonge 17). It certainly is not revolutionary for an athlete to recognize the importance of "feel," but Tiger had been taught to trust his feel from a very young age and to rely on it through every aspect of the game. When an athlete combines that trust in the subconscious with the heightened awareness of the body resulting from intense physical training, that player can develop a very powerful physical advantage in competition.

Of course, a question that must be posed, in 2012, is whether that particular advantage is still relevant. Of course, Tiger's overall physical fitness has been hampered by knee injury, and there are countless examples of elite athletes who were never able to fully recover their past dominance after a significant injury. Working in Tiger's favor is the fact that golf is not a contact sport, and it does not place the same kind of strain on the body that long distance runners or tennis players experience. That is not to say that a physical injury is less debilitating or distracting in golf; however, there is less likelihood for re-injury, which means that an aggressive rehabilitation program has a better chance of success. Additionally, Tiger has won despite injury, most famously in his "one-legged" victory at the 2008 U.S. Open, a win that only contributed to the "supernatural discourse" surrounding him. The biggest impact his injury will likely have on his game is it has necessitated Woods to adjust his swing to his knee's new limitations. Once again, however, Tiger has shown that he can completely change his swing and still find success, a process he has undertaken two other times in his career. With the previous two swing changes, an expected "slump" (by his standards) was eventually followed by a return to dominant form. Although the slump following the most recent knee surgery has been longer and more dramatic than in previous years, he has shown of late that his comfort and form may be returning. Of course, in December 2011 at the Chevron World Challenge, he earned his first win since the knee surgery, but he also had strong showings at the Australian Masters and the Presidents Cup in previous months.

More so than the knee injury, the biggest factor that could undermine his previous physical advantage is from the "Tiger Effect." An advantage only remains as long as an athlete has something that others do not. Tiger's own success has caused others to begin emulating him, and now that his competition has recognized the importance of physical training, the advantage he once had is now shrinking. Steve Gomen, editor of *Golf Fitness*, points to Woods as the primary force behind the fitness revolution in golf, claiming that "it wasn't until this past decade in which Tiger Woods' influence and domination forced a real and permanent change in the way professionals train and the way the golfing public will learn, practice and play for evermore." Professional golfer Retief Goosen, who recently enjoyed a career resurgence, attributes much of his success to Tiger's influence on his physical fitness:

"I started working hard in the gym and I figured instead of being totally out of shape and struggling I might as well be totally in shape and struggling. I feel better about myself and a lot of it has to do with what Tiger has brought to the Tour. I think the whole Tour has learned a lesson from Tiger" [qtd. in Berlinicke and Gomen].

For the newest generation of professional golfers — a generation that grew up watching and idolizing Woods — physical fitness is an integral part of training. What was once a distinct advantage for Woods is now a prerequisite for competition.

Overwhelming the Competition

Just as Woods' success helped to erase his physical advantage, his struggles after the sex scandal also weakened an equally important advantage he once had over his competitors. As they say, success breeds success, and few golfers have seen as much success from such an early age as Woods. His early history is well documented: from the attention he received on *The Mike Douglas Show,* to beating adult players on Earl's home course before he could even carry a golf bag, to the success he had at the junior and amateur levels. Of course, much of that occurred while he was competing against players with far inferior ability. Tiger's natural affinity for the game combined with Earl's shrewd perceptiveness and determination (how many other athletes have a sports psychologist on staff before they hit puberty?) created a player that was far ahead of the competition, leading to early success on the golf course. As long as a player can cope with the pressures that success brings (no simple task), two things result: confidence within that player and doubt in the competitors. Many have commented that Tiger seems to thrive under pressure, including his high school coach, who said that even at that young age Woods actually played better when surrounded by crowds and cameras (Crosby and Dale 13). Who knows whether the confidence led to the success or the success led to the confidence, but it is clear that by the time Woods reached the professional level, everyone in the golfing community knew who he was and the aura of invincibility that surrounded him. That only grew as he continued to win professional tournaments.

At the height of his success, everyone, including his competitors, *knew* they were playing for second place. In a 2000 article, sports columnist Thomas Boswell writes, "Woods doesn't just win. He tries to imprint on the mind of every opponent that resistance is useless. The military calls the tactic 'overwhelming force.' You paralyze the enemy to the point where he doesn't even try to fire back" (149). In "The Lost Generation," Frank Deford laments the plight of the "second-best golfer in the world" (a generic reference to all other professional golfers) because he would never be able to escape Tiger's shadow. At about the same time, Jim Murray compared telling the general public that Woods is beatable to telling them there is an Easter bunny (126). Professional golfer Tom Watson admitted in 2000 that the rest of the tour are "all playing for second place," and he was just one of many professionals that expressed similar thoughts (Boswell 145).

It would be a mistake to underestimate the impact that belief has on performance. Over the past thirty years, strong research, most notably the Processing Efficiency Theory, have explained and quantified the significance of such factors as anxiety and stress on performance. On the most basic level, these studies all demonstrate that if athletes believe they are going to lose, a number of physiological and psychological effects occur: muscles stiffen up, adrenalin pumps, heart rates increase, palms sweat, focus drifts, perception changes. All of these are detrimental to a golf game and will cause the competitor to lose. It is similar to a placebo effect. When people believe they are receiving medication, their body responds positively even when the pill is a placebo. In much the same way, when a golfer believes he is playing for second place, his body responds in a way that diminishes performance potential. For many years, Tiger's competition believed both consciously and subconsciously that he was going to win, and that equated to a significant competitive advantage on the course.

Since the sex scandal, Woods has struggled like no other time in his life. The psychological strain and physical injuries have taken a toll on his performance. It is not just the two-year gap since he won a tournament; it is also the way his golf has slumped. During that time, he dropped from the number-one ranking (a position he dominated from 1997 to 2010) to number fifty-eight, his lowest since beginning his professional career. The majority of his stats (driving accuracy, greens in regulation, putting percentage, etc.) all plummeted, but more telling than the numbers is simply observing his demeanor on the course. Not only has he failed to make the kind of "miraculous" shots that the golfing community has come to expect, but he also has not exuded the kind of confidence and focus that made his competitors wilt on the final day of a tournament. Logically, the slump will have had an impact on his own confidence, leading a lot of commentators to speculate if and when he'll get his "mojo" back.

A more pertinent question might be whether getting his mojo back will even be enough. Now that his competitors have seen his vulnerability, the rhetoric of invincibility fades with each passing tournament. They are no longer just playing for second, because Tiger has shown that he is not a lock for first, and when athletes are playing to win, they play differently than when they play to compete. As sports psychology expert Dr. Chris Stankovich claims,

The number one problem Tiger is facing is that other golfers no longer fear him, which has allowed them to play more freely and confidently, while Tiger's game has "tightened up" as a result of no longer having the psychological edge that he had on the competition for the last ten plus years. The days of the field playing scared and to "not lose" rather than playing to win are long gone. Once a titan on the golf course, Woods is still respected today, but he is no longer feared. Professional golfers have seen over a year's worth of pretty average play from Tiger, giving them less worry and more confidence when competing against him. The result? A hard fall for Woods — going from nearly invincible to just another good golfer competing along with everyone else.

As Stankovich acknowledges, fear is a powerful ally when overwhelming the competition, but fear can only be maintained as long as the dominance does not waver. Over the past two years, Tiger's aura of invincibility has been assaulted in two ways: first, his competitors have witnessed him laboring on the golf course, and second (due to both his on- and off-field struggles), they are no longer inundated with messages from the media and society that Tiger is the "chosen one" and that his abilities are supernatural.

If Tiger can string together a series of impressive victories, there is a chance that he could begin to reestablish his aura of invincibility. However, that will be more difficult than in the past for many reasons, not the least of which is that his competition will fight harder because they have witnessed his struggles over the past few years. Woods is, after all, a human being now, and human beings, unlike their supernatural counterparts, are fallible.

Do not misunderstand; a Tiger Woods in the hunt on day four in a tournament is still a psychological hurdle for any competitor because the specter of the miraculous Woods still remains. Just ask Zach Johnson, who jockeyed with Tiger for first place on the last day of the Chevron World Championship. Down the final stretch, Johnson claimed that Woods exhibited "some superhero strength" (Crouse). Additionally, Woods could benefit from a sports media that is just itching to write a redemption story. It probably will take several impressive performances in a short amount of time, but any inkling that he is returning to form will quickly result in proclamations of the second coming of Tiger, and the rhetoric of invincibility (and perhaps spirituality) will erupt once again, filling the competition with self-doubt. At least, that is what the cult of Tiger is hoping for.

The Kool-Aid Factor

Whether they were commenting on his supernatural ability to drive the ball or proclaiming the he would bridge the racial divide in golf, the media certainly played a significant role in creating the cult of Tiger. However, no one contributed to and perpetuated this spiritual discourse more so than Earl Woods. In the now famous *Sports Illustrated* profile where Earl proclaimed Tiger "The Chosen One," Earl opened the floodgates for the cult of Tiger to flow.

> "Tiger will win because of God's mind. *Can't you see the pattern?*" Earl Woods asks. "*Can't you see the signs?*" "Tiger will do more than any other man in history to change the course of humanity," Earl says.
>
> *Sports* history, Mr. Woods? Do you mean more than Joe Louis and Jackie Robinson, more than Muhammad Ali and Arthur Ashe? "More than any of them because he's more charismatic, more educated, more prepared for this than anyone" [qtd. in Smith, G., original emphasis].

Many parents *hope* their children will change humanity for the better. Some may even *believe* that it will happen. But how many educated, experienced parents are going to *proclaim* their child as humanity's savior to a major media outlet, knowing that every word would be recorded, printed, and meticulously scrutinized? Before the *Sports Illustrated* profile, the media had already constructed Tiger as a racial unifier bridging the black/white divide so apparent in professional golf, but Earl's rhetoric opened the conversation to include all humanity. Additionally, he added a spiritual mystique to the cult of Tiger with language of predestination. Not only did he sprinkle his talk with words like "signs" and "patterns," but he also explicitly claimed that every aspect of his own life had been carefully crafted to lead to his son's success, from Earl's own sports and military careers to his first failed marriage and eventual second marriage to Tiger's mother. With the predestination rhetoric, Earl added a level of inevitability to his son's success, essentially creating the image of a golfer who simply was living out a script written by supernatural forces.

Of course, Earl was a shrewd and intelligent man, and he knew how to manage (some might say manipulate) the media. This is, after all, a man who trained his three-year-old son how to deal with reporters' questions. As described by Gary Smith,

> FATHER (EARL): Where were you born, Tiger?
>
> SON, age three: I was born on December 30, 1975, in Long Beach, California.
>
> FATHER: No, Tiger, only answer the question you were asked. It's important to prepare yourself for this. Try again.
>
> SON: I was born in Long Beach, California.
>
> FATHER: Good, Tiger, good [original emphasis].

One might wonder how much of Earl's rhetoric was a deliberate attempt to manufacture a myth of invincibility. As a Green Beret, he would have known the effect that this sort of psychological warfare could have on both the soldier and the enemy. He would have seen it firsthand. Charles Pierce, writing a controversial article for *Gentleman's Quarterly* that both perpetuated and deconstructed the cult of Tiger, claims that late in his life Earl admitted to creating the mythology around his son and discussed the reasoning behind it: a two-fold hustle to both help prepare Tiger for fame and to create a much larger narrative of his son ("The Man"). Still, it would seem that at least a part of Earl's predestination and "healer-of-nations" rhetoric was heartfelt. If it was all a con, it should go down in history as one of the greatest.

More to the point, one must ask how much of this "chosen-one" rhetoric Tiger, especially the young, impressionable Tiger, could hear before buying into it himself. How often can a father whisper into his son's ear, as Earl did before the final round of the U.S. Amateur Championship, "Let the legend grow," before it becomes a part of that son's identity (qtd. in de Jonge 16)? When Earl made his now-famous comments before the Fred Haskins Award dinner, Tiger did not flinch at the claims that he would change humanity. He did not balk at the notion that he was chosen by God himself (G. Smith). He did not approach the podium and say, "My father likes to be dramatic, but I'm just a golfer." Instead, Tiger appeared very comfortable with the rhetoric, embracing his father after the speech and never contradicting the statements. Also, it is useful to consider the father/son bond between them. The close relationship between Tiger and Earl is well documented, and Tiger has been quoted as saying, "I basically respect everything he does. We're best friends" (qtd. in de Jonge 23). If Tiger looked up to his father as much as has been reported in the media, it is logical to assume that Earl's words — including the spiritual/predestination rhetoric — would have been strong enough to help shape Tiger's self-identity.

It is impossible to know the extent to which this rhetoric affected Tiger, but it is hard to imagine that it did have a profound impact. If it did, even to a small degree, the advantage it would give him on the golf course is incalculable. This would no longer be *confidence,* which wavers. Instead, this moved past cockiness or swagger that might disappear the first time an athlete misses the cut. This would be an individual who believes at his core that God has predestined him to win at golf. This would be the Mother Theresa of tee boxes and greens, unflappable faith that what he is doing is inspirational and miraculous. And throughout the majority of Tiger's life, all he had was success after success to reinforce that belief. If Woods drank the Kool-Aid, if he was consciously or subconsciously a devout member of the cult of Tiger, he would certainly have a powerful psychological and competitive advantage over the "mere mortals" he competed against. Perhaps the discourse of spirituality that Earl set out to create had achieved everything and more than it was intended to accomplish because, when athletes believe they are untouchable and the world does nothing but reinforce that belief with something akin to religious fervor, the competitive advantage would be incalculable. The spiritual/supernatural discourse may have been Tiger's greatest advantage ... at least until it was gone.

Reimagining the Cult

Nothing shatters a spiritual icon like a sex scandal. After the events unfolded in late 2009, Tiger came under a scrutiny that he was both unfamiliar with and unprepared for. Of course, Woods' career has been under a spotlight since he began winning tournaments as a child, but his personal life was never splayed open like it was during and after the scandal. The tabloid media was a different breed of animal than the tame sports media he was familiar with and had controlled for so many years. For so long he was untouchable, but he was now completely exposed. The spiritual discourse disappeared overnight, and the harsh criticism began. Even two years after the scandal broke, the articles discussing his on-field performances still featured the sex scandal as a predominant theme. Nearly every article covering his victory at the Chevron World Championship addressed the scandal in some way, creating a sense that it may remain an asterisk staining the rest of his career. Just as modern baseball records hardly can be discussed without the taint of steroids creeping into the conversation, it is likely that Tiger will never fully escape the shadow of his infidelities.

Plenty of sports superstars have emerged from scandal once their on-field performance proves them "worthy." Michael Vick is a recent example. But in most of those situations, the fall has not been as dramatic as Tiger's. Vick plays what many see as a violent, gladiatorial sport (American football), and the dog fighting he went to jail for does not seem a far cry from his sport of choice. The narrative is altered in that there is a new chapter to Vick's story, but the basic discourse remains the same — a gladiatorial character is attracted to brutal, competitive activities. There is no hypocrisy here, no shattering of the underlying themes. Woods, on the other hand, participated in the type of lurid sexual scandal that cannot exist simultaneously with the spiritual discourse that had been so carefully crafted over many years. According to Pierce, "the promulgation of Earl's gospel is as much at the heart of Tiger's appeal as is his ability to go long off the tee" ("Tiger Woods Creation"). When this kind of central discourse is questioned, it does more than simply alter societal views. Destroying the cult of Tiger could undermine the sense of predestined invincibility that contributed powerfully to his competitive advantage.

Former professional golfer and commentator Nick Faldo believes that what Woods went through has changed him forever.

> "He's quite a sensitive guy, so to try to come out after global humiliation with (affairs) comments, let alone the criticism, it's pretty difficult. He won't have the dominance back ... because he was a totally clear-thinking man on a mission, a rampage. Once that gets chipped away, he's not the same on the golf course" [qtd. in Cherner].

When he mentions something getting chipped away, Faldo appears to be referring to Tiger's drive to win. But that drive stems from a deeper source; it is part of Woods' psyche and part of his identity. When an athlete's identity is chipped away, as it was with several of the baseball/steroids scandals, that player is much less likely to be able to compete at the same level again.

A significant question is yet to be answered. Just how much of Woods' identity relied on the spiritual discourse? If he was fully aware of Earl's rhetoric and managed somehow to avoid internalizing it, then it is likely that an elite Tiger could emerge once again. He has shown the ability to adapt to new swings and pull himself out of slumps in the past. However, it is difficult to imagine that Tiger did not internalize the rhetoric at all, especially since Earl admitted that the discourse was created in part to affect Tiger. If that is the case, Woods may never again dominate the tour because *that* Woods no longer exists either psychologically or, in an odd but real sense, spiritually. Yes, he certainly will win more tournaments and probably some majors. Woods is too experienced a golfer and driven a competitor to be denied that. However, it is far less clear whether he will regain the winning percentage that made him "the Man" for over a decade.

Tiger has always been known as a guarded figure, and after the scandal, he understandably pulled back even more. However, his televised apology offers a few insights into how much the scandal may have affected his identity. In the closing lines, he pleads, "there are many people in this room and there are many people at home who believed in me. Today, I want to ask for your help. I ask you to find room in your hearts to one day believe in me again" (Woods). "Believe" is a complex word, and it is often used synonymously with "support" or "accept." However, the tone here suggests more than simple fan support. He is asking his fans to make room in their hearts for him, a phrase that has obvious religious undertones. The "belief" here is more like a type of "faith." Additionally, he asks for their belief in order to help him. In public apologies, the speaker often expresses a desire to return to normalcy. It is a hope more than a central need. But Woods is not simply hoping for a return to the way things were; he is pleading for belief. It is as if Woods understands that on some level he cannot believe in himself or *be* himself without the cult of Tiger as part of his identity. And finally, it is important to note that this was the last statement he made in the speech. Unlike all the various apologies, self reflections, and requests for privacy that dotted the speech's body, Tiger's beseeching call for belief was placed as the final utterance for emphasis; it is the last thing his audience will hear and therefore the first thing they will remember. Of all the things he wanted his audience to take away from the apology, the need for belief was the one he wanted to stick in their minds the most.

There is no way to know how much of the Tiger Woods who has dominated the golf course was built upon the spiritual, predestined discourse created and perpetuated by his father. But what does seem clear is that, in Tiger's darkest moment, he appears to be a man desperately needing to be believed in so he can believe in himself.

Works Cited

Berlinicke, Jeff, and Steve Gomen. "Paradigm Shift ... Tiger Woods Changing the Perception of Golf." *Golf Fitness*. n.d. Web. 15 Oct. 2011.

Boswell, Thomas. "With the Course He's On, Things Can Only Get Better." In Stout. 143–148.

Cherner, Reid. "Faldo Says Tiger Could Be Marked Man." *USA Today*. 4 Nov. 2011. Web. 5 Nov. 2011.

Crosby, Don, and James Dale. *Tiger Woods Made Me Look Like a Genius*. Kansas City: Andrews McMeel. 2000. Print.

Crouse, Karen. "After Two-Year Drought, Tiger Wins with Flourish." *The New York Times*. 4 Dec. 2011. Web. 5 Dec. 2011.

Deford, Frank. "The Lost Generation." In Stout. 119–123.

de Jonge, Peter. "A Zone of His Own." In Stout. 15–27.

Glassman, James K. "A Dishonest Ad Campaign." In Stout. 45–49.

Gomen, Steve. "About Us." *Golf Fitness*. n.d. Web. 15 Oct. 2011.

Johnson, Roy S. "Tiger!" *Men's Fitness*. 29 June 2007. Web. 10 Oct. 2011.

Kaplan, Erin Aubry. "Falling for Tiger Woods." In Stout. 131–135.

Karp, Josh. "The Spirituality of Golf." *The Huffington Post*. 14 May 2010. Web. 28 Oct. 2011.

Kindred, Dave. "So Young to Have the Master's Touch." In Stout. 83–87.

Lipsyte, Robert. "One Writer's Tiger Woods Problem." In Stout. 181–184.

Murray, Jim. "Wait! It's Not Supposed to End This Way, Is It?" In Stout. 125–129.

Pierce, Charles P. "The Man. Amen." *Gentleman's Quarterly*. Apr. 1997. Web. 1 Aug. 2011.

_____. "The Tiger Woods Creation Myth." *Esquire*. 25 Mar. 2009. Web. 14 Aug. 2011.

Smith, Earl. "The Mundanity of Excellence: Tiger Woods and Excellence in Golf." *Sociology of Sport and Social Theory*. Ed. Earl Smith. Champaign, IL: Human Kinetics, 2010. 173–186. Print.

Smith, Gary. "The Chosen One." *Sports Illustrated*. 23 Dec. 1996. Web. 1 Aug. 2011.

Stankovich, Chris. "Tiger Woods Has Lost His Mojo, and It's Not Coming Back." *Examiner*. 1 Feb. 2011. Web. 24 Aug. 2011.

Stout, Glenn, ed. *Chasing Tiger: The Tiger Woods Reader*. Cambridge, MA: Da Capo Press, 2002. Print.

Woods, Tiger. "Tiger Woods' Apology: Full Transcript." *CNN*. 19 Feb. 2010. Web. 29 Oct. 2011.

Branding: At What Price?

Michael V. Perez

Tiger — now that is a name with potential. A marketer's dream. Not only is this largest of all cats distinctively beautiful, sleek, and graceful, but it is also a swift and deadly predator. Banking on those powerful images, a great many sports organizations have identified themselves as "tigers": Australian rugby; Canadian ice hockey; Indian cricket; American collegiate football; American, Japanese, Korean, and Israeli baseball. The gleam (probably in the shape of dollar signs) in marketers' eyes must have been patently obvious as Tiger Woods was about to break into professional golf. With that name and those looks, Tiger was obviously not another Davis Love III, whose watching-paint-dry demeanor matched his staid, pompous name. Nor was he going to be a Freddy Couples, a likeable guy whose intimidation quotient was quite limited. This was a golfer who could be marketed like none before him. He would come to be known, almost exclusively, by that potent first name, Tiger.

Author of *The Wicked Game* Howard Sounes argues that branding sells a part of the whole person through "the exploitation ... of name, likeness and image" (136), and a considerable number of corporations have "branded" Tiger. They have essentially "owned" and sold various aspects of his being to assure that particular products would become synonymous with his youth, power, and charisma. Consistent with other celebrity endorsements, Tiger's branding has arisen from an essentially symbiotic relationship, wherein the celebrity brands the merchandise, and the merchandise brands the celebrity. As a result, both entities thrive. Indeed, enormously successful marketing campaigns in some sense "created" at least the public Tiger. In doing so, they simultaneously developed one of the most powerful brands ever known.

Tiger's brand was different from others in a number of ways. For example, Woods' sponsors received nearly instant gratification because their campaigns did not feature a celebrity who slowly surfaced from oblivion, gained gradual recognition, and finally realized full-blown notoriety. Instead, Woods garnered tremendous notoriety from his father's early "marketing" efforts and his own accomplishments as an amateur. Once Woods turned pro, a marketing campaign of enormous proportions enabled Brand Tiger to rise, nearly instantaneously, to meteoric heights. In addition, Tiger's early marketers promoted the figurehead and merchandise not to American golf or culture in general, but to the world. In *We First*, branding expert Simon Mainwaring describes the importance of international branding. As he notes, "What defines a brand nation is the quality of consumer loyalty and the diversity of its global consumers. In today's world, brands are properties with increasingly multinational markets" (44). Woods' handlers obviously understood the desirability of globalization and employed a number of strategies to place Tiger's name, face, and body in front of the world to crystallize the brand.

For nearly two decades, Brand Tiger fared extraordinarily well, selling not only golf equipment and attire but also cars, watches, sports drinks, global consulting services, razor blades and men's grooming products, premium credit cards, and especially anything covered with the emblem that became synonymous with Woods, the Nike swoosh. With every purchase, no matter how small, people owned a piece of Tiger. Some may have even bought that particular sleeve of golf balls, obviously Nike, in the hope that they could be like Tiger on the course.

Brands imply much more than simply hawking products, however. As University of Melbourne English professor John Frow asserts, products imply "a set of meanings and values" (64). Mainwaring also emphasizes the intersection of marketing and values as he writes, "Even when addressing specific countries or cultures, companies are seeking to maintain a consistent voice and set of values" (44). By design, celebrity endorsements invite the transfer of the spokesperson's purported "meanings" to the merchandise, and Tiger's marketers obviously projected him as a set of values, on and off the course. As Charles Pierce points out in his article, "The Man. Amen," the young Woods embodied elements of humanness and godliness, but early marketers displayed little of Tiger, the mere human. Rather, they featured a superhero who performed incredible feats on the golf course. Tiger was never marketed as merely a golfing gentleman selling gear; strategists mixed in a healthy dose of the sacred, or at least what passes for sacred in the golfing world. Tiger was a man, actually *the* man, a superhero with a somewhat other-worldly edge. A close analysis of several commercials and a "stray" music video illuminate how Tiger's brand presented that superhero to the public.

Images and claims that originally sold Woods also set up a precipitous drop for the brand when the world learned that the man was not, and probably never had been, a near-god superhero. After the scandal, Woods' brand machine attempted to construct a new image by highlighting his humanness. A now infamous advertisement pointed out that he had some fairly significant flaws, implicitly claiming that he had learned from his mistakes. When that strategy fell flat, his public brand virtually disappeared from American media, at least for a time. Overall, Brand Tiger was left in disarray, quite a substantial problem. However, after having come through a fairly lengthy dark period, Brand Tiger, like its spokesperson, seems to be resurgent as Tiger has begun to sign new sponsors.

Training Ground for Brand Tiger

Tiger Woods became the figurehead of such a powerful brand, in large part, because his father had a vision and plan. Sounes reveals how the elder Woods employed more than words of wisdom as training tools for the budding player:

> In preparation for tournaments, Earl began to toughen his son mentally around the age of six. Tiger was given audiotapes with subliminal messages such as "My Will Moves Mountains!" To get the boy used to distractions, Earl would drop the golf bag when Tiger was about to swing. Tiger was forbidden from saying anything when his father was playing tricks like this [129].

Biographer Tom Callahan additionally notes that Tiger's half-brother Den understood that Earl's training was only the beginning of something significant. As Den asserts, "You know, during those early 'Let The Legend Grow' days, I never laughed at it…. I believed it. I knew how good Tiger was compared to the other little kids, and I knew my dad would carry him forward. I still remember the little boy who used to say 'sand twap' and 'wa-wa,' meaning 'water hazard'" (45). Tiger seems to have cut his baby teeth on the golf course, with self-help audiotapes playing in the background. This was great training for a future superstar and merchandise spokesman.

Further paving the way for Brand Tiger, Earl and Kultida, Tiger's mother, booked a number of key television appearances. In 1978, for example, an adorable two-year-old Tiger toddled onto *The Mike Douglas Show* as a fully developed child prodigy. Directed by his father to swing for the camera, Tiger also shared an amusing exchange with special guest Bob Hope. The banter with Hope amounted to a bet that young Woods could make a certain putt. He did, much to the audience's delight (Callahan 42). By age ten, Woods had appeared on a number of other nationally televised programs, including *That's*

Incredible, the *Today Show*, and *Good Morning, America* (Sounes 126–7). Tiger was well on his way to becoming a brand.

Sounes adds that Tiger nonetheless was a shy child and that he viewed the branding game as an interruption to his "fun time" of playing golf. As Woods' former coach Rudy Duran reports, media events and interviews were distractions: "'So Tiger never really liked [marketing].... Then he actually learned it's part of the business. His parents were training him to be a touring pro and deal with the media'" (qtd. in Sounes 127). Obviously Woods, in more ways than one, was a *nurtured* natural for a brand. The toddler deftly quipping with Hope on a variety show eventually became the figurehead of one of the most potent brands in advertising history. Interestingly, Tiger had little, if any, control of the brand, at least at first. He attended to the game, and Earl focused on brand development. In order for the brand to thrive, Tiger just had to cooperate. He did just that.

Introducing Brand Tiger to the World

Tiger's brand was first unveiled at a press conference in 1996. As *New York Times* reporter Larry Dorman writes, the young man stood on the platform, "bedecked with the Nike logo ... flashed his impossibly toothy smile, and almost sheepishly intoned his first words since turning professional." Dorman claims that Tiger's "I guess, hello world." seemed "sweet" and "unaffected" ("Woods Says"). The tentative "I guess" might indeed imply that this untested professional was a bit shy and thus endearing. Turning pro before finishing college is a big step, after all, and professional golfers expect at least a bit of humility from newcomers. But everyone soon discovered that the other part of that sentence, "hello world," delivered the real message of the day. With two simple words that stood as the "hook" for the entire campaign that followed, Tiger was not simply introducing himself to American golf or to American culture at large. Rather, he announced his arrival, almost like the "first coming," and he broadened his audience to include the entire world. As well, those words simultaneously and unambiguously proclaimed his sponsor's global marketing intentions. Brand Tiger was thus born, possibly the first sports brand to emerge fully globalized. As Dorman notes, the press conference provided a mere glimpse of the Nike "blitz" that included "30- to 60-second spots ... flooding the airwaves" ("We'll Be"). The "Swoosh Heard 'Round the World" resonated from the start.

In essence, Brand Tiger sought nothing short of a paradigm shift. Marketing expert Stephen Johnson offers a four-stage model that describes "how social transformation evolves." In stages one and two, people recognize that a new idea does not adhere to their current world view. By stage three, they understand that the new and old perceptions must be reconciled, and in stage four, people "believe in the new idea and change their behavior to align with it, or they reject the new idea and retrench themselves in their current beliefs" (Mainwaring 153). All of these stages apply to Nike's initial campaign because the commercials not only celebrated, but also elevated, ethnicity. UCLA history professor Henry Yu asserts that in the twentieth century "racial identity was itself increasingly a commodity which might or might not have value (25–26). In the case of Brand Tiger, racial identity was an important part of the package, if not the entire commodity.

One of those first Nike commercials clearly illustrates that racial identity heralds a new product, if not a new day, for golf and possibly the planet. In a series of fade-in, fade-out vignettes, a broad range of Benetton-like children utter both a call to arms and a pledge of unity. Spartacus-like, they declare, "I am Tiger Woods." Some children clutch golf clubs in their hands or carry them slung over their shoulders. Others practice putting. All of the short clips are accompanied by African-inspired world beat music in the background. The diversity implies that the next generation may be just like Woods — and not necessarily like Arnie Palmer or Jack Nicklaus. It is noteworthy that Woods does not speak during the entire spot. Rather, he first appears in a Cecil B. de Mille-esque close-up, briefly glowering toward the camera and his audience. Looking into the "invisible" lens, Woods "breaks the fourth wall." This technique, borrowed from theater (for example, the narrator of Thornton Wilder's *Our Town* who talks directly to the audience), adds a riveting effect to an already compelling advertisement. The commercial asks its audience to "interact" as they view the ad, not as a passive event, but as an act of engagement and acknowledgment of Woods and the youth he ostensibly inspires.

In one portion, a young boy is seated next to a window displaying a list of golf rules, indicating that the new guard is here and he will obey the rigorous expectations of the gentleman's game. Young girls also figure prominently in the ad, joining in the "I Am Spartacus-Woods" declarations. In essence, the entire ad answers an unstated question. No one asks, "Who is Tiger Woods?" The absence of the question implies that it need not be asked. Instead, Tiger announces, with a simple assertion of identity, that *he* has arrived. He is simultaneously the golf world's heir apparent and the unrivaled inspiration for future boys and girls of all ethnicities. Woods' full body is shown briefly, functioning as a slow-motion-swing placeholder for his brand's product, a white mock-turtleneck that displays Nike's trademark swoosh at Woods' neckline. Here is Brand Tiger as it enters *and* arrives at the top, fulfilling the legacy of the tot who, according to Woods' half-brother, said "wa-wa" and meant something entirely different from what most two-year-olds intend.

As Mainwaring and Frow note, this commercial relays a set of implicit values. The most obvious is Woods' identity as a superhero. By echoing Tiger's announcement, the children claim their rightful places in the world, whether they play golf or not. The ad also extends that option to any viewer who might choose to say, tacitly, "I am Tiger Woods." Unlike so many celebrity golf endorsements, this commercial offers a very different superstar, inviting everyone, regardless of race or ethnicity or gender, to identify with and share in his future successes.

That first Nike campaign birthed a brand that would grow to powerful proportions. A year later, in October 1997, *USA Today* reported that Nike's "Hello World" campaign was by far the most popular advertising effort of the year (Yu 24). *Forbes* columnist Lisa DiCarlo argues that "no company has capitalized on the appeal of the good looking, clean-cut, articulate, scandal-free golf whiz more than Nike.... For its money, Nike has purchased almost every aspect of the Tiger Woods brand, and a piece of almost every marketing appearance of the golf star." In essence, Brand Tiger filled the space that television coverage of tee and green could not. Commercial breaks sold Woods, not simply as a great golfer, but as a multi-ethnic global contender that children could admire and emulate.

Developing Brand Tiger

Many more commercials, vending a plethora of products, projected a wide variety of images to sell Tiger. In one ad, Woods embodies both superhero and "every-dude." He is simultaneously quite ordinary and exceptionally dazzling as he performs a playful "bouncing ball" act. At first glance, he would seem to be just like that all-too-familiar playground wise-guy who could beat anyone at hacky-sack. Instead of the little beanbag, however, Tiger bounces a golf ball, always a Nike, off an iron. Tiger's bounces are cadenced and varied, and he maintains superb control, even when he shifts the club behind his back and between his legs. Obviously, this regular guy has nothing better to do than spend time perfecting these vital "skills." Like the dude striving to impress, Woods then lifts one leg off the ground. With seemingly little effort, he balances himself on one foot while deftly pop-pop-popping the ball in rhythm between his legs, like a very daring game of ball-and-paddle. The "paddling" shifts again as Woods pops the ball higher into the air, ultimately balancing it on the end of the club, bringing both iron and ball gracefully to rest for just a moment. Then, he flicks the ball up one last time. Suddenly transforming himself from Clark Kent to Superman, Woods winds up for a mighty swing and smashes the ball before it hits the ground. In a blink, the ball rockets into the horizon.

The background music is a jaunty calypso, faux-"Rat Pack" tune with background singers infectiously scat-singing syllables. The overall effect is quite bubbly, its message "I can hang out and be cool, too. Do not be mistaken, however. I am in control; I am also raw power." Nike might have altered its tag line, just for this ad: *Just Bounce It.* This clip, posted on YouTube, has garnered nearly two million views and apparently has inspired more than a few young men and women to mimic Woods. As many as twenty imitators have posted their own version of the feat. Because the act could be potentially painful, the clip possibly should have come with a disclaimer: *Kids: don't bounce this at home.*

Also wordless in a PGA Tour commercial, Tiger does absolutely nothing extraordinary. At the start, the spot shows only the shoulders, arms, and lower body of a guy tying his shoes in a club locker room. Of course, by 2009, when the ad was first aired, those arms and shoulders were entirely recognizable. To confirm Tiger's identity, the camera quickly pans up to show his head. Although shoe-tying hardly seems worthy of being captured on film, the soundtrack delivers the fundamental message. Throughout the thirty-second clip, Tiger is whistling — what else? — "Eye of the Tiger," the theme song from the *Rocky* films. Working on the first shoe, Woods casually whistles the opening bars. As he taps his foot to the beat, this everyday guy whistles the chorus and shifts to tie his other shoe. Shoes tied and ready to go, Woods simply gets up and leaves as the real power chords kick in, ostensibly so that viewers everywhere can play along on their air guitars.

Once again, this Tiger is simultaneously a regular guy and superhero. The seemingly carefree Woods prepares to play golf just like everyone else, by sitting in the locker room to tie his shoes. Nothing special. The commercial nonetheless also declares that Woods is an incredible tiger and a champion. He is as mentally focused and driven as a boxer, even if the boxer suggested is a cinematic one. In one fell swoop — or lack thereof because this is a PGA Tour commercial — Woods' most mundane activities conjure images of Sylvester Stallone in triumph, pumping his arms while jogging in place at the top of the Philadelphia Library steps. Nothing more needs to be said about this superhero. He simply whistles while he works wonders.

Walking on Water

Woods' half-brother claims that "Dad never said Tiger was the second coming of Jesus. He just said he was going to change the world. Well, didn't he? He put a whole new face on one small piece of it, anyway" (Callahan 45). By commenting on his young son's legacy so early and with such frequency and vehemence, Earl seems to have, with stunning prescience, previewed one of his son's most famous commercial coming attractions, the "Walk on Water" commercial. In a noteworthy interview, the proud father claimed, among other amazing things, that Tiger would "accomplish miracles" (Smith 33). Twelve years later, with the help of cutting edge video technology, Brand Tiger offered images of Tiger performing just such a miracle.

This famous ad arose from a "dialogue" between an on-line gamer, Bryan Levi (aka "Levinator25"), and EA Sports, an enormous corporation that develops and distributes sports video games. Levi discovered what he believed was a glitch in the PGA Tour '08 videogame. During one portion of the game, Woods' avatar appears in the middle of a pond. Not only does Woods stand on water, but he also successfully launches a ball that has come to rest atop the surface of the pond. The video then segues to a blank screen with the word "PAR" in the center. The crowd roars in the background. "Levinator25" dubbed this the "Jesus Shot" and became "virtually" famous by posting his own video identifying the glitch. Although Levi's video produced 50,000 hits on YouTube, that number would seem like nothing in a very short time.

EA Sports responded to Levi's public accusation by producing a commercial that actually features the gamer's claim, showing the amateur video as the prologue. As Levi narrates his findings, the screen fades and bold text appears: "Levinator25, you seem to think your Jesus video was a glitch in the game." The rest of the ad "proves" there was no glitch. What follows is an almost silent movie clip of Woods removing his shoes and, yes, testing the waters with his toes. He — finally — walks onto the surface of the pond, never sinking. Because the ball has "safely" landed on a lily pad, Tiger addresses it. The humor of the clip largely rests in Woods' immediate reaction to the situation — that of course he would immediately remove his shoes and walk on water in order to swing to victory. He has no doubts; he knows what he has to do and just does it. Woods hits the ball perfectly, lands it on the green, and seemingly wills it to roll into the hole. A tag line accompanies his return to solid land: "It's not a glitch. He's just that good." The video went viral immediately, garnering over six million hits on YouTube.

Although the ad might seem to proclaim Tiger as a latter-day Jesus in the flesh, the tone is clearly ironic. Woods is not supernatural, but he is superheroic and cannot be reduced to a "glitch." The Walk on Water commercial synthesizes Brand Tiger quite effectively. He is an "every guy" who hits bad shots, as evidenced by his ball landing atop a lily pad in the first place. Yet he also performs extraordinary feats on the golf course, even if those achievements sometimes defy reason. That is, after all, what a superhero does, and Tiger is obviously "just that good."

"Tigershack": Failing to Cohere

As marketers discovered in one unfortunate commercial misstep, Brand Tiger was not so resilient that they could ignore the implicit values Woods had always brought to the tube. A two-and-a-half-minute American Express ad attempted to pay homage to the low-comedy film classic *Caddyshack* by presenting an almost shot-by-shot (pun intended) re-enactment of Bill Murray's war with the exasperatingly resilient gopher. Of course, Tiger assumes the role of the frenzied greens keeper, and he seems to be more than a bit crazy. No longer the spit-and-polish exemplar of the gentlemanly golfer and certainly not a superhero, Woods is half-shaven and disheveled. His eyes register that fanatical gleam of unreasoned passion. Not simply looking like a lunatic, Tiger acts crazed as well. Wildly rolling his eye, he mutters, "I hate gophers," and uses the same strategies Murray did in the film to outwit the varmint. With apparent sadistic glee, Tiger flushes the gopher out and then dynamites it.

The clip suddenly detours to a weird moment as Woods plays with clay figures, a tiger and gopher, of course. Verbalizing both critters' voices, Woods says, "Hello, Mr. Gopher.... This is Mr. Tiger" and then reverses the introduction. This commercial marks quite a marketing departure from "Hello World." Like Bill Murray, Tiger inevitably gets the gopher; unlike Murray, he's not the least bit funny. Most people would never think of Murray and Woods in the same breath, unless, of course, marketers assumed that the brand was so stable that anything offering images of Woods would be a hit.

American Express may have intended to reveal a funny, fun-loving, accessible, and approachable Woods; instead, the "Tigershack" commercial offers a "Hello, Mr. Gopher" puppet show that plays out like some bizarre private moment one wishes not to have witnessed. That moment, indeed the entire production, is antithetical to Brand Tiger as Woods exhibits extreme emotions — albeit as parody — that brand him as a hapless psychopath, no superhero in sight. The commercial strayed so far from the brand's implicit values that it was received with shock and dismay. Realizing their mistake, marketers pulled the spot after only a month.

The video's lack of success can be verified by the paucity of views (fewer than 1,500) on YouTube. Comparisons of the "Walk on Water" spot to the "Tigershack" ad reveal how powerfully Brand Tiger had crystallized and how resistant that brand was to modification. In essence, the failure of the latter commercial demonstrated that Tiger had to remain within the confines of his branded identity, the superman who performed extraordinary feats on the course.

Unintentional Exposure

Clinical psychologist and golf enthusiast Dr. Rafael Parlade asserts that "Wood's brand has brand awareness outside of the actual arena, which makes him even more significant." Evidence of how quickly that far-ranging awareness sprang up, rappers Notorious BIG (posthumously), Ma$e and Sean "P. Diddy" Combs produced a 1997 music video that prominently features "Tiger Woods." The video of the rap-pop single "Mo Money Mo Problems" starts with a deft bit of recycling by offering an infectious percussive guitar and drum break from Diana Ross' hit, "I'm Coming Out." That beginning cleverly reiterates and remixes Brand Tiger's primary message nicely: "Hello World, I'm Coming Out," indeed.

In the video clip, P. Diddy, fashioned as a facsimile of Woods, appears in a prologue. The rapper takes hyperactive mock interviews and erupts in a trademark Woods burst of celebratory emotion when he sinks a long putt. Exaggeratedly performed by P. Diddy, this "Woods" takes a "victory lap" around the edge of the crowd and pumps his fists as the rap song kicks in. These "Woods-bursts" appear throughout the video clip, integrated with more conventional late '90s pop-rap scenarios (inside a large metallic cylinder, for example).

Produced only a year after Tiger's professional "coming out," the video stands as a testament to Woods' rapid ascension as an icon in American culture. The creators of this clip, as well as the rap artists, may have thought they were "playing" with Woods' image just for fun, but the production offers interesting cultural commentary. The spot revels in golf stereotypes, showing the "gallery" (other rappers) in nerd regalia, complete with thick glasses. The "mainstream" fans are stolid and reticent, in sharp contrast with Diddy/Woods' antics. Rather than frowning on Tiger's obviously anti-gentlemanly behavior, the video applauds his exuberance. Although Diddy's rendition of Woods is clearly a caricature, the golfer is always depicted as fully on top, cool enough to be portrayed by Diddy just as Diddy is cool enough to play Tiger.

By virtue of Woods' exposure in this production, Brand Tiger earned more than money. Although many in the golf world may never have seen the video, Tiger's image was displayed to people far beyond the typical tee-to-green set. The very popular song and video hit #1 on the *Billboard Hot 100* in August 1997 ("Mo Money") and was the #20 song for the entire year ("Billboard"). Although Brand Tiger might not have initiated a comic parody of the figurehead, the production afforded Woods an edge of coolness and even street credibility. Experiencing a second coming out a year after Woods announced his arrival to the world, the video unexpectedly exposed him to an unmistakably young, hip, and hot audience.

The Fall and Aftermath of Brand Tiger

Prior to 2009, Brand Tiger maintained an unprecedented peak, experiencing no cold or even lukewarm period. That was soon to change, and a Nike commercial that aired just before the scandal broke might be perceived as previewing the reason for the brand's unfortunate drop. The ad displays Woods as a literal split-personality as three Tigers test new golf clubs at The Oven, Nike's research and development facility. Initially, one Tiger, decked out in a white Nike shirt, strolls in as two other Tigers, both attired in black, follow. All three examine clubs, and then one of the "black-shirts" examines an iron as the other two look on. The implicit message is clear: The Oven has manufactured golf clubs that interest Woods —*all* of them, that is. By the commercial's end, all three Tigers are wearing his "signature" colors as a voiceover states "from the most demanding eye in the game ... comes the most refined irons in golf." This moment essentially proclaims that not only one, but three Tigers approve the club. A duplicated Woods, in other words, would have especially exacting eyes for a product that will perform triply well on the course. Without doubt, three Tigers are better than one, and in a market that simply cannot get enough of Woods, clones are most welcome.

In light of Woods' accident and the subsequent exposure of his extramarital affairs, however, this clip displays more than marketers probably intended. The three Tigers reveal the stark difference between the public and private man. Interestingly, two of them wear black in the spot rather than white. In a literal sense, the ad was accurate because Tiger seldom wears white. Obviously aware that black is a "power" color, Woods always wears his signature outfit, black slacks paired with a red shirt, on tournament Sundays. In this way, he presents himself as a predator, the guy who intends to slaughter his foes. Tiger's choice of black attire to annihilate the competition is not only acceptable, but also desirable as he fulfills fans' hopes and expectations. However, the public had also been "sold" on a very different reality, that Tiger is a good guy off the course. He does wear white, so to speak, at least sometimes. But, in retrospect, when two of the three Tigers arrive in black, the reality of his deception and duplicity are displayed clearly. Then, when all of them morph into his competitive guise, no other Tiger seems possible. He is entirely predator.

The brand was unexpectedly faced with the dichotomous Tiger that Pierce highlighted years before. No longer could marketers ignore the fact that Tiger was the kind of guy who told sexist, juvenile jokes and behaved badly. No longer could they sell him solely as the superhero capable of otherworldly feats accompanied by a fist pump and a "hell yeah" grin. As *New York Times* columnist Charles McGrath astutely points out,

Woods has become a public figure not just in the way that most great athletes are public figures, but also in a way probably unparalleled in the history of publicity itself. He has made far more money from selling himself, or his image, than he has made from playing tournaments. That image, partly genuine and partly sculptured, has been one of decency, modesty, filial devotion and paternal responsibility, and not of mysterious car crashes and evasive explanations.

The crash and evasion confirmed that the all-too-perfect package was terribly flawed. Although McGrath notes that portions of the old image were genuine, many believed that those former values no longer adhered at all. As a result, Brand Tiger was "marked down." Gatorade, Accenture, and AT&T fled quickly. Tag Heuer and Gillette scaled back their Woods marketing and then dropped him as well. According to ABC News columnist and advertising executive Larry Woodard, Woods likely lost $50 million in endorsements (qtd. in Gomstyn and Arnall 2). Suddenly, Woods was *a man*, as opposed to *The Man*, the figurehead of a brand in disarray.

Dressing Down

Tiger Woods has long been a component of Nike, as Frow claims, and both Nike and Tiger would obviously benefit from carefully controlling the "consistency and integrity" of his brand (68). Since consistency was lost as a result of the scandal, Nike attempted to regain the integrity by staging and delivering a public dressing-down in the aftermath of the crisis. Aired for the first time during the run-up to the 2009 Masters, the thirty-second black-and-white Nike commercial created a lively debate. The sales aspects of the spot are minimized, but Nike merchandize is subtly displayed throughout. The camera remains tight on Woods' head and torso, and two strategically-placed white swooshes — one on his vest and a larger one at the center of his cap — not only sell the brand but also signal Nike's constancy to the beleaguered figurehead.

This commercial aims to do much more than selling a few hats or vests, however. The primary goal is to show that Woods really *is* a regular good-guy who messed up badly and is very sorry for his sins. During the entire ad, Tiger remains silent and virtually motionless, purportedly contrite. None other than Earl Woods, the *pater familias* who could rightfully be credited with carefully selecting and scripting the superhero Tiger, delivers the verbal message. Earl's voice starts to drone, and Tiger blinks several times as the camera tightens in on him, all sad eyes and stoically-clenched jaw. His face remains expressionless. Earl's slow monotone appears to acknowledge the seriousness of his son's transgressions: "Tiger, I am prone to be more inquisitive ... to promote discussion ... I wanna find out what your thinking was ... I wanna find out what your feelings were ... and did you learn anything." The elder Woods thus sets himself up as the grand inquisitor.

Prioritizing thought over feeling, the solemn father proclaims that he is "inquisitive" and claims he intends to "find out" what his son was "thinking." Earl essentially endorses an analytical process to isolate and identify the problem and solution, indicating that he is interested in understanding Tiger's thinking before he even mentions anyone's feelings. As the elder Woods indicates, learning occurs only by pursuing rational inquiry and discussion. Apparently, because Tiger has subjected himself to this public humiliation, he did learn. As this spot tacitly asserts, the contrite son has not been entirely duplicitous; he simply forgot himself, lost control, and abandoned his real values for a time.

Certainly, Nike hoped that Tiger's willingness to broadcast a difficult *mea culpa* moment would demonstrate that he understood the errors of his ways and signal that he would never make those mistakes again. Unfortunately for Nike and Tiger, the ad was met with mixed reviews. Some commentators declared that they believed that it showed Tiger's true remorse. *International Sports Association* correspondent Matt Trueblood, for example, describes the commercial as "moving and meaningful," showing "real remorse." Trueblood then claims that "it shows a far more tender and meaningful remorse than any of his public apologies or press conferences have." Although some agreed with Trueblood, other commentators have expressed skepticism, clearly doubting the sincerity of this public display of repentance. Among them, *Daily Beast* reporter James Othmer declares that the commercial is neither poignant nor moving. As far as he is concerned, the spot "isn't just odd, it's creepy." Much of the "creep factor" doubtlessly arises from the reality that the beloved father died long before the scandal. Earl Woods, no longer really able to guide his son to do better, had been resurrected to do just that — publicly. Here, Brand Tiger took a terrible misstep in its attempt to restore a once-powerful brand.

Disarray and Resurgence

Musing about the post-scandal Woods, actor Donald Sutherland states that "Tiger had an easy life and a very hard life. A child prodigy — going through all that crap to please his father. Suffering through all the dilemmas, the contradictions. He made himself an angel, only he wasn't an angel." The perceptive Sutherland asserts that Tiger was, in fact, a "made" angel. Although he seems to understand that Earl had a huge influence on Tiger's life, the actor nonetheless proclaims that Tiger is solely responsible for creating that "angel." Sutherland also asserts, "Then came the humiliation of that angelic persona being shattered in front of him ... and suddenly he's cast out in the desert" (qtd. in Fussman). Here, the actor shifts from one otherworldly reference, angel, to another as he adopts a metaphor that harkens back to Biblical references of the savior cast to the desert, possibly implying that Woods is about to be crucified. As Sutherland implies, fame exacts a price. Ironically, as early as 1996, commentator Gary Smith predicted that the Madison Avenue "machine" would bring Woods down. As he argues, "Let's be honest. The machine will win because you can't transcend wearing 16 Nike swooshes, you can't move human hearts while you're busy pushing sneakers. Gandhi didn't hawk golf balls, did he? ... Who or what will save Tiger Woods?" (72). Like Sutherland, Smith understands that branding sometimes results in terrible consequences, and he predicts that Tiger would need to be saved from himself.

Sutherland's desert metaphor is very perceptive, but he never mentions what might happen to the multi-billion dollar brand. Was it cast into the desert as well? Where could Woods' brand go, in between a trap and a wet place? Could the brand succeed by embracing a very human Tiger? Might consumers balk if Woods' marketers sought to capitalize on the player's failures in the same way they had capitalized on his successes? Quoting marketing specialists, *USA Today*'s Nancy Armour points to a possible future for Brand Tiger:

> "Nike's brand equity is not really about sports or athletic performance ... but about the emotion of sports," said DeBiase, now chairman of Reboot Partners, a growth advisory consulting firm. "They sell what drives people to watch or participate — the fact that sports is the ultimate drama in which no one, not even the participants, knows the outcome. They are not standing by [Tiger] as much as standing by his reality, delivering the drama that makes sports so compelling.... But Woods has something equally powerful working in his favor right now, Ries said. "We love stories of redemption. We want that happy ending," she said. "That's what Tiger has going for him, because we are rooting for him now."

These experts indicate some possible avenues for Woods and the brand to flourish. In order for one green to foster another kind of green, the brand must sell a post-fallout Woods whose credibility lies in the heart of the American Dream. Although the public will likely never perceive him as the nearly flawless superhero of yore, Tiger can project himself as something even more compelling, a regular dude with one hell of a swing and an even stronger will to succeed. Woods needs to pick himself up by the bootstraps and succeed, again and again and again. Although the purgatory of disgrace was quite long and doubtlessly difficult, Tiger seems to be enacting that redemption story. Ending the longest winless spell of his professional career in December 2011 at the Chevron World Challenge, Woods closed down a bad year on a positive note. The tournament was not official, nor was there a full field of contenders, but the win bears an implicit promise that Tiger will continue to try and will probably thrive.

Even before his latest victory, Tiger had signed several new sponsors, including Kowa (signed June 2011), a Japanese company that produces heating rub; Rolex (signed October 2011); and Fuse Science (signed November 2011), a company that develops energy and nutrition products that are purportedly more easily absorbed by the body (Badenhausen). Although Rolex is certainly the most recognizable and prestigious of the new sponsors, the two others may be more significant for Brand Tiger in some ways. As *Benzinga* commentator Gary Cassady writes, after closing a deal for their name to appear exclusively on Tiger's bag, the little-known Fuse Science has marked an extraordinary surge in stock prices, "gaining about 50 percent on its value" in only a few days. Perhaps Tiger, the regular dude who could use some extra energy and nutrition, is just the right guy for this company. The same concept applies to Kowa. As the spokesperson of these corporations, Tiger can be frankly down-to-earth. Although being less than flawless might be unchartered territory, Woods no longer needs to appear as a superhero. He can be just what he is, a guy who gets sore muscles and joints, just like everyone else. And when that happens, he can use some Kowa deep heating rub.

WORKS CITED

Armour, Nancy. "Coming Soon to Ads Near You? Woods May Pitch Again." *USA Today.* 22 Nov. 2011. Web. 28 Dec. 2011.

Badenhausen, Kurt. "Tiger Woods Adds First Sponsor Since Scandal." *Forbes.* 29 June 2011. Web. 23 Nov. 2011.

"Billboard Top 100 Songs of 1997 — Year End Charts." Bobborst.com. n.d. Web. 10 Dec. 2011.

"[Bouncing Ball] Tiger Woods Golf Commercial." Nike Television Advertisement. YouTube. 27 Feb. 2007. Web. 18 Oct. 2011.

"Caddyshack Tiger Woods Commercial." American Express Television Advertisement. YouTube. 27 Aug. 2010. Web. 24 Oct. 2011.

Callahan, Tom. *His Father's Son.* New York: Gotham Books, 2010. Print.

Cassady, Gary. "Fuse Sciences: Hole in One or Tiger Woods Gold Digger?" *Benzinga.* 13 Dec. 2011. Web. 15 Dec. 2011.

DiCarlo, Lisa. "Six Degrees of Tiger Woods." *Forbes.* 18 Mar. 2004. Web. 14 Dec. 2011.

Dorman, Larry. "'We'll Be Right Back, After This Hip and Distorted Commercial Break.'" *New York Times.* 1 Sept. 1996. Web. 2 Nov. 2011.

_____. "Woods Says Hello to New World." *New York Times*. 29 Aug. 1996. Web. 2 Dec. 2011.

Frow, John. "Signature and Brand." *High-Pop: Making Culture into Public Entertainment*. Ed. Jim Collins. Malden, MA: Blackwell, 2002. 56–74. Google Books. n.d. Web. 21 Nov. 2011.

Fussman, Cal. "Donald Sutherland: What I've Learned." *Esquire*. 16 Feb. 2011. Web. 12 Nov. 2011.

Gomstyn, Alice, and Daniel Arnall. "New Tiger Woods Nike Commercial Debuts Today." ABC News. 7 Apr. 2010. Web. 20 Nov. 2011.

Mainwaring, Simon. *We First: How Brands and Consumers Use Social Media to Build a Better World*. New York: Palgrave MacMillan, 2011. Print.

McGrath, Charles. "Not Playing by the Rules." *New York Times*. 5 Dec. 2009. Web. 13 Nov. 2011.

"Mo Money Mo Problems — The Notorious B.I.G." Billboard.com. n.d. Web. 27 Oct. 2011.

Othmer, James. "How Nike Exploits Tiger Woods' Dead Father." *The Daily Beast*. 8 Apr. 2009. Web. 16 July 2011.

Parlade, Dr. Rafael. Personal Interview. 30 Aug. 2011.

Pierce, Charles P. "The Man. Amen." *Gentleman's Quarterly*. Apr. 1997. Web. 1 Aug. 2011.

Smith, Gary. "The Chosen One." *SI Vault. Sports Illustrated*. 23 Dec. 1996. Web. 8 Aug. 2011.

Sounes, Howard. *The Wicked Game: Arnold Palmer, Jack Nicklaus, Tiger Woods, and the Business of Modern Golf*. New York: HarperCollins, 2003. Print.

Sutherland, Donald. "What I've Learned." *Esquire*. 16 Feb. 2011. Web. 13 Nov. 2011.

Trueblood, Matt. "Tiger Woods Watch: New Nike Commercial Embodies Best of American Sports." *Internationaled*. International Sports Organization. 8 Apr. 2010. Web. 30 June 2011.

Woods, Tiger. "Earl and Tiger." Nike Television Advertisement. YouTube. 7 Apr. 2010. Web. 24 Oct. 2011.

_____. "Eye of the Tiger." PGA Tour Television Advertisement. YouTube. 25 Feb. 2009. Web. 18 Oct. 2011.

_____. "I Am Tiger Woods." Nike Television Advertisement. YouTube. 13 Mar. 2008. Web. 13 Oct. 2011.

_____. "Nike Golf— Split Personality." Nike Television Advertisement. YouTube. 24 Feb. 2009. Web. 21 Oct. 2011.

_____. "Walk on Water." EA Sports Television Advertisement. YouTube. 19 Aug. 2008. Web. 24 Oct. 2011.

Yu, Henry. "Tiger Woods at the Center of History: Looking Back at the Twentieth Century through the Lenses of Race, Sports, and Mass Consumption." Adapted from essay in *Sports Matters: Race, Recreation, and Culture*. Eds. Michael Williard and John Bloom. New York: New York University Press, 2002. n.d. Web. 8 Aug. 2011.

Showing Us the Money

Joe Gisondi

Americans were transfixed. Tiger Woods somehow limped around the 7,643-yard Torrey Pines Golf Course in the 2008 U.S. Open with a torn anterior cruciate ligament and a double-stress fracture to his left tibia, grimacing after shots and gnashing his teeth when his legs buckled in mid-swing. At one point, he used his clubs as crutches to climb out of a sand trap.

Yet Woods was in the lead for most of the third and fourth rounds, pleasing NBC's executives because ratings had increased through the day. Millions were mesmerized by Woods' torturous journey across the San Diego course. The pain proved nearly unbearable during the final nine holes when Tiger lost a three-stroke lead to Rocco Mediate, a veteran golfer who had never won a major tournament. But Woods rallied on the final few holes, moving to within one stroke. Woods launched his second shot on the par-5 No. 18 to the edge of the green, leaving him a long putt for eagle and the tournament title. Birdie would force a tie and an eighteen-hole playoff the following day with Mediate — a bonanza for the United States Golf Association, the Professional Golfers Association, and the TV network.

Fans surrounding the green screamed ecstatically as Woods rolled his putt just past the hole. When Woods sank the four-foot birdie to force the playoff, nobody cheered more loudly than United States Golf Association president James Vernon. Tiger's performance would help the USGA earn an extra $40 million in TV revenues during the five-day event.

PGA commissioner Tim Finchem was also excited. TV ratings, he knew, always spike when Woods has a chance to win. But this kind of drama, where the world's top-ranked golfer is fighting to survive an injury for a major championship? Epic. The ratings proved him correct. Nearly 8 million people watched the U.S. Open, making it the third highest rated Open in history.

Tiger's victory at Bethpage, New York, six years earlier remains the most highly watched U.S. Open, attracting a whopping 10.75 rating. The playoff between Woods and Mediate would be the most-watched cable golf event of all time, with 4.8 million viewers — at least, until viewers flocked to watch Tiger return from exile in the 2010 Masters ("2008"). Finchem and Vernon were ecstatic, knowing the ratings would please network executives who would soon bid on new TV contracts. Nobody elevated golf's profile like Tiger Woods.

Nike CEO Phil Knight was equally thrilled. He knew golfers would want the same Nike Method 003 putter Tiger had used, imagining they also would drop lengthy eagle putts. Tiger's Nike Victory Red Tour driver and Nike Victory Red Blade irons would also be hot items among the roughly 25 million golfers in the United States. The Nike One Tour golf balls would move quickly off the shelves, too. More importantly, casual fans would snap up black Nike swoosh caps and red Nike dry-fit shirts, happy just to identify with the world's best golfer and most identifiable athlete, a man who was on the verge of becoming the first person to earn one billion dollars from sports, thanks to sponsorship deals with Gillette, Buick, AT&T, Accenture, EA Sports and Rolex.

Many players have contributed to golf's growth through the decades — Walter Hagen, Byron Nelson, Arnie Palmer, Jack Nicklaus, Tom Watson. But none have affected golf's bottom line like Tiger Woods, something not fully appreciated until after Tiger hobbled off Torrey Pines and out of sight for most of the 2008 season.

Everybody knew Tiger's resume.

- His U.S. Open victory now gave him fourteen major titles.
- He had sixty-five total victories (increased to seventy-one the following season).
- He had won a career grand slam earlier than anybody at age twenty-five, when he won the British Open in 2000. (The Masters, U.S. Open and PGA Championship are golf's other major tournaments.)
- He had been the youngest Masters champion at age twenty-one.
- He had also been the youngest to win the U.S. Junior Amateur at age fifteen and the youngest to win the U.S. Amateur at eighteen.

Few people fully understood how much Tiger had elevated golf's profile and funding. But there would be plenty of time to evaluate Tiger's impact once he slowed down or retired. At the U.S. Open, Woods looked like he had the world in his grasp even while hobbling along Torrey Pine's fairways. After all, he was only thirty-two years old. He had been ranked No. 1 for an astounding five hundred weeks by 2008. Tour players feared him. Fans adored him, flocking to events and tuning in even if they never played. Single-handedly, Tiger had made golf seem cool. No player has exalted his sport more than Tiger Woods — TV ratings soared, TV contracts skyrocketed to nearly $1 billion, galleries swelled dramatically, sponsorship money poured in at a record pace, and prize money for PGA events more than quadrupled after he joined the PGA Tour in 1996. Tiger has been an economic superstar.

"There's been nobody in sport that has done what Tiger has done to a sport," said Brett Ogle, a golf commentator and former PGA player (qtd. in Walsh).

"Tiger wields more power than Arnold Palmer or Jack Nicklaus," said NBC golf commentator Roger Maltbie (qtd. in Jackson).

Said PGA Tour veteran Kenny Perry: "Tiger is our Tour" (qtd. in Potter).

When Tiger eventually sank a short putt to win the 2008 U.S. Open on the 91st in sudden death, there was no reason to believe anything would change in the near future. After all, golfers play far longer than other athletes, often into their early 50s. But two dramatic events would rattle the world of golf and underscore Tiger's monumental influence over the business of golf— his surgery and withdrawal from the Tour after he won the Open and his self-imposed exile in early 2010, following a scandalous marital split from his wife the previous fall.

Television Ratings

Television ratings slip when Tiger is not in contention. They tumble when he is not playing. So imagine the PGA Tour's plight after Woods withdrew from all future events following his 2008 U.S. Open triumph. Fans could no longer hope to catch a glimpse of Woods, meaning casual observers would not even check in for the rest of the season.

On average, 2.2 million fewer people watched golf events in 2008 and early 2009 before Tiger returned to the Tour. Nielsen ratings dropped by nearly 50 percent overall, from a 3.3 share of total audience to 1.7. Barely one million people tuned into the third round of the BMW Championship, a 65 percent drop compared to the previous year's event that Woods had played. Ratings dropped 61 percent for the final round. Even golf's major championships suffered, none worse than the PGA Championship played two months after Woods' epic U.S. Open victory. Fewer than 1.3 million watched the third round, a 78 percent decrease from the previous year's event won by Woods. The final round's ratings decreased by 57.6 percent from the year before, a drop of more than 5 million viewers ("Tiger's Return"). That made it the least-watched major in thirty-six years (Shaw). If anything, these numbers prove Tiger's effect on golf viewership.

Generally, Tiger's presence in a golf event is worth a full ratings point, which equates to 1 percent of the nation's TV audience. In September 2010, for example, a ratings point translated to 1,159,000 households. NBC estimates that ratings increase by 56 percent when Tiger is playing, even more when he is contending (Hosford). CBS found that ratings increased by 171 percent for events where Tiger finished in the top five, compared to those he did not enter or when he never truly contended (Fitzpatrick). As most TV executives realized, there were three types of PGA golf events — those where Woods is not entered, is entered, and is in contention in the final rounds. The ratings for each increase significantly. The ratings for the end of the 2008 season reveal Woods could affect ratings as much as 1.6 points.

"There's no question that Tiger dominates our PGA Tour coverage," said Golf Channel president Page Thompson. "He's a once-in-a-lifetime talent. The ratings indicate people want to watch him, and it's a privilege for us to cover Tiger and devote as much attention to him as we do.... When Tiger's in the field, he is the story" (qtd. in Rubenstein).

The PGA took another hit in early 2010 when Tiger withdrew from the Tour in order to try and salvage his marriage following frenzied media coverage. Woods did not play for the opening four months. When Tiger decided to return for the Masters, though, people tuned in at near-record numbers, eager to see how he would handle the media after a self-imposed exile. Hardcore golf fans, meanwhile, wanted to see if he could mentally prepare for the sport's first major event. Tiger finished fourth in the Masters, but he struggled the rest of the season. Subsequently, viewership for the final rounds of PGA events fell 16 percent compared to the season before. Some events dropped much more seriously. The Wells Fargo Championship drew 42 percent fewer viewers, while 800,000 fewer people watched the Memorial Open, where Woods had won the season before. At the AT&T National, viewership was half that of 2009, when Woods had competed (Sandomir).

"When Tiger plays or is in contention, he spikes ratings off a very healthy base," said Ty Votaw, the PGA Tour's executive vice president of communications. "When the No. 1 most-recognized athlete isn't playing, there's a falloff" (qtd. in Sandomir).

Tiger has always elevated television ratings. Even before he turned pro, viewers were enthralled by the kid who had once driven tee shots on *The Mike Douglas Show* at age two. Americans tuned into the U.S. Amateur in record numbers, far more interested in watching Tiger become the youngest amateur champ than viewing the World Series of Golf. In fact, the amateur event attracted a larger audience than all but three PGA events in 1996, outdrawing that year's British Open and PGA Championship. Several months later, Tiger helped the Skins Game practically double its ratings from the year before and attract a larger audience than the Notre Dame-USC football game (Strege 225).

Grand Slam and Other Tournaments

In Grand Slam events, Tiger is a major ratings winner. Tiger's wire-to-wire victory in 2002 is the only U.S. Open to attract more than 10 million viewers, making it the most viewed in the history of that major championship. Tiger's epic battle against Mediate in 2008 ranks an all-time third. U.S. Open ratings are nearly 40 percent higher when Tiger wins compared to when he does not, 6.3–4.6 ("In 2008").

In his first full season on the Tour in 1997, nearly 14 million people watched the 21-year-old *wunderkind* blister Augusta National to win his first major by twelve strokes, good enough for a 15.8 rating and a 32 audience share and by far the best TV ratings ever for the prestigious Masters ("TV Ratings Rise"). The Masters, on average, has the highest ratings among all golf tournaments. When Tiger won in Augusta between 1997 and 2008, ratings increased even more, spiking by 20 percent for final round coverage — a bump of about 2.5 million viewers for an 11.9 million average and an increase of two ratings points to 9.5 ("When Tiger Wins"). Tiger's return to the Tour in 2010 ranks as the second most-watched Masters, followed by Woods' victory at Augusta in 2001, when he completed the Tiger Slam by winning his fourth golf major event in a row. These are also the three highest-rated final rounds for any golf tournament since 1986, as far back as TV records go (Sandomir).

Tiger's playoff victory over Bob May in 2000 earned the PGA Championship its highest viewership ever, attracting 46 million viewers during the final two rounds. An estimated 38.5 million people watched Woods battle May during the final holes before winning his fifth major in a sudden-death playoff. That was the second highest-rated PGA Championship, trailing Jack Nicklaus' 1971 victory. Woods' playoff victory in 2000, though, ran over its prescribed time slot and into primetime, which starts at 7 P.M., when it surpassed Nicklaus' 12.1 rating by three points. The 2000 PGA Championship garnered a 15.1 rating that peaked at 16.0 for a 32 percent audience share between 7 and 7:30 P.M. that was, remarkably, 25 percent higher than the combined ratings for shows airing on NBC, ABC, FOX and the WB during the same time slot. As with the other majors, Tiger's success on the course translates to a substantial ratings increase for the PGA Championship — 33 percent, for a 6 rating ("In 2008").

Tiger's late charge to challenge Rich Beem in 2002 helped the PGA Championship record its second largest audience, delivering 40.8 million viewers during the final two rounds. That included 30 million for the final round, worth a 7.5 rating and an 18 audience share. Tiger's victories in 2006 and 2007 are also among the most-watched PGA Championships. Thanks largely to Tiger, ratings for the PGA Championship from 2000 to 2007 increased by a full point compared to the previous decade, jumping to 6.3 ("PGA Championship").

Woods' blowout victory in the 2000 British Open yielded the second-highest rating and audience in the past thirty years of the fourth major event, a 5.9 that attracted more than 7 million viewers. Lee Trevino's one-shot victory in 1972 that halted Nicklaus' string of three straight major wins remains the most-watched British Open. Overall, ratings at the British Open increase by about 1.2 points when Tiger wins, the smallest increase among all majors for this comparison, probably because it is regularly the lowest rated Grand Slam event in the United States. Americans clearly had lost interest in the British Open during the early 1990s, when ratings dipped below 3.0 three times between 1990 and 1996. Since 1997, Tiger's first British Open, ratings remained mostly above 4.0 when Woods competed (Gorman).

A month after Woods won the 2008 U.S. Open, the British Open suffered its smallest audience in seventeen years without Tiger, recording a 3.5 rating. Two years later when Tiger finished thirteen stokes behind little-known South African Louis Oosterhuizen, the British Open fared even worse, posting a 2.1 rating for the final round despite some strong early-round ratings. That's about half what Tiger helped deliver for the pedestrian Buick Open he had won in 2009. The 4.0 rating was nearly three times higher than the previous year's audience when, injured, Tiger was unable to play. Ratings, overall, nearly doubled in the four tournaments Tiger won in 2009, compared to the season before, proving further that viewers would much rather see an iconic golfer than an unknown South African golfer, no matter how prestigious the event (Ballengee). "The casual golf viewers are not going to tune in," said Jim Spence, a former senior vice president at ABC Sports. "Like very few athletes during our lifetime, Tiger transcends sports. He's like Muhammad Ali or Michael Jordan. These are athletes with larger-than-life talents and personalities" (qtd. in Buteau, "No Tiger").

Tiger's presence has also dramatically lifted ratings for numerous other non-majors. "His impact is mind-boggling," said Larry Novenstern, director of sports marketing at advertising agency BBDO. "His presence at a golf tournament drives the price (of commercials) up artificially" (qtd. in "Tiger Draws").

Even comedians understand Woods' importance to golf. "Mathematicians at Stanford have calculated the smallest number known to man," said Jay Leno, a day after Woods won the 2008 U.S. Open. "It's the Nielsen ratings golf will get without Tiger Woods" (qtd. in Hiestand).

PGA Television Contracts

In early 2011, PGA Tour officials braced for contract negotiations with the networks. The PGA had twice negotiated lucrative TV deals thanks to Woods' popularity — after Tiger blew away the field to win his first Masters in 1997 and after he had won four successive majors over two seasons, and seven over three years. In both cases, the PGA Tour had dramatically increased total revenue from its broadcasts. The four-year $575 million contract from 1998 to 2002 tripled the previous deal worth $160 million. The PGA then struck a deal for a reported $850 million for the 2003–07 contract, followed by one for $3 billion for 2008–12. However, the next contract, PGA officials feared, could yield a decrease in fees paid for TV rights. Tiger had played only seven tournaments in 2008. He won four titles in 2009, but then his game fell apart as horrifically as his personal life in 2010, the first year Tiger failed to win a PGA event. He even missed the cut once. That season, TV ratings, along with network profits, plunged. The average TV audience dropped by 22 percent in 2010, a loss of about 800,000 viewers for the weekend's final two rounds compared to 2008, when roughly 3.2 million watched (Futterman). Advertising revenue also decreased by $8 million for the first three months of 2010, when Tiger hid away from the paparazzi. Media analysts like SNL Kagan predicted the Golf Channel could lose 20 percent of its ad revenue (Smits). "The future is murky and unless Tiger gets it back, we may be looking at an interregnum like the period between Jack Nicklaus and Tiger," said Brad Adgate, a senior vice president of research for Horizon Media. "Tiger has been one of those few athletes, like Muhammad Ali or Michael Jordan, who lives up to the hype" (qtd. in Smits).

So PGA officials were clearly concerned when TV executives like Sean McManus, CBS Sports president, started saying publicly that he would monitor Tiger's progress before negotiating another contract. McManus said he assumed no golfer would dominate as Tiger had in the past. Tiger's winless streak had reached twenty-two months by the time McManus cautiously finalized a contract that appeared to include negligible increases, at best. Neither the PGA nor networks disclosed the final figures; however, Finchem said the new contract would result in modest increases for prize money, an indication the contract increased only slightly. Said McManus: "We were very conservative with respect to Tiger's effect. If Tiger plays well that will be a big bonus for us. We have not counted on that in respect to our business model" (qtd. in Buteau, "PGA Extends").

Prize Money and Endorsements

Incidentally, when Tiger slowed down, so did the PGA's growth. Prize money remained flat, increasing by just 3 percent over five years to $279,750,000 in 2011, an overall increase of $9 million. Part of this can be attributed to the Tour's first reduction in prize money since 1975. The PGA Tour strongly denies the notion that Tiger's absence had anything to do with three events being canceled and purses dropping by $8 million for the 2009 season. But fans tuned out and turned away from most Tour events the remainder of the season. Conversely, purses had grown at a record rate once Tiger joined the Tour. Prize money doubled in Tiger's first four seasons, soaring from $65,950,000 in 1996 to $134,950,000 in 1999. A lucrative new TV contract enabled purses to grow by an amazing $38 million between 1998 and 1999, by far the largest monetary increase in the history of the Tour. Purses quadrupled during Tiger's first ten years, nearly the same rate as during Jack Nicklaus' initial decade when purses increased from $1.79 million to $7.1 million between 1962 and 1971. No doubt, the Tour was healthy before Tiger entered the field, growing steadily through the years. Between 1990 and 1996, prize money had increased by 40 percent; however, those increases pale in comparison to the millions injected into the Tour's purses after Tiger joined the Tour in 1996.

Tiger Woods is reportedly the first athlete to earn $1 billion, an impossible feat without endorsement deals. Like many athletes, Woods earns far more off the field than on it. According to *Forbes*, Woods has earned most of his billion from endorsement deals that have regularly been worth more than $40 million a year. In 2010, Woods earned $60 million from the likes of Nike, Buick, AT&T and EA Sports, which was $10 million less than 2009 when several sponsors dropped him after a scandalous marital break-up (Freedman). Yet, Tiger remained No. 1 on *Sports Illustrated*'s list of top-earning American athletes that year for the eighth consecutive year. But that was not his most profitable year. Tiger made an astonishing $115 million in 2007, including an estimated $90 million from endorsements (Baker).

Tiger, the world's most recognizable athlete for almost a decade, has drawn the highest TV ratings, attracted the largest galleries at events, and won the most golf titles since 1997. So it follows that he should attract the most lucrative sponsorships — although marketing directors and business leaders still shake their respective heads at how much Tiger earned so quickly through his deals. He signed endorsement deals worth $43 million right before he entered the PGA Tour. But Tiger's influence extends beyond his soaring bank accounts. Thanks to Tiger's ability to engage fans beyond golf's base, all PGA golfers have profited.

Before Tiger joined the Tour full-time in 1997, few golfers earned $1 million either on or off the course. Curtis Strange was the first Tour player to earn $1 million, the only to do so in 1988. In 1996, nine golfers earned more than a million on the PGA Tour, led by Tom Lehman at $1,780,159. Tiger Woods raked in more than $2 million the following season, while eighteen players also earned $1 million on the course. In 1997, Tiger also won the highest-rated Masters event, helping the PGA Tour, subsequently, negotiate a TV contract worth a reported $575 million. Purses for PGA events then increased dramatically, and players earned much more. Twenty-six players broke the $1 million barrier in 1998, thirty-six in 1999, and forty-five in 2000. By the time Woods completed his Tiger Slam of winning four majors in a row in 2002, sixty-one players earned more than $1 million, including twenty-three who earned more than $2 million ("2002 PGA").

The PGA negotiated another four-year contract worth $850 million in 2003 right after Tiger went on a freakishly successful run to win seven of eleven majors played between August 1999 and June 2002 (Stewart). In 2007, after Tiger won several more majors and numerous regular-tour titles, the PGA Tour parlayed an even more impressive four-year contract reportedly worth $3 billion (Futterman).

The PGA Tour continued to increase its revenue, from $141 million in 1989 to $316.8 million in 1996 and $661.9 million in 2001. The PGA passed along the revenues to players by increasing prize money. By 2007, nearly one hundred golfers earned a million bucks. By 2010, thirty-nine golfers earned more than $2 million ("2002 PGA"). Player earnings more than quadrupled between 1994 and 2009, from $111 million to $461 million. "I've thanked him profusely," said Phil Mickelson, who earned $52 million in endorsements in 2010, "not only for what he's done for the Tour but for the game of golf" (qtd. in Sirak, "Golf's First").

Players profited from Tiger's off-course financial dealings as well. Before he ever played a professional event, Tiger had signed sponsorship deals worth $43 million, a figure that shocked players and agents alike. But soon other Tour players negotiated their own lucrative deals, thanks to increased exposure on TV and in the media. By 2001, businesses were spending more than $400 million endorsing players worldwide, including $200 million on American golfers, according to *Golf World* (Sirak, "Funny Money").

Unlike baseball and football players, golfers can wear logos on their attire. Like NASCAR drivers, PGA players sell spots on their clothes for fees. Tiger's cap, for example, is part of a clothing deal with Nike worth an estimated $29 million. English golfer Luke Donald, meanwhile, earned about $1 million a year to wear Mizuno's logo on his hat, while veteran Jim Furyk, the 2003 U.S. Open champion, signed a three-year, $2 million deal to wear a Johnnie Walker menswear logo on his collar. Golfers can earn anywhere from $25,000 to $250,000 for placement on the chest pocket, another $10,000 to $30,000 for shoes, and anywhere from $10,000 to $1 million for a right sleeve, which is far less valuable because it gets less time on TV except on a player's follow through ("How It Works"). The right shoulder is hidden as the player prepares to make a shot, unless he is a lefty, like Mickelson, whose endorsement income of $50 million-plus has been second only to Tiger the last several years. Non-golf companies now realize a logoed player on TV for several hours is worth millions in advertising dollars. Golf's profile rose so much that a National Hockey League team bought sponsorship on Jeff Quinney, placing a Phoenix Coyotes logo on his shirt ("Coyotes Announce"). Sports marketing directors and agents say Tiger's domination and worldwide recognition have enabled golf to stave off the typical whims and volatility associated with endorsement deals. Despite the recession, companies still sought Woods and other Tour players, mostly because golfers were considered a safe investment because they are typically educated and articulate, don't strike, and rarely get arrested.

Even in disgrace, Tiger set the standards for endorsements. Tiger's scandalous marital breakup in 2009 changed the way endorsements were devised. No longer would companies pay millions to athletes up front and hope for the best. After Tiger crashed his Cadillac Escalade at Isleworth, companies started to insert breach language and moral clauses, spread payments out over long periods, or back-loaded them as a bonus for players who fulfilled their obligations off the playing field. "This is all the Tiger Woods effect," said Mark Zablow, senior director of marketing at Platinum Rye Entertainment. "The 'You don't EVER have to worry about him' sell doesn't exist anymore" (qtd. in Lefton, original emphasis). Said Subway chief marketing director Tony Pace, whose company uses athletes such as Phillies first baseman Ryan Howard and Olympic swimmer Michael Phelps to endorse its products: "Because of what happened to Tiger, everyone now gives a third and fourth look at an endorsement prospect, as opposed to just a first and second look before." Tiger's the example that all marketing directors reference now, said Matt Delzell, group director for Omnicron's Dave Brown Entertainment, whose agency helped land Tiger deals with Gillette and AT&T. "As much good as Tiger originally did for golf endorsements and golf ratings, he may also have done that much harm," Delzell said. "If you asked me whether the recession or Tiger had more impact on endorsements and sports marketing in general, I'd tell you the recession, but not by much." Consequently, athlete endorsements declined by more than 50 percent (qtd. in Lefton).

Still, most PGA Tour players receive substantial endorsements, enough to make nearly every PGA member a millionaire. Titleist sponsors more than six hundred players worldwide. Fans checking scores on PGA.com see this logo below players' names on each tournament's online leaderboard. Typically, more than two-thirds of all players use Titleist golf balls. Within four years of Tiger joining the Tour, most players ranked between 50 and 75 on the PGA Tour earned as much as $100,000 to $150,000 a year in endorsements. Agents confirmed that some deals ranged as high as $450,000 annually. By 2005, more than twenty-five golfers earned $5 million a year from both golf events and endorsements. Ben Crane, at No. 50 on the annual list, earned $3.3 million. More than forty current PGA players earned more than $1 million in endorsements in 2010, according to *Golf Digest*. Twenty players earned more than $3 million. Tiger remained atop the list by accumulating $74.29 million in endorsements, despite his personal problems, followed by Mickelson with $36 million. Average earnings increased by 11 percent overall from 2009 to $26.2 million (Sirak, "Golf's First").

"Do some people turn off the TV if Tiger isn't playing?" said Fred Couples, two-time PGA player of the year. "Sure they do. That's true in other sports. That's why the Chicago Bulls were on in prime time so much when they had Michael Jordan. That's why they never showed the Cleveland Cavaliers on prime time until they got LeBron James" (qtd. in Brown).

Future Economic Prospects

Rory McIlroy had not even finished his final round at the 2011 U.S. Open before the comparisons to Tiger Woods started flooding in. The announcers marveled at McIlroy's deft iron shots and lethally accurate putting. Masterfully, he used a 6-iron to drop a tee shot between a large pond and multiple sand traps at Congressional Country Club's tenth hole, landing it three inches from the cup. He had hit a wedge on another hole from 117 yards out that rolled into the cup for eagle. Earlier, he had hit a 7-iron from 175 yards that barely cleared the bunker and rolled straight at the flag, leaving him a fifteen-foot putt for another birdie. No doubt, McIlroy was in another zone, one usually occupied by Tiger Woods. Like Woods in the 2000 U.S. Open, McIlroy had an insurmountable lead through three rounds. Tiger had won the 2000 in Pebble Beach by fifteen strokes; McIlroy was about to finish eight shots ahead to become the youngest champion since the legendary Bobby Jones in 1923. Like Woods, McIlroy set a U.S. Open record for lowest score, breaking Tiger's twelve-under score by three shots.

In many ways, McIlroy has Tiger to thank for his success, having followed

Woods' approach to golf by playing early and often as a youth. As a result, McIlroy also earned the silver medal for lowest amateur score at the British Open right before turning pro. McIlroy also studied Woods' 2000 Open performance as inspiration. Like Tiger, McIlroy dominated a major golf tournament at a young age. At twenty-two years old, McIlroy looked to be Tiger's heir apparent. The golf world yearned for someone to fill the void in case Tiger never returned to his dominating ways. Perhaps that's why golf announcers and PGA players were so quick to coronate the curly-haired young Irishman. Former U.S. Open champion Mark O'Meara declared: "Better than Tiger Wood at this age." Said 2006 Open champ Geoff Ogilvy: "Rory is by far the best young player I've ever played with" (qtd. in Huggan). Padraig Harrington, a two-time British Open champ, predicted that McIlroy, not Woods, would surpass the record of eighteen Grand Slam titles held by Jack Nicklaus, audacious given that Tiger had thirteen more major titles than the new Open champ (Kay). Tiger also praised him, calling it a "heck of a performance" (qtd. in Boren). *Golf Magazine*, meanwhile, tabbed McIlroy's performance as "transcendent" (Morfit).

But viewers were not extraordinarily impressed so ratings decreased by 26 percent from the previous year to 5.1. That is a number Tiger pulls in for events at Bay Hill and the Buick Invitational, not for a Grand Slam. In 2000, Tiger attracted 60 percent more viewers during his record run. Twice as many people watched Tiger win again in 2002. In 2011, recurring knee injuries kept Tiger from playing. McIlroy may be the most exciting and talented young golfer on the Tour, but he does not have Tiger's invincible aura, illustrated when McIlroy blew a four-shot lead in the final round of the Masters held two months earlier. McIlroy had shot a horrific eight-over 80 to finish well behind the leaders. Tiger, conversely, rarely wavered in critical situations, having won fourteen straight majors where he held a lead. Fans took notice.

McIlroy is a gifted golfer, but few athletes have the talent or charisma to carry a professional sport. Babe Ruth resuscitated baseball after the Black Sox scandal, Muhammad Ali elevated boxing's profile, and Michael Jordan raised basketball's status worldwide. It is unfair to expect McIlroy, or any other young golfer, to do the same. But that is precisely what Tiger has accomplished. If golf is to continue to grow, Tiger Woods needs to get healthy, regain his assassin's approach on the links, and win a few more majors. If he does not, golf should expect a decrease in both popularity and wealth in the near future.

"Look at team sports," said Brad Faxon, an eight-time winner on the PGA Tour. "The most popular team is the Yankees, and the most hated team is the Yankees. People love to see Tiger win, and they love to see Tiger get beat. As long as Tiger's around, people will always pay attention" (qtd. in Brown, "Tiger Is Human").

WORKS CITED

Baker, Andrew. "Tiger Woods, the $1 Billion Man." *The [London] Telegraph.* 11 July 2008. Web. 10 Oct. 2011.

Ballengee, Ryan. "Tiger Nearly Tripled the Buick Open's Ratings." *Sports Media Watch.* 4 Aug. 2009. Web. 9 Oct. 2011.

Boren, Cindy. "2011 U.S. Open: Rory McIlroy Win with History-Making Performance." *Washington Post.* 11 June 2011. Web. 14 Oct. 2011.

Brown, Clifton. "Tiger Is Human, and the Golf World Wonders If That's Good or Bad." *New York Times.* 13 June 2004. Web. 28 June 2011.

Buteau, Michael. "No Tiger Woods Means Lower Ratings, More Bets for British." *Bloomberg.* 15 July 2008. Web. 14 Oct. 2011.

_____. "PGA Extends Television Deals with CBS, NBC Nine Years Through 2021." *Bloomberg.* 1 Sept. 2011. Web. 14 Oct. 2011.

"Coyotes Announce Sponsorship Agreement with PGA Tour Golfer Jeff Quinney." *NHL.Com Network.* 29 Jan. 2008. Web. 10 Oct. 2011.

Fitzpatrick, Michael. "Tiger Woods' Absence Means the PGA Tour Will Suffer." *Bleacher Report.* 19 June 2008. Web. 14 Oct. 2011.

Freedman, Jonah. "The 50 Highest-Earning American Athletes." *Sports Illustrated.com.* n.d. Web. 9 Oct. 2011.

Futterman, Matthew. "Still Waiting for That Golf Apocalypse." *Wall Street Journal.* 29 Jan. 2011, A18. Print.

Gorman, Bill. "British Open Ratings Debacle Looms as Tiger Misses Cut." *TV by the Numbers.* 17 July 2009. Web. 28 June 2011.

Hiestand, Michael. "Shark Sighting Gives ABC a Boost in British Open Ratings." *USA Today.* 20 July 2008. Web. 14 Sept. 2011.

Hosford, Christopher. "Marketers Playing Through Pain of Losing Tiger." *BtoB: The Magazine for Marketing Strategists.* 14 July 2008. Web. 18 Sept. 2011.

"How It Works — 'PGA Player Endorsements.'" *My Golf Spy.* 1 March 2010. Web. 13 Sept. 2011.

Huggan, John. "U.S. Open 2011: Rory McIlroy Hailed 'Better Than Woods.'" *The [London] Guardian.* 19 June 2011. Web. 9 Oct. 2011.

"In 2008, We Learned What Happens to Ratings When Tiger's Not Around." *Golf.com.* 22 Dec. 2008. Web. 9 Oct. 2011.

Jackson, Barry. "Florida's Finest: Tiger's Tops in Golf, Yes, But His Influence Extends Much Further." *Miami Herald.* 15 Dec. 2002. C4. Print.

Kay, Emily. "Rory McIlroy Is the New Tiger Woods." *Waggle Room.com.* 18 June 2011. Web. 14 Oct. 2011.

Lefton, Terry. "Endorsements Remain Buyers Market." *Sports Business Daily.* 20 Sept. 2010. Web. 26 June 2011.

Morfit, Cameron. "With Heart-Wrenching Loss at Augusta and an Explosive Win at the U.S. Open, Rory McIlroy Transcended Golf in 2011." *Golf Magazine.* 1 Nov. 2011. Web. 4 Nov. 2011.

"PGA Championship on CBS Ratings Notes." *CBS Sports.* n.d. Web. 16 Oct. 2011.

Potter, Jerry. "Woods' Sport Faces Void with Its Star Out for Season." *USA Today.* 19 June 2008. Web. 14 Oct. 2011.

Rubenstein, Lorne. "Is There Such a Thing as Too Much Tiger?" *The [Toronto] Globe and Mail.* 31 Jan. 2008, 52. Print.

Sandomir, Richard. "PGA Says Viewership Decline Shouldn't Be Costly in TV Talks." *New York Times.* 19 Aug. 2010. Web. 26 June 2011.

Shaw, Lucas. "Tiger Woods: Without Him, U.S. Open Ratings Could Land in the Sandtrap." *The Wrap.* 17 June 2011. Web. 28 June 2011.

Sirak, Ron. "Funny Money." *Golf Digest*. 9 Feb. 2001. Web. 2 Oct. 2011.

_____. "Golf's First Billion-Dollar Man." *Golf Digest*. Feb. 2006. Web. 19 Oct. 2011.

Smits, Gary. "With Tiger Woods' Struggles and TV Deal Looming, PGA Tour Faces a Challenging Course." *Florida Times-Union*. 14 Aug. 2010. Web. 10 Oct. 2011.

Stewart, Larry. "PGA Agrees to $850 Million Television Deal." *Los Angeles Times*. 17 July 2001. Web. 28 June 2011.

Strege, John. *Tiger: A Biography of Tiger Woods*. New York: Broadway, 1997. Print.

"Tiger Draws Those Who Don't Normally Watch." *Associated Press*. 7 Apr. 2000. Web. 9 Oct. 2011.

"Tiger's Return Expected to Make PGA Ratings Soar." *Nielsen Wire*. 25 Feb. 2009. Web. 28 June 2011.

"TV Ratings Rise for Masters, Fall Short of Record." *Golf.com*. 13 Apr. 2010. Web. 16 Oct. 2011.

"2008: A Record-Breaking Year of Sports Viewing." *Nielsen Wire*. 4 Dec. 2008. Web. 10 Oct. 2011.

"2002 PGA Tour Money Leaders." *PGA Tour*. 30 Dec. 2002. Web. 28 June 2011.

Walsh, Scott. "How Tiger Woods Saved a Sport." *[South Australia] Sunday Mail*. 8 Nov. 2009, 50. Print.

"When Tiger Wins in Red, The Masters See Green." *Nielsen Wire*. 8 Apr. 2009. Web. 28 June 2011.

Faithful Fandom

Donna J. Barbie

Why would an otherwise modest young man suddenly don a giant wedge of orange foam cheese and scream at the top of his lungs in a public place? Why would anyone curse at and then pelt the television with pizza crusts simply because a player missed a free throw? Why, indeed. Even though these kinds of antics are commonplace, sports fandom,[1] it would appear, is not about reasoning, but emotion, and often too much of it. *New York Times* writer Michael Elliott is a perfect example of a "fanatical" sports fan. Recounting his own tearful emotionality when Liverpool won a championship, Elliott claims that watching his team has provided him some of the "really walloping emotional highs and lows" of his life. Elliott deems himself "Hopelessly Devoted" in the title of his article, pointing to his conviction that he has no choice in the roller-coaster of ecstatic wins and despairing losses.

Sports Fan Psychology and Golf Fandom

Of course, some sports aficionados are more ardent than others, and a number of psychologists, most notably Daniel Wann, have studied the fandom phenomenon, primarily focusing on people's sometimes violent attachments to sporting teams. According to Wann, Melnick, Russell, and Pease, intensely involved or "highly identified" fans establish and maintain significant emotional responses to a team for a variety of reasons, including the need for affiliation, enjoyment of the game's aesthetic, desire for entertainment, and thirst for eustress (30). Often referred to as "positive stress," eustress produces excitement and arousal that may be missing from the average person's everyday life. Another study concerned with spectator satisfaction concluded that fans

55

achieve the highest levels of gratification when their team wins and they can engage in BIRGing, or basking in reflected glory (Van Leeuwen, Quick, and Daniel 100).

Although some skeptics might think it impossible to be a highly-identified *golf* fan, many people do establish powerful connections to specific players and "invest" in their particular success. Although *all* athletes are subject to the vagaries of life and are especially vulnerable to aging, there are significant differences between rooting for a team and cheering on an individual player who is not part of a team. When team sports superstars retire, the team continues, quite possibly forever. Beloved teams often become celebrated social institutions, and highly identified fans take great pleasure in being part of the tradition throughout their lives. Most initiate their children and grandchildren into the pleasures of fandom. On the other hand, when superstars of a singly-played sport inevitably fade, fans must transfer their attentions to a different player or give up their passion. Despite the clear time-criticality of golf, fans of the sport have long supported their favorites with gusto.

Al Barkow, author of *The History of the PGA Tour*, points to a unique aspect of golf that increases the potential for bonding. As he writes, "Even with the restraining ropes that line the fairways, people ... can stand within a few feet of a player and overhear him discuss strategy, or note such minute details as worry beads of sweat trickling down his nose" (7). Golf, alone, allows such close player/observer proximity. Because immediacy occurs during a uniquely slow-paced game, fan experience, whether garnered directly on the course or delivered through television, is obviously intensified. As a result, observers witness acutely a golfer's shot-making prowess, the ability (or inability) to handle adversity and loss with grace, and the capacity (or incapacity) to show humility in victory. Myriad golfers have excelled in their sport over the past century, but only two American players have clearly captivated huge numbers of fans, Arnold Palmer and Tiger Woods.

Arnold Palmer and Other Pre-Tiger Superstars

Although golf aficionados admired and appreciated the skills and showmanship of a considerable number of players prior to the mid–1950s, Barkow asserts that a significant American fanbase would never be established until a home-grown player could really excite the galleries (29). Arnold Palmer was that player. *Sports Illustrated* commentator Jim Gorant claims that Palmer was "a bolt of lightning" that "made golf the coolest sport on the planet." A nexus of factors, including the rise of the American middle class after World War II, a population who had sufficient time and money to play the game, as well as increased television coverage of tournaments and golf "challenges," helped to catapult Palmer into the hearts of golf fans.

Palmer was no country club brat who flaunted his pedigree and perfectly crafted swing. Born into a lower middle-class family and reared during the Great Depression, the Coast Guard veteran was a scrappy and often erratic player. Barkow argues that Palmer was "Everyman, making mistakes, making up for them" (127). Emphasizing Palmer's "everyman" quality, Curt Sampson, author of *The Eternal Summer*, asserts that this player "made a hard game look hard" (102). Here was a man that other regular guys could relate to, one of their own — but with excellent skills. His galleries demonstrated their adoration and familiarity by calling him Arnie. Although seemingly contradictory and counterintuitive, Arnold Palmer was special because he was *not* special in most ways.

Palmer was more than a guy that galleries called by his first name, however; he was also the most exciting player fans had ever seen. Palmer rose to national and international fame when he won the 1958 Masters. Gorant argues that a specific "transformational moment" served as the "catalyst" that changed the game forever. Golf fans, not the play, were the centerpiece of that transformation. As the *Leaderboard* website notes, Palmer enjoyed a "legion" of fanatic followers who looked like "advancing infantry" supporting their "general" ("Arnie's Army"). These military references are not happenstance metaphors chosen to relay the essence of intense competition. Instead, they reflect quite literal images. Soldiers from Camp Gordon, near Augusta, were given free admission to the prestigious event for the first time in 1958. Many carried placards, and others tended the scoreboards. According to Gorant, "Palmer won over the troops" during the first three rounds, and by "Sunday morning, Arnie's Army was officially born, and its enthusiasm helped carry Palmer to victory." In fact, the scoreboards provided an opportunity for the "Army" to display their support. As Sampson notes, someone posted on the corner of the scoreboard the message "'GO ARNIE. ARNIE'S ARMY'" (88).

Television audiences were also "sold" on Palmer. Gorant recalls a conversation with CBS producer Frank Chirkinian, who claimed he "knew golf would succeed as a televised sport the moment Palmer appeared on screen, coming over a rise, silhouetted by the light ... his thick forearms hitching his pants like some long-forgotten cowboy." Here was a true American hero. Not some namby-pamby, stiff-necked aristocrat, Arnie embodied powerful and cherished stories of American pioneering spirit and intrepid masculinity. Although people in the galleries likely never perceived Arnie as a latter-day cowboy, those potent meanings clearly resonated with the masses.

People who write about Arnold Palmer claim he exuded charisma, the single most important quality that creates ardent fans. As *Orlando Sentinel* sports columnist Larry Guest notes, Palmer was a "flamboyant winner" whose magnetism emanated from his "'go-for-broke' style" (5). In "Palmer in His Prime," Tom Callahan quotes Gary Player, who asserts that Arnie "fell out of bed with all this great charisma, just fell out of bed with it." That is high praise, indeed. Most commentators argue that Arnie's play was not the sole, or even necessarily the critical, element that generated his charisma. They all focus on Palmer's ability to connect with fans. As Barkow notes, Arnie "actually communicated" with his galleries in an "easy, comfortable way" (128). The word "actually" clearly indicates that Arnie's interactions with galleries were far from the norm. Guest narrows down the unique aspect of Palmer's inter-actions to one act, the "simple little statement of mutual respect: eye contact" (7). Callahan quotes another famous golfer, Raymond Floyd, who affirms that Palmer was "able to focus in on everyone in the gallery individually."

Although he was no longer competitive by the time I saw Palmer for the first time at the 2000 Bay Hill Invitational, I witnessed his charismatic warmth. Waiting to tee off at a par three, Palmer congratulated his playing partner's caddie because it was the young man's birthday. On-course inter-actions among players and caddies are not unusual, but what happened next seemed extraordinary. Palmer looked directly at me, grinned slyly, and then declared that the caddie was "just a young pup." Everyone laughed. Later in the day, I was positioned on another hole when Palmer strolled to his ball. He didn't make his way down the middle of the fairway, far from the galleries, but instead walked no more than two feet from those of us who were just outside the ropes. He looked, really looked, at us as he nodded and smiled and sometimes offered a greeting. Guest notes that Arnie was "like a beacon producing an afterglow that moved along the row of spectators in a wave. Chests would rise and faces beam as The King made eye contact, acknowl-edging each person behind the ropes" (8). He was certainly the "King," but he was not the typical imperious being. He was the beloved royal who knew how to connect with his people, not just as spectators, but as humans.

Arnie's warmth no doubt contributed to the reality that his "Army" was extraordinarily faithful. Long after he was able to compete at the highest levels, long after his fans could possibly believe he might win, they followed and cheered. Howard Sounes, author of *The Wicked Game*, claims that Arnie's "enduring popularity" defied logic (87). True fans, however, are not born of logic, nor do they live by logic. Guest provides examples of the Army's illogical loyalty, describing an incident when a disruptive man in the gallery called out to Palmer during the Houston Open: "'Give it up, Palmer! ... You're getting too old, just like me'" (60). Gasps of "shock and embarrassment" quickly became "white-hot disdain" (60). No one was allowed to disrespect their beloved Arnie, even if he was telling the truth, perhaps especially *because* he was telling the truth. As Sampson confirms, Palmer "made fans for life" (101). Palmer created lasting connections, but his fans inevitably had to satisfy themselves with recollections of past glories. Apparently those memories proved to be enough for some.

Jack Nicklaus challenged The King's status on the links all too soon for members of Arnie's Army, and some of them, including my father, called the inevitable usurper "Nicklouse." Many aficionados nonetheless joined Nicklaus' growing galleries as he tallied up the wins. According to Barkow, golf fans are like any sports fanatics who need "at least one athlete they can rely on to perform at a certain level" (143). Fans could count on Nicklaus for a long time. Although he stands as one of the best players of all time, if not the absolute best, he simply did not inspire unbridled fan enthusiasm or loyalty as Palmer had done. Perhaps Nicklaus, who emerged on the national scene as a pudgy, Germanic-looking guy in a passé crew-cut, was simply not blessed with enough intangible magnetism. Other winning players have come and gone since Nicklaus surrendered his crown, including Tom Watson, Seve Ballesteros, and Nick Faldo, superstars all. Despite their amazing skills and ability to perform, none of them captured widespread adoration and enthusiasm of golf fans.

Tiger Woods: Fandom Approval

No golfer did, that is, until Tiger Woods appeared on the scene. For more than fifteen years, Tiger has been the darling of the golf world. His successes on the course, along with the power of his positive brand, translated to national and international celebrity. Prior to the fall from grace in 2009, Tiger achieved the highest favorable ratings of any sports figure on national polls. According to *USA Today*'s Michael McCarthy, Tiger's approval ratings stood at an unprecedented 88 percent on the 2000 Gallup poll. Such high positives, when coupled with very low negatives (8 percent unfavorable responses recorded in 2005), signaled that Woods clearly enjoyed widespread approbation of the American public.

After the revelations of 2009, Tiger's approval ratings plummeted, and negative reactions skyrocketed, as might be expected. McCarthy notes that Woods' favorable ratings tumbled to 33 percent and unfavorable responses rose to 57 percent in a December 2009 Gallup poll. According to a poll conducted shortly before his televised apology in March 2010, Tiger's approval ratings remained low, at only 40 percent, but the negatives had decreased to 33 percent (Langer). This slight improvement in unfavorable ratings might seem to result from Americans' legendarily short attention spans and/or their inclination to forgive. The findings of a poll conducted by *Forbes* Sports Business in January 2011 would seem to counter those assumptions, however. In a *Forbes* poll measuring the extent that respondents disliked currently active sports figures, Tiger Woods garnered a 52 percent dislike rating, fourth on the list of "shame" for the year (Van Riper).

Although surveys of general populations may offer important insights, teasing out responses from particular cohorts can also be informative, and this certainly was the case in both the December 2009 and February 2010 Tiger Woods polls. Women, as might be anticipated, recorded lower approval ratings in comparison to men. The biggest differentials, however, were between people who identified themselves as golf fans and those who did not, resulting in 62 percent and 35 percent approval ratings, respectively.

These ratings prompt a number of questions. For example, why have people found Tiger so very compelling? In addition, why has a considerable percentage of golf fans persisted in their "approval" of Tiger, despite his precipitous drop in other Americans' estimations? Although many commentators have predicted that Tiger would lose, or will yet lose, large numbers of fans, that has not yet happened. Written commentaries, as well as on-course observations, help to verify the magnitude and avidity of his fanbase, to identify some reasons Tiger Woods has developed such a strong following, to illustrate the adoration that children have clearly demonstrated for the player, and to confirm that many of his ardent fans persist in their attachment.

Tiger Woods' Fans Before the Scandal

Throughout his career, Tiger Woods has attracted huge and diverse galleries. Author of *A Biography of Tiger Woods* John Strege asserts that Tiger generated media and fan attention even before he turned pro. In his third bid to win the U.S. Amateur, a record number of people came "to see the prodigy who had become the most formidable marquee name in golf" (174). Very quickly, Woods' galleries became even larger. Strege recounts a tournament early in Tiger's professional career, reporting that Fred Couples, a perennial fan favorite, attracted 20 percent of on-course observers while Tiger drew about 75 percent even though he was not in contention (231). Tiger's hordes increased as he tallied the wins. Bob Smiley observed Woods play every hole during his truncated 2008 season and subsequently published *Follow the Roar* to document that experience. As he notes, anarchy reigned during the Dubai Desert Classic "as fans duck under ropes and run toward the tee box to beat Tiger there" (50). A great many commentators also report the unique composition of Tiger's fanbase. Unlike other players' galleries, typically comprising mostly middle-aged white men, Tiger's followers instead have consisted of people of various ages, ethnicities, and genders. As Smiley claims, Tiger's fans at Torrey Pines were as diverse "as the pictures on Girl Scout cookie boxes" (10), the phenomenon doubtlessly arising from Tiger's youth, good looks, obvious athleticism, and ethnicity.

Although Woods has drawn huge and diverse crowds, the number of people who attend tournaments is minuscule in comparison to those who watch golf on television. Hundreds of articles verify that viewership rises significantly when Tiger is playing. Nearly three million homes tuned in to watch Woods win the 2000 Canadian Open, for example, resulting in ESPN's highest ratings for a golf telecast to that point (Anthony). Although drawing an audience to cheer a victory seems less than extraordinary, Woods has attracted viewers even when he has not scored well. The Golf Channel, for example, played and recapped Tiger's less than stellar round on a Thursday afternoon in 2000 even though top contenders were still playing. When quizzed about this, spokesman Dan Higgins said they tried to "deliver what the viewer wants," claiming that they received few fan complaints ("Do You Suffer"). Networks would be foolish to eschew opportunities to draw big audiences.

Because of increased television coverage, some of Woods' most avid followers have never previously been interested in, nor have they played, the sport. Blogger Jamie Samuelsen, in fact, claims that Tiger's most important impact on golf has been the "mom effect." Samuelson explains that his mother had never watched a tournament, but during the 1997 Masters, when "all of America was riveted," his mother called from California to ask "what time golf came on TV and what time Tiger was going to win." No one can deny that Woods generated new audiences. My mother has been a long-time golf lover, but many of her friends were not, at least not until Tiger came into the picture. As my mom reports, Thelma, a bowling friend who has *never* watched golf, "glues herself to the set when Tiger is playing."[2]

Sometimes Tiger's new fans have been captured by surprise, and Bob Smiley is a perfect example. Recounting his journeys in 2008, Smiley is transformed from Tiger-skeptic into a true believer. At first, he is intrigued by the impact Woods seems to have on "everyone else" (xv) but becomes nervous when Tiger makes a charge at the Dubai tournament early in the season. Smiley attempts to explain away his emotionality as a "spike of nationalism" but then admits that he is beginning to hope that Tiger will win (61). Later, at the Accenture Matches, Smiley concludes that his feelings for Tiger are akin to the fixation he held for Pink Floyd (82), and at Bay Hill he concludes that observation has turned to obsession (109).

By July, Smiley is in the grips of full-blown Tigermania. As he watches the U.S. Open, the tournament that many claim was the most exciting golf event in history, Smiley understands the nature of true fandom:

> For most of the year, I have been merely cheering for Tiger, wanting to see exciting things happen because I enjoy good golf and he is the surest bet to provide some.... How much you cheer is inherently connected to how entertained you feel. And when it's over, there's no emotional attachment to whatever you just witnessed. But ... I've begun rooting for him. Rooting goes deeper. It doesn't ebb and flow when good things or bad things happen. Wins and losses can't change its strength. It's constant and selfless, and when your guy is hurting, it hurts you, too [241].

Now a fanatic, Smiley experiences the "walloping highs and lows" of the highly-identified fan, and his journey has not yet ended. When Tiger makes a long putt on his campaign to get into a play-off, Smiley releases a "primal scream," joining others who create the "sustained blast of complete and utter joy" (244). He agonizes and prays throughout the torturous 18-hole playoff, cursing the misses, hugging strangers when Tiger sinks a long putt (260). Claiming that he has cried only three times when watching professional sports events, Smiley discloses that he wept openly "after watching a broken Tiger Woods summon the will to win his fourteenth major championship" (271). Overcome with emotion, Smiley basks in reflected glory of the win.

Most people argue that Woods has the necessary charisma, enabling him to draw enormous audiences. Sounes contends that when he was only sixteen Tiger exuded "star quality" (160). Even with the power of charisma, Woods, like Palmer, had to bring fans' imaginings to life in order to solidify and maintain their loyalty. That meant he had to play exciting and extraordinary, even breathtaking, golf. A considerable number of fans attest to Tiger's ability to deliver. Responding to a website post, Evangeline Brackett writes, "He's Secretariat, and while I am not a golfer (yet?), I find it inexplicably exciting to see him play." Although Immer Chriswell claims that he is still as interested in watching tournaments even when Tiger is not playing, he does admit that "watching Tiger Woods is a thrill. He makes the unthinkable possible, he has turned clichés into realities." My mother does not even claim to be a Tiger Woods fan, but reports, "I *don't* want Tiger to win every tournament. And I *hate* to admit it, but it's just not the same when he's not playing. The spark of excitement, that potential 'explosion' is just missing."

Despite Tiger's charisma and amazing play, a question still lingers. In light of his infamous lack of interaction with galleries, how has he created and maintained a fanbase? Unlike Arnold Palmer, who was celebrated, at least in large part, *because* of his accessibility and *because* he was perceived to be one of the guys, Woods has been revered for entirely opposite reasons. Ironically, Tiger has been celebrated *because* he has been removed. He has never treated his fans as if he were anything other than their imperious King. The surprise, perhaps, has been that his fans have accepted that reality. As Sounes observes, Tiger "ignores" fans after he hits a shot and exudes "a coolness that borders on rudeness" (200). Anyone who has ever watched Tiger play can attest to these behaviors. He has seemed intent on maintaining a distance, determined not to interact.

Smiley asks a significant question at the beginning of his book: does Tiger not owe "his loyal fans a lot more love than he gave" (5)? Prior to his conversion to Tiger fan, Smiley claims that he could not understand how people "could happily root for someone who seemed to go to great pains to ignore each and every one of them" (276). According to Wann, Melnick, Russell, and Pease, however, fans can become emotionally attached even in the absence of "meaningful interaction" (79). Smiley begins to understand this when he meets Njaaga at the Dubai tournament. Flying from Kenya solely to see Tiger play, Njaaga proclaims that he wants "to connect" with the famous golfer and later reports that he experienced true connection. Based upon his observations, Smiley concludes that very few of Tiger's fans "felt his coldness" (276), counting himself among them. Reporting that Tiger had never acknowledged him directly—no eye contact, not a single smile, nor a nod during those 604 holes of observation—Smiley nonetheless asserts, "But that doesn't mean I don't know him. And with every tournament he wins, he reminds me of what can be achieved when someone does what he loves the best that he possibly can" (277). For Tiger's fans, his absolute connection to the game would seem to be enough to sustain their admiration.

Of course, a great many golf lovers have never cheered for Tiger Woods, and quite a few have openly disliked him. As Samuelsen claims, Tiger has fostered "strong opinions, both positively and negatively," even from the start of his professional career. I have met a considerable number of Tiger detractors over the years. Most of them, prior to the scandal, cited his arrogance as the cause of their antipathy. This includes Bill, who joined me when I played a round of golf at a local club. A young man in his mid- to late-twenties, very formal in his language and posture, Bill was instantly recognizable as a military guy. Indeed, he reported that he was an Air Force officer, and he also asserted that he hated Tiger because he has always been such a "jerk."

Despite the number of people who have never cheered for Tiger, many others have taken great pleasure by doing just that. Author of the infamous article "The Man. Amen." Charles Pierce documents the crowd's response, for example, as Tiger won a sudden-death playoff against the popular veteran player Tom Lehman at the 1996 Mercedes Tournament. When Woods hit an amazing shot, the crowd did not cheer for a "brief, precious slice of time in which the disbelief was sharp and palpable.... Then the cheers came, and they did not stop until he'd reached the green" (6). This young up-start had the power to sweep away old loyalties.

The infamous "loose impediment" incident of the 1999 Phoenix Open perhaps best illustrates the extreme enthusiasm of some Tiger fans. When his tee ball nestled up to a giant boulder in a desert area, Tiger asked an official to determine if the rock was "solidly embedded" ("Mediate Holds Off"). Wendy Uzelac reports that the boulder was the "size of a steamer trunk," weighing nearly a ton. Eventually, the official ruled it a "loose impediment," akin to other natural objects like leaves, twigs, and stones, so Tiger asked members of his gallery to "help him" move the boulder. As Uzelac assets, "after much heaving, pushing," a group of young men moved the rock out of Tiger's way, and other members of the gallery cheered. Although Uzelac and others express no alarm at the ruling, Phil Mushnick decries Tiger's "unnatural advantage" and disparages his fans, calling them "toadies." Granted, not all players enjoy such dedicated and demonstrative galleries. Tiger merely took advantage of their adoration.

During a great many tournaments, I have observed Tiger's enormous and enthusiastic galleries. The fans hoped to witness extraordinary golf, and Woods has often fulfilled those desires. The 2001 Bay Hill Invitational is a perfect example. I was sitting on the par-five sixth monster hole that encircles a big lake. Like the previous day, the wind was strong, full into the players' faces on the tee shot. The first twelve players I saw used an identical strategy. Trying to avoid penalties, they "bit off" less water on the tee to land the ball safely in the fairway. Their second shots were irons, again evading the lake and laying up short of the green. Most were on the green in three; some had a chance for birdie. They used their heads, thought it through, stuck with reasonable course management.

Then Woods arrived, with multitudes in tow. Although I was too far from the tee to see exactly who was hitting, it was soon obvious. Woods' drive was forty yards ahead of the others. Already in place as Tiger fans approached, and not about to surrender my spot despite a little shoving, I was in perfect position to see his second shot. Murmurs of "Is he going to go for it?" ran through the crowd. He grabbed a wood, but seemed hesitant. When he put the club back in the bag and chose an iron, a man beside me whispered, "Rats, he's going to lay up, too. Wind is just too strong." Then Woods stopped, went back to his bag, and retrieved the wood. The gallery applauded. He had not even hit the shot, but they were thrilled with his confidence and dynamism. Here was a player with heart. Woods hit the ball, hard, landing it on the green. The crowd loved it. As one fan said to his friend, "You gotta admit; he's exciting!" Indeed he has been just that.

Tiger Woods' Fans After the Scandal

Tiger sustained large and appreciative galleries and television audiences even during some fairly lengthy "slumps" in his career, most notably when he changed his swing in 2003–04. Despite that history of fan loyalty, many commentators, including Tom Tomashek, predicted that Tiger's followers would be repulsed by reports of his infidelities and would "desert" him in great numbers. As Wann, Melnick, Russell, and Pease note, some people enjoy the fall of "tall poppies," celebrities who have achieved much in their careers (88), and a considerable number of people doubtlessly relished the exposure of Tiger's secrets and his subsequent travails. Tiger's fans may not have celebrated, but some lost faith. Gwen Knapp, sports writer for the *San Francisco Chronicle*, argues that fans who "turned on" Tiger saw his infidelities as evidence that he has always been a "narcissistic jerk," and she predicts that they may never return to his galleries.

Steve Elling, commentator for CBS Sports, declares that Tiger has been the "most irrefutably crowd-pleasing player in the game" but asserts that he has become a "magnet in cleats. He attracts, he repels." The scandal clearly magnified polarized positions. That polarization became more obvious once Tiger returned to play in 2009. As Gola, Obernauer, and Siemaszko observe, some fans openly heckled Woods at Quail Hollow. Despite this example, some polls, as previously noted, indicate that many of Tiger's fans have continued to support him. Wann, Melnick, Russell, and Pease argue that highly-identified fans often search for justifications that allow them to remain loyal (89). Summing up post-scandal gallery responses, ESPN commentator Bob Harig claims that observers cheered Woods "at Augusta, Sawgrass, Pebble Beach, St. Andrews." Apparently, Woods' followers seem to have found some adequate justifications.

Of course, Tiger's faithful supporters want to see him play great golf again. Not long after Tiger's relatively successful performance at the 2010 Masters, I observed his galleries at the Players Championship. They were practically *willing* him to win. Although Tiger made the cut to play on the weekend, he was far out of contention by Sunday. Clearly in denial about the significance of an early morning tee time, two men stood near the practice putting green, discussing the odds that Tiger could prevail. One guy stated, "OK, if he shoots seven or eight under par today, he could still win. He *could* do it, you know." The other looked a bit skeptical but finally nodded, agreeing that it was "not impossible." Here is a great example of fan faith, a belief probably arising from Tiger's history of astonishing victories. The sense that "anything is possible" persisted at the first tee. Although the area had been virtually deserted moments before, the place was mobbed as Tiger's tee time approached. Everyone wanted to be in place before he arrived. His playing partner Jason Bohn, a "nobody," appeared first. When Bohn saw the throngs, he ironically thanked everyone for coming out to see him play, and the crowd laughed and then applauded, but not nearly as thunderously as when Tiger arrived.

Tiger didn't play the first few holes well; in fact, it was a clear case of butchery. The galleries seemed determined to see him perform, however, as people packed onto the amphitheater-like grassy areas surrounding the ninth green. They waited for him to do something, *anything*, spectacular. Then the golf cart drove by, and Tiger was inside. When a marshal announced that Woods had withdrawn because of a neck injury, the disappointment was palpable. As one young woman declared loudly, "Well, *that* sucks! He's the only reason I came today. Now what?" Throughout the day, even after Tiger was long gone, his presence loomed large in conversation and speculation.

Tiger did not regain his form in 2010, but his fans still did not lose faith. In early 2011 at the Arnold Palmer Invitational, Tiger continued to draw the biggest galleries on the course. In "Tiger Rocks Bay Hill Crowd," one of three feature articles presented in the Sunday Pairing Sheet, golf writer Dave Shedloski asserts that Tiger's galleries were "electrified" by Friday's round (5). Sunday's fans were just as excited. Hordes were stacked four deep, hoping to catch a glimpse of him at the practice putting area. Later, I was positioned at number three green, and I saw masses of people moving down the cart paths, coming toward me. Like a giant amoeba, the gallery flowed with seemingly singular purpose and conviction. As I left the green, I walked backwards towards the players that were actually leading the tournament, and I saw far fewer observers. At one of the greens, two marshals were talking about the crowds that had passed by them. One shook his head, commenting to the other, "All they care about is Tiger. It's amazing that they don't even seem interested in the ones who might win this thing."

Tiger did not win, of course, doubtlessly disappointing his fans. But he sparked renewed hope when he showed flashes of brilliance during the 2011 Masters. *AOL Sporting News* columnist David Whitley describes reactions to Tiger's Sunday charge: "When he rolled in the five-foot eagle putt on No. 8 to move within one shot of the lead, it sounded like a sonic boom.... Since running is not allowed at Augusta National, people scurried like ducks to see Tiger.... There's nothing like Tiger being in the hunt." Far greater numbers watched the tournament on television, and AP sports writer Chris Singleton was among them. Claiming that he was "into every stroke," Singleton thanks Tiger for making golf fun to watch again. Matt Krummel also tuned into the drama. Reporting that he slid "closer and closer to the edge of his couch," he claims that "It was as if Tiger's expanding gravitational pull was sucking me in," and he literally fell off his seat after the spectacular eagle. Then he argues that "No other golfer in the world has that effect on me (or anyone else I suspect). You may not want to admit it, but I'll bet you were sucked in too. We all were." Although many of Tiger's fans would deny that they have been "sucked in," there is little doubt of their enthusiasm.

Child Fans Before and After the Scandal

One of the most remarkable aspects of Tiger fandom is the connection that children have felt with him. Asserting that the attraction began at the very start of Woods' career, Strege compares Tiger to the "pied piper" (226). Although he likely did not intend to conjure the negative aspects of that fairy tale, Strege certainly verifies the potency of the children's attraction to Tiger. I have witnessed that attraction at every tournament I have attended. At the 2000 Bay Hill, for example, I was near a food court on the front nine, and many people were under canopies in the heat. Not there simply to eat or drink, they wanted to glimpse Woods playing through. One little boy, no more than three, wandered around waving a huge orange plastic golf club while his grandparents sat in the shade. He strolled up to me and boldly announced, "I am going to see TIGER!" I am not positive he really understood who Tiger was, but he was excited. At the 2001 Bay Hill on Sunday, I overheard a conversation between a father and his teenage son. Obviously tired and dragging, the bedraggled father shook his head, finally caving in: "Ok, Ok, we'll stay to see Tiger for a while, and then we go home." These displays of overt admiration, even adoration, could certainly be viewed as a reflection of their parents' or grandparents' affinities, just magnified because children have not yet learned to adhere to cultural expectations of decorum.

After the scandal broke, children's fervor for Tiger seems to have endured. If children's emotional ties to Woods have been simply a reflection of their parents' support, at least some adult fans have apparently felt little discomfort in continuing to show their enthusiasm in the presence of their children. Greg Wiseman, for example, was not the least troubled as he geared up for the 2011 U.S. Open by watching clips of Tiger's most "extraordinary and unbelievable" shots with his son. As Wiseman asserts, their celebration was "magical." Although Wiseman never addresses the issue of whether he should celebrate a disgraced sports figure's achievements with his son, ESPN sports columnist Bill Simmons does just that. He describes how his very young son had never shown the least interest in watching golf, until the 2011 Masters. When the little guy yelled "*AGAIN!*" several times, Simmons reran Tiger's eagle putt over and over. Unapologetic for allowing his son to admire Tiger's skills, Simmons declares that no one is perfect, that people can learn from their mistakes, that they have not really won until they have fought back. He continues, "I want my son to know that great athletes are meant to be appreciated, not emulated," and then declares that he will be his son's role model.

At the 2010 Players Championship, I observed quite a few parents who made no attempt to stifle their children's enthusiasm for Tiger. Just after getting past the ticket gates, I was walking in the midst of the masses, moving toward the course. Suddenly, four children, from about four to six years old, raced ahead of their parents. Clearly golf tournament veterans, the kids ran to the box that held the pairing sheets, but only one was tall enough to retrieve the document. Hopping up and down and screaming Tiger's name, they impatiently waited for a father-reader to arrive. They were interested in seeing only one player. Later, when Tiger's tee time approached, one little girl and her father waited at the practice putting area. Whining loudly, she asked, "But *where* is he? *Why* isn't he here?" When Tiger failed to practice his putting, she was clearly upset. Even later, when Tiger's group was approaching the second green, a little boy looked anxious as he wormed his way through the crowd to get close to the ropes. His mother hung back beside me, explaining, "Tiger is his favorite, by far. Tommy doesn't even care if he plays well. He just wants to see Tiger play." Long after Tiger withdrew from the tournament and left the course, I witnessed a scene remarkably reminiscent of the 2000 Bay Hill. An extremely tall man, presumably the daddy, held his tiny son's hand as they walked around the course. The little guy carried a stuffed animal, chanting "Tiger, Tiger, Tiger." His father just grinned.

Future of Tiger Woods' Fandom

Children probably do not understand why Tiger might not deserve their adoration, because their parents might not feel comfortable discussing the scandal or do not believe that Woods' personal life is an issue. Revelations of his infidelities did nonetheless cause some of Tiger's fans to question their dedication and flee. Others, however, have remained loyal. That loyalty continued to be tested in 2011 when Tiger was sidelined because of injuries. Then, when he finally returned to play, his game seemed to be in shambles. Although he comments about sports fandom in general, Michael Elliott's assertions certainly apply to Tiger's hardcore fans as well: "We fans like to describe our passion in religious terms.... you give yourself up to something bigger than yourself, not just because your individuality is rendered insignificant in the mass of the crowd, but because being a fan involves faith." He adds that "belief is all."

A considerable number of fans provide testament to the depths of their belief. In a satirical article, Timothy Miller claims that he really is on the path to shedding his identity as a Tiger fan but also admits that he has "oscillated, vacillated, hesitated, dithered, wavered and just been plain old indecisive" on his journey to abstinence. Posting a response to Wiseman's article, Judy Knight offers most convincing evidence of her dedication:

> I will never, ever give up on Tiger. I never even watched golf until my husband said you have to come watch this young boy play back in 1997. I haven't missed a tournament since that he has played in. I pray for him to do good again. I have never seen the shots this man has made by anyone before or since, but I haven't given up on seeing him come back.

Hers is true faith, belief that may defy reason but nonetheless is intensely felt.

As these commentaries and observations would indicate, Tiger Woods continues to rouse extraordinary fan support. He has been a golfing phenomenon, and many fans have adopted him and cheered him on to many victories and even in defeat. Such was the case with Arnold Palmer, but few other golfers in history have enjoyed that kind of fanbase. Barkow asserts that the emergence of a superstar golfer is an infrequent "happening" and adds that "Golf people understand that and are willing to wait for the next messiah" (214). Despite Barkow's unfortunate hyperbole, many people who love golf have seen Tiger Woods as that once-in-a-lifetime "happening." Using less elevated language, former NBC sports executive Dick Ebersol discusses why Woods has been so compelling, claiming that "People want to watch history. And Tiger is history" (qtd. in Rosaforte).

I know that I have seen history as I have joined Tiger's galleries: when he won Bay Hill for the third time even though he was retching his way around the course because of food poisoning, when he won the 2005 British Open shortly after his father died, even when he fell short at the 2010 U.S. Open. However, one of the most memorable moments I have witnessed had nothing to do with tournament play. The magic moment involved three golf fans. As I sat near the midpoint of a hole during the Disney Classic, I watched a number of spectators getting into position because Tiger was on his way. Among them, I noticed an African American woman and her two children: a boy, about five years old, and a girl, about four. The kids busied themselves, with matchbox trucks and cars, a little way off. Their mother was watchful but let them play. Tiger's group was next. Gathering the children, the woman steered them to the ropes, right next to me. She said to them, "OK, *this* is *it*. This is something I want you to remember your whole life!" They sat quietly, waiting for the event, for the "giant" man to pass. The little girl's eyes widened as Woods came into view. Then she exclaimed, "Momma — he looks like *us*!" The mother smiled, looking at her children and said, "Yeah, I know." This mother no doubt wanted her children to witness history. Indeed, they will likely never forget that moment — not because they watched, but because they were *part* of history. There is little doubt that they will be Tiger fans for life.

NOTES

1. The word "fan" evolved from "fanatic," meaning "possessed" or "frenzied," most commonly associated with religious zealotry by the early 1500s. "Fan" became part of sports vocabulary in late 19th century America, initially describing baseball enthusiasts. As these derivations indicate, a fan has always been viewed as someone who feels, and often demonstrates, extreme fervor.

2. Portions of this chapter, primarily on-course observations gathered prior to 2008, have been reprinted here. They originally appeared in *Horsehide, Pigskin, Oval Tracks and Apple Pie: Essays on Sports and American Culture*, James A. Vlasich, ed., and have been reprinted by permission of McFarland, Box 611, Jefferson, NC 28640, www.mcfarland pub.com.

WORKS CITED

Anthony, Michael. "Golf Tip: The Tiger Woods Appeal." *Golf Digest*. 24 Sept. 2000. Web. 30 Sept. 2000.

"Arnie's Army." *Leaderboard: Glossary*. n.d. Web. 25 July 2011.

Barkow, Al. *The History of the PGA Tour*. New York: Doubleday, 1989. Print.

Brackett, Evangeline. Abuzz Message Board. *Abuzz*. July 2000. Web. 23 July 2000.

Callahan, Tom. "Palmer in His Prime: As Arnold Turns 80, It's Time to Savor the Skill and Charisma that Changed Golf." *Golf Digest*. Sept. 2009. Web. 14 Feb. 2011.

Chriswell, Immer. "Tiger Woods: Does the Honda Classic Miss Him?" *Bleacher Report*. 4 Mar. 2011. Web. 15 Mar. 2011.

"Do You Suffer from Tiger Overkill: All Woods All the Time?" *Golf Digest*. Oct. 2000. Web. 12 Oct. 2000.

Elling, Steve. "Love Him or Hate Him, Tiger Occupying Perfect Purgatory." *CBS Sports*. 27 Apr. 2011. Web. 30 Apr. 2011.

Elliott, Michael. "Hopelessly Devoted." *Time*. 30 May 2005. Web. 17 Aug. 2011.

Gola, Hank, Michael Obernauer, and Corky Siemaszko. "Tiger Woods Gets Heckled for the First Time since Comeback at Quail Hollow Championship in Charlotte." *New York Daily News*. 30 Apr. 2010. Web. 13 May 2010.

Gorant, Jim. "1958 Masters: Arnie's Army Is Born." *Sports Illustrated.com*. 20 Aug. 2008. Web. 25 May 2011.

Guest, Larry. *Arnie: Inside the Legend*. Orlando: Tribune Publishing, 1993. Print.

Harig, Bob. "Let's Stop Rehashing Tiger Woods' Fall." *ESPN Sports*. 22 Nov. 2010. Web. 13 Dec. 2010.

Knapp, Gwen. "Knapp: Tiger's Spin Lost on Fans He Won't Win Back." *San Francisco Chronicle*. 30 Nov. 2010. Web. 20 Jan. 2011.

Krummel, Matt. "Tiger Woods: Power Ranking the Young Guns Who Could Keep Tiger from No. 1." *Bleacher Report*. 20 Apr. 2011. Web. 24 Apr. 2011

Langer, Gary. "Poll: Tiger Woods Censure Eases, But It's a Bogey for Golf." *ABC News*. 19 Feb. 2010. Web. 29 Apr. 2010.

McCarthy, Michael. "Tiger's Favorability Showing Record Decline." *USA Today*. 14 Dec. 2009. Web. 21 Sept. 2011.

"Mediate Holds off Leonard, Woods for First Win Since 1993." *Golf Today*. n.d. Web. 21 June 2011.

Miller, Timothy. "FORUM: Path to No Longer Being a Tiger Woods Fan." *North County Times-Californian*. 27 June 2010. Web. 3 July 2011.

Mushnick, Phil. "Tiger's 'Pals' are Toadies." *New York Post*. 3 Dec. 2009. Web. 12 Feb. 2011.

Pierce, Charles. "The Man. Amen." *Gentleman's Quarterly*. April 1997. *Gentleman's Quarterly*. Web. 12 Apr. 2010.

Rosaforte, Tim. "The Power of Tiger: Tiger Continues to Put Golf on the Front Page." *Golf Digest*. 22 June 2000. Web. 18 Aug. 2000.

Sampson, Curt. *The Eternal Summer: Palmer, Nicklaus, and Hogan in 1960, Golf's Golden Year*. Dallas: Taylor, 1992. Print.

Samuelsen, Jamie. "Why Is Tiger Woods So Much More Compelling than Rory McIlroy?" *Detroit Free Press*. 20 June 2011. Web. 22 June 2011.

Shedloski, Dave. "Tiger Rocks Bay Hill Crowd." *Daily News and Pairings: Arnold Palmer Invitational Tournament*. 26 Mar. 2011. Print.

Simmons, Bill. "The Gift of Tiger Woods." *ESPN*. 11 Apr. 2011. Web. 12 Apr. 2011.

Singleton, Chris. "Tiger Is Still Golf's Top Star." *[Lafourche Parish, LA] Daily Comet*. 14 Apr. 2011. Web. 18 Apr. 2011.

Smiley, Bob. *Follow the Roar: Tailing Tiger for All 604 Holes of His Most Spectacular Season*. New York: HarperCollins, 2008. Print.

Sounes, Howard. *The Wicked Game: Arnold Palmer, Jack Nicklaus, Tiger Woods, and the Story of Modern Golf*. New York: William Morrow, 2004. Print.

Strege, John. *Tiger: A Biography of Tiger Woods*. New York: Broadway Books, 1997. Print.

Tomashek, Tom. "Tiger Mania Lingers, But for How Long?" *Newark Post*. 8 Feb. 2011. Web. 12 Feb. 2011.

Uzelac, Wendy. "Marking the 10th Anniversary of the Most Famous Incident in Rules of Golf History." *US Golf Association*. 10 Jan. 2010. Web. 23 Apr. 2011.

Van Leeuwen, Linda, Shayne Quick, and Kerry Daniel. "The Sport Spectator Satisfaction Model: A Conceptual Framework for Understanding the Satisfaction of Spectators." *Sports Management Review* 5 (2002): 99–128. Print.

Van Riper, Tom. "The Most Disliked People in Sports." *Forbes: Sports Business*. 27 Jan. 2011. Web. 20 Feb. 2011.

Wann, Daniel, Merrill Melnick, Gordon Russell, and Dale Pease. *Sports Fans: The Psychology and Social Impact of Spectators*. New York: Routledge, 2001. Print.

Whitley David. "Missed Opportunities Leave Tiger Woods Unsatisfied." *AOL Sporting News*. 10 Apr. 2011. Web. 12 Apr. 2011.

Wiseman, Greg. "Tiger Woods, Our Hopes and Our Doubts Gear Up for the 2011 United States Open." *Bleacher Report*. 28 May 2011. Web. 24 June 2011.

Celebrations and Conniptions in the "Gentleman's" Game

Donna J. Barbie

Since its inception, golf has been called the "gentleman's" game. That label has doubtlessly perpetuated the conviction that golf is sexist and elitist, but some argue that the sport has evolved from its discriminatory origins. Others contend, however, that the supposed change is not so clear because all golfers must be gentlemen, no matter their sex or class. The word "gentleman" entered the English lexicon during the Middle Ages, but the concept of gentleman was not fully delineated until the 16th century. Born of the landed gentry, a gentleman was blessed with sufficient wealth that protected him from the necessity of having to work. He socialized with people of equal, or higher, station and occupied himself by hunting and other suitable pastimes. Great Britain gave birth to the game of golf during the same period the ideal gentleman was being established. Because only gentlemen belonged to links clubs, golfers and gentlemen were essentially an identity, bound by the same codes. A gentleman, for example, always spoke properly, never using words that sullied his reputation or called his status into question.

Appropriate diction has typically served to signal identity and social position, especially for the higher classes, but nonverbal behaviors offer even more, and often richer, information. As Ray Birdwhistle, Albert Mehrabian, and other researchers argue, nonverbal cues account for as much as sixty-five to ninety percent of all meanings sent and received in face-to-face communication. Nonverbal information "centers" include appearance, posture and body orientation, as well as gestures, eye contact, and facial expression. Clusters of nonverbal behaviors often coalesce into unambiguous affect displays indicating a person's emotional state, as well as the intensity of those emotions.

72

Such representational displays often arise at critical moments when someone is overwhelmed with joy, sadness, anger, or disgust. Although a sudden flood of emotion often prevents individuals from hiding or modifying felt emotion, pioneering researchers in nonverbal communication Paul Ekman and Wallace Friesen argue that people can and do learn to shape affect displays. Most adults become adept at deintensification and masking, as well as other affect-management techniques, for a variety of purposes, including aligning with cultural expectations.

Nonverbal Cues in the "Gentleman's Game"

In light of the necessity of displaying "correct" nonverbal cues, golfers of the past rigorously governed their appearance and behaviors. They dressed appropriately and presented themselves with decorum, which included managing affect displays. Even under the most stressful circumstance, they could not reveal extreme emotion. Despite the passage of centuries, the gentlemanly code persists for professional golfers, as they are expected to "respect" the game by being thoroughly courteous and, of course, never out of control. Oliver Brown, commentator for the online United Kingdom newspaper *The Telegraph*, writes that Bobby Jones, founder of the Masters and the Augusta National Golf Course, prized gentlemanly behavior. The back of every Masters pairing sheet bears Jones' conviction that "In golf, customs of etiquette and decorum are just as important as rules governing play." The commentary continues with an admonition: "Excessive demonstration by a player is not proper." As Jones emphasizes, "proper" golfers are never "excessive."

Some of golf's most revered professionals, Arnold Palmer, Jack Nicklaus, Gary Player, and Tom Watson were gentlemen on the course, even in the most trying circumstances. Although they celebrated good shots and agonized over missed opportunities, their displays were restrained. Contemporary players Jim Furyk, Steve Stricker, and Davis Love III have "respected" the game as well. Spectators following them on the course or watching them on television can verify the appropriateness of their responses. Photographs that have captured key moments during their play, such as sinking a long putt, attest to each player's self-possession. One oft-used photo of Furyk, for example, was taken during a Ryder Cup team competition, when golfers' emotions run very high (Chaney), and a similar photo portrays a victorious Stricker (Rosaforte). In these shots, Stricker and Furyk are obviously energized by making their putts, as evidenced by smiles and raised arms. When isolated from the rest of the body, the arm gestures might appear to indicate flooded emotion. Other nonverbal cues, however, reveal that they are properly restrained. Both players display relaxed postures, their shoulders down, and their necks show no evidence of unmanageable intensity. Perhaps even more importantly, both players' faces disclose their happiness, but reasonably so. Their eyes glint with pleasure, and they are smiling, but their mouths remain closed. As these photos illustrate, even when celebrating significant moments of success, Furyk and Stricker have adhered to the rules of appropriate decorum.

Granted, golf has had its share of "bad boys" storming around the professional circuit. Sports journalist Al Barkow contends that "Golf has a way of exciting the temper of men, especially when they are put under the pressure of high-grade competition." He adds that some have even shown "vituperative" personalities and tempers (115). Howard Sounes, author of *The Wicked Game,* names a few of those characters, including Tommy Bolt, also known as Terrible Tommy or Thunder Bolt. According to Sounes, Tommy, a contemporary of Arnold Palmer, entertained galleries with powerful driving and "displays of ferocious temper." He routinely tossed clubs and once smashed an iron nearly nine inches into a damp fairway (39). Although the golfing world has typically disdained "bad boys" and applauded players who show restraint, the Professional Golf Association has also faced a dilemma in its quest to engage more people in following, and playing, the sport. For golf aficionados, high quality shot-making and close competitions create suspense and excitement, but many fans of other sports have long believed that watching golf, a game reliant on absolute physical control being played by gentlemen, is numbingly boring.

An Unconstrained Tiger in Triumph and Frustration

The PGA's fan-boredom problem seemed to have disappeared when Tiger Woods rose to dominate the links in the mid–1990s. Unlike the majority of players, Tiger was not constrained. In the heat of competition, he pumped his fist and grimaced. He quite literally roared. Despite these ungentlemanly behaviors, Tiger was celebrated by those inside and outside the golfing world for nearly fifteen years, no doubt because he was largely responsible for an enormous surge in viewership and tremendous increases in tournament purses. Tiger's popularity rose not simply because of spectacular shots and even more spectacular wins, but also, at least for some observers, because he was *not* controlled, because he has *not* always been a gentleman. As Frankb03 verbalizes in a post to *Bettors Chat Forum,* "Personally, I like when Tiger displays his emotion.... I prefer Tiger over the other robots that play the game." Tiger was certainly not robotic on his way to winning dozens of tournaments, including the most majors since Jack Nicklaus, and many spectators were entranced.

Without doubt, Tiger Woods has delivered some of the most memorable triumphant moments in sports. *AOL Sporting News* columnist David Whitley admits, with some shame, that he is still a "Tiger-holic." Writing in defense of his addiction, Whitley declares that Woods "can make golf deliriously exciting." Mike Imrem of the *Daily Herald* concurs. As he notes, "Let's face it, without Tiger Woods the PGA Tour is just golf. With him it's show business — for better and worse." Robert Lusetich, author of *Unplayable*, offers numerous descriptions of Tiger's "dramatic, theatrical" play (49). Detailing the last moments of Tiger's 2009 Bay Hill Invitational victory, as he sank a lengthy putt in near darkness, Lusetich declares that flashbulbs lit up the green as Tiger "struck a pose that would lead every newspaper's sports page — if not front page — the next day" (49). The phrase "struck a pose" hardly captures the intensity of Tiger's physical response to that, or any, win. This man was excitable and thus exciting to watch. Instead of maintaining the sometimes eerily flat affect of his press conferences, Woods was unconstrained on the course and never showed any inclination to change.

PGA authorities, as well as those who thrived as a result of Tiger's successes, may not have exerted themselves to convince him of the necessity of toning down his displays, however. When he hit a spectacular shot, Tiger's emotion was transparent. Here, finally, was the real person, showing the fire that drove him, the passion that fascinated and exhilarated observers. Photographs of Tiger's celebrations contrast sharply with those of Furyk and Stricker. Although still photographs may not illustrate the mental and physical control required for successful execution of a shot, they have often succeeded in capturing Tiger at the instant of triumph, showing a completely flooded affect. Over and over, they reveal Tiger's tensed body, his raised hand and clenched fist, and his extraordinarily animated face. Here was potent felt emotion. One of the most famous sequences of stills was taken during the 2008 U.S. Open. After he chipped in, on his quest to qualify for a playoff, Tiger's emotion was manifest. As the final shot of the series reveals, he is charged by adrenaline, springing off the ground, a mass of taut muscle and sinew. His face is completely alive, filled with power and elation. This was no gentleman who, regardless of stress or circumstances, remained under control.

Other contemporary players, even the most "gentlemanly" ones, have occasionally shown enthusiastic celebrations, as Jim Furyk did when he won the 2010 Fed Ex Cup, but the majority have managed to avoid exposing extreme frustration and anger. Not Tiger. He has not filtered emotional responses during great triumph, nor has he suppressed displays of anguish, anger, or exasperation. When a shot failed to rise to his standard, Tiger reacted, seemingly without restraint. According to Tom Callahan, author of *His Father's Son*, Tiger carries his father's passion "gene," causing him to "overload" when he hits a bad shot (113). As Callahan notes, Tiger's passion was often evident on the course, but his commentary offers no description of how "overload" has translated into particular behaviors. Callahan, an ostensible apologist, instead employs a word that conjures images of circuits or fuses, inanimate objects that have no volition when too much power courses through a system. John Strege, author of *Tiger: A Biography of Tiger Woods,* supports the possibility that Woods may have little choice in his on-course tantrums. As Strege recounts, Tiger was disqualified from a junior tournament for tossing a club into the air and failing to catch it before it hit the green. Tiger's mother perceived the ruling as unfair despite his having clearly broken the rules. Rather than chastising him for his show of temper, she purportedly told him that he should use his most important weapons, his golf clubs, to "speak" for him (24). Apparently, Tiger learned that lesson well.

Whatever the reasons, Woods never trained himself to stay within the constraints of gentlemanly decorum when he was disappointed with his play. He grimaced, growled, and gnashed his teeth. He often swung clubs wildly and even threw them. Tiger's anger and frustration are exemplified in nearly as many photos as those of celebration. Brent Kelley, a "guide" for the on-line website About.com, provides almost a dozen photos of Tiger throwing clubs, proclaiming in the five-sentence text that readers should not mimic Woods' actions. Even those who might defend Tiger's club-throwing as a signal of his intensity and passion for the game must admit that such behavior is hazardous. Perhaps the potential dangers of the game, of the clubs themselves, as well as the balls set into motion by those clubs, necessitated golf's code of etiquette at its inception. No one, including a few senior players, could persuade the pre-scandal Woods to curb his displays, and even hefty fines for clearly unacceptable behaviors failed to provide that impetus.

Fan Reactions to the Unconstrained Tiger

Since Tiger showed little restraint on the course, people who have watched him play witnessed exuberant celebrations, as well as perilous tantrums. Yet, throngs followed him on the course, and the networks broadcast his play disproportionally to other players, even when he was not in contention. Tiger was compelling, after all. As seen in the background of the previously mentioned final photo of the 2008 U.S. Open series, the crowd goes wild, astonished and clearly intoxicated by Tiger's achievement and emotionality. Sports writer Bob Smiley comments frequently in his work *Follow the Roar* about the connection between Tiger's displays and their affect on galleries. Describing Tiger's lengthy winning putt at the 2008 Bay Hill tournament,

Smiley writes, "The moment he hits it, the crowd starts to cheer, sounding like a distant wave that won't stop breaking.... As the putt banks to the right, the cheers from those with better views continue to swell and we take our cues from them, screaming the ball down toward the cup" (130–1). Smiley later claims that "If there were only a way to harness the energy released around that green, it would power the city of Orlando for a week" (130–1). This player, like few others, was capable of exhilarating galleries.

Because Tiger has historically hit more good shots than bad and won so many tournaments, many have overlooked the bad-boy tantrums in order to witness great golf and to share in the celebrations. Such is not true of everyone, however. When I traveled to California to walk Pebble Beach to witness the 2010 U.S. Open in person, I also spent a few mornings at local courses. One day, I played with a man and his teenage son, and I asked the young man what professional golfers he admired most. He instantly said "Tiger" and then mentioned a few others, including Phil Mickelson. His father agreed, added other names, and then stated that his brother, who attends tournaments and avidly watches golf on television, refuses to watch Tiger. When I asked why, the man stated that his brother could not abide Tiger's fits of pique. He would rather not watch his favorite sport than subject himself to those displays.

This man's brother has not been the only person who recoiled from Tiger's excessive demonstrations. According to Callahan, Nick Price took Tiger to task for his behaviors at the 2000 U.S. Open, declaring that if Woods had "enough control" over his emotions to play the game well, he should be able to keep himself in check even after bad shots (112–3). Rick Reilly, an award-winning writer for ESPN's *The Magazine*, joins the small chorus of early critics when he proclaims that Woods was at his worst at Turnberry in 2009, when the player acted out two days of "Tiger Tantrums." Reilly concludes the article by noting that Tiger was "the most talented golfer in history," but then adds, "I just thought we'd be over the conniptions by now." Employing language dear to the game, golf blogger Lawrence Donegan argues that Tiger's behaviors were "disrespectful to the game," expressing hope that someone would tell Tiger that such outbursts are unacceptable. Reacting to Donegan's blog, Jingothai writes that it has been "an open secret ... that Tiger can behave like a petulant child." These commentaries were in the minority, however; most kept silent as they celebrated Woods' victories.

Pledge After the Scandal

After Thanksgiving 2009, everything changed. When the high drama of multiple infidelities surfaced, his carefully shaped public image disintegrated. In early February 2010, a story that had long been held from publication appeared in *Vanity Fair*. The spread included a series of Annie Leibovitz photographs. Known for her abilities to penetrate and reveal, Leibovitz produced "edgy" shots of an unambiguously ungentlemanly Tiger. On the cover of the magazine, Tiger appears, bare-chested, heavily muscled, with beads of sweat on his torso. He glowers, staring straight at the camera, challenging the voyeur/viewer. In no way does he resemble a gentleman golfer. Instead he looks like a thug, wearing a prison-wear knit cap, engaging in weight-lifting, just like so many prisoners whose "time" is spent in endless, narcissistic body sculpting.

As these kinds of images conjoined with so many memories and illustrations of his behaviors during play, Tiger's negative on-course behaviors suddenly became an integral part of his bad-boy "storyline." No longer were his tantrums an occasional "minor" unpleasantness. These displays suddenly helped to define the fallen man. In an attempt to resurrect something of his life and career, Tiger offered a televised apology in February 2010, marking his first public appearance since the damaging stories had broken. During that apology, Tiger stated that he intended to continue to play, noting, "When I do return, I need to make my behavior more respectful of the game." Alan Shipnuck, writer for *Sports Illustrated*, focuses on the word "respect" in his commentary, claiming that Tiger had always played the "gentleman's game in a controlled rage." Shipnuck later declares that Woods had suddenly been confronted with the reality that he was "not exempt from golf's code of conduct." Although one might argue that Tiger's rages were not necessarily "controlled," Shipnuck's prediction that Tiger was "on notice" to change proved absolutely accurate.

Shaken by the scandal and resulting media frenzy, constrained by his own pledge, Tiger Woods was subsequently forced to try to redefine himself, especially through modifying nonverbal cues during play. Using different strategies from what had worked in the past, he clearly needed to interact with galleries more freely and to ameliorate, even eliminate, emotional outbursts. One might speculate that Furyk and Stricker, as well as other gentlemanly players, have controlled emotional displays because of inherently less intense personalities. Such an assumption would seem incorrect, however, because both men have been tenacious and hugely successful in a very competitive environment. Another possibility might explain how they have managed to maintain composure even in extraordinary circumstances. Perhaps they, like so many players of the past, have suppressed extreme representational displays through discipline and practice.

For more than a decade, Tiger's passion for competition was manifest, often revealed in unacceptable behaviors. If he were to pursue behavior modification, some very important questions lingered. Could Tiger change engrained actions and exert his legendary will to conform to the gentleman's code? Although interacting with galleries would probably be relatively easy, could he train himself to curb or eliminate "excessive" displays? Altering seemingly instinctive responses during competitions could certainly prove far more difficult. Take, for example, people who have changed their accents, another learned nonverbal behavior. These people typically establish new vocal patterns by expending great effort. Desired results come from practice and continued vigilance. Very often, however, even after the new voice seems to be the norm, many "reformed" speakers revert to old accents when they are tired or angry or under a great deal of stress. Tiger's emotional displays have been like those accents, his norm.

Other questions loomed even larger. If Tiger could transform his on-course actions, from representational displays to consciously shaped presentational displays, by will and vigilance, would he still be able to perform to previous levels? As well, would flattening his affect, to reflect the restraint expected of all gentlemen golfers, diminish or even eradicate Tiger's fire and passion, the very qualities that people have craved and celebrated? In an interview that occurred before he was dismissed as Tiger's caddie, Steve Williams expresses skepticism about whether Woods could ever succeed in such an elemental change. Tiger's passion, Williams claims, has been one of his greatest assets. He also argues that showing anger has not only been Tiger's mechanism for expelling fury, but it is also Tiger's "makeup.... It's always going to be the same; that's the way it is" (Lusetich 183). Shipnuck concurs that this transformation would be "Easier said than done." How correct he and Williams have been.

Disastrous Return to the Masters

Tiger Woods' hiatus from golf ended at the 2010 Masters. During a pre-tournament press conference, Tiger reinforced the message of his intent to show more "respect" for the game. When asked what changes he would make, Woods responded, "I'm actually going to try and obviously not get as hot when I play.... I made a conscious decision to try and tone down my negative outbursts.... Just trying to be more respectful of the game and acknowledge the fans like I did today." These comments, which were doubtlessly carefully crafted in anticipation of such a question and delivered in a moment of calm, imply that Woods was aware of the importance of nonverbal cues on the course. He confirmed that his negative "outbursts" had been contentious and signaled his understanding that behavior modifications arise from "conscious decision." Signaling his realization that transformation would not be easy, Woods used some form of the word "try" three times in a few short sentences.

During the press conference, Tiger also recognized a common source of celebratory and frustration behaviors. He remarked, "But then again, when I'm not as hot, I'm not going to be as exuberant either. I can't play one without the other, and ... consequently I'm sure my positive outbursts will be calmed down, as well." Here he verbalized a most important quandary. If Tiger could tame the negative outbursts, which he seemed to understand he must, would his passion dissipate or disappear altogether? In addition, would his game, without the "heat," rise to his and everyone else's expectations?

Woods' nonverbal cues, especially affect displays, were indeed a center of much commentary before, during, and after the Masters. Callahan notes that he showed up in sunglasses, speculating that Woods did so to protect himself from scrutiny (229). That protection may not have been necessary, as the patrons were very receptive. ESPN broadcaster Mike Tirico states that Woods was trying to "remake his image" by being "friendly with the fans, his fellow golfers and even the press." People everywhere, even as far away as India, were fed information about Tiger's behavior during the Masters. According to the *Times of India*, "he initially engaged with the fans at every opportunity. For the first two rounds, Woods continually tipped his cap to acknowledge his supporters, repeatedly saying 'Thank you'" ("Tiger Struggles"). Although many other commentators offered similar praise for these transformations, some skeptics noted that interacting with patrons should not really have been such a strain in the first place.

Despite a few nay-sayers, Tiger clearly achieved some success in reformation during the first two days of the tournament. Unfortunately, he also displayed several fits of pique when good play deserted him on the weekend. After he hit one bad shot, he grimaced and spun to the side, exasperated. He seemed inclined to throw his club. Although Tiger was obviously trying to contain his fury and curb his behaviors, he also swore loudly, "Tiiiiiigerrrrrr, you SUCK.... God Dammmmmmit!" As might be anticipated, Tiger was ripe for criticism. Mike Cormack of Sportsnet, for example, stated that the "new, kinder-gentler Tiger is a work in progress," claiming that he might have forgotten his promise because he "sure looked and sounded like the same old Tiger on the course." CBS lead analyst Jim Nantz leveled the harshest condemnation. In an appearance on *Mike and the Mad Dog*, hosted by Mike Francesa, Nantz expressed his disappointment that Woods had failed to live up to his pledge. Although Nantz's criticisms primarily centered on the use of profanity, he and others also chastised Woods for untoward behaviors.

All of this coverage fueled a storm of responses. When Tom Weir reported on Nantz's comments in his *USA Today* column, nearly six hundred readers responded. Many attacked Nantz for being hypocritical, based upon his purported adultery. Some contributors attempted to deflect the criticism, including Tbone5656, who asks, "Can we please leave this man alone and let the majority of us who could not care less about his anger on the course enjoy watching him play?" Despite Tbone5656's plea, many respondents agree that Tiger's behaviors were unacceptable. Maxie, for instance, writes, "I don't expect him to smile on bad shots but he is just a spoiled baby and pouts if he's not winning." White Shadow admits that "Yes he slipped a couple of times" but nonetheless contends Tiger had indeed improved, citing that "You could see on numerous occasions that he held back from any kind of outburst." Emphasizing a critical word in Tiger's promise, one which seemed to have escaped Nantz's notice, White Shadow insists that Tiger said he would "try to improve and he is!!!!!!!" If White Shadow appears adamant in defense of Woods, the use of seven exclamation points certainly confirms that perception.

In apparent agreement with White Shadow and other apologists, ESPN's Stephanie Wei reiterates that Tiger pledged to *try* to change, explaining that he was engaged in a process that would take time. Tapping into Tiger's declared reconnection to his Buddhist upbringing, Wei observes that Woods had shown more restraint in his play, his celebratory displays toned down and his frustration more contained. She argues that "this Tiger stopped himself" from throwing clubs and stomping about, but she also admitted that he showed "less poise and composure" as the week progressed when "mental fatigue caught up" with him. It seemed that Tiger, who was almost never off-camera, struggled with his mission to reform, and people watched and judged freely.

Another Tiger incident during the 2010 Masters week prompted additional debate. In a post-tournament interview with CBS sports analyst Peter Kostis, Tiger failed to capitalize on a perfect opportunity to advance his reimaging. Kostis asked him to put the week into perspective. Woods, who finished tied for fourth place, stated that it had not been good. Elaborating on missed shots and his inability to meet his own expectations, Woods called the tournament "unsuccessful," declaring that he "didn't get the job done." Not only did he sound peevish, but he looked irritated, even angry. He frowned and pursed his lips; his arms remained crossed tightly across his chest. This was not a man grateful to be back on the course playing his beloved sport.

Hundreds of commentators feasted on Woods' interview, many noting his nonverbal behaviors. Shannon Bell, for example, refers to Woods sardonically as "pal," claiming that he acted as if he were owed the win. In Bell's judgment, Woods had earned no redemption, because he had shown no humility. Sports columnist Tim Kawakami agrees. As he argues, Woods' week-end actions in general, and the Kostis interview in particular, signaled that Tiger had not changed. Kawakami adds, "Pressure reveals who you really are and ... we saw ... who Tiger is.... He's a golfer, and not a charming one ... and when he didn't win, he was furious." Mike Lopresti, columnist for *USA Today*, penned a satiric piece that offers several short letters or blogs Tiger had purportedly written during his Masters experience. One is addressed to the Augusta patrons: "I tried to be appreciative. I tried to be respectful, most of the time, anyway.... This isn't going to be easy. Sometimes, my game showed it. My face showed it. So did my voice and vocabulary. You're probably wondering where I go from there. Me too." As these commentaries reveal, Tiger Woods was on display and had clearly failed to convince everyone that he was a new man, or even a person intent on remaking himself.

Kostis, who provided the most extensive analysis of the interview and its ramifications, describes what Woods should have said in those few critical moments. As Kostis notes, "The 'New Tiger' could have talked about how much the fans' support meant to him, how the Masters is only a first step in a long road back, and how he tried his best to win but came up short," adding that if he had, "Tiger would have been golden." Tiger didn't say any of those things, and he came out leaden.

Although one of Kostis' questions garnered far less scrutiny than other portions of the interview, the query was critical to Tiger's effort at transformation. Kostis first asserted that there is a "fine line ... between controlling your emotions and eliminating them." Then he asked Tiger if it would take some time to "control" his emotions and yet "not eliminate them on the golf course" as he pursued change (Woods, Tiger Interview). This reporter clearly understood the connection between Tiger's passionate play and affect displays on the course. Perhaps not unexpectedly, Tiger seemed completely oblivious to myriad redemptive possibilities this question offered him. He could have emphasized the difficulty of modifying deep-seated behaviors. He might have repeated his intention to keep trying, acknowledging that he would likely backslide again. And most of all, he could have connected with the viewers by showing some vulnerability and even asking for more time to achieve these important changes.

Unfortunately, he responded with, "I think people are making way too much of a big deal of this thing." This thing? Clearly, Tiger did not understand, in his immediate disappointment of not winning the tournament, the enormity of "this thing." Obviously, he did not comprehend that he had actually invited this scrutiny when he initiated the discussion about "this thing" of "respecting the game" not once, but twice, in very public venues. Certainly, he did not grasp any of these realities. Once again, Kostis' later analysis is insightful. He bemoans Tiger's failure to "open up," but he also softens the criticism by asking for patience. As he writes, "Change takes time. Let's give him some." Clearly, Kostis understood the magnitude of Tiger's pledge and was willing to afford him some time to retrain.

Although Tiger played relatively well during the Masters, he actually set back the effort to remake himself. He verbalized his intentions to reform, promising to try to change and to earn redemption through action, but his behaviors indicated that he failed to understand the difficulty of altering such a wide spectrum of behaviors. Nor did he seem to have an idea or plan of how to effect those changes. One might claim, and perhaps justifiably, that Tiger thought that he could appear before the masses, speak a few words of apology to signal his remorse, and then just revert to his regal, removed, and ungentlemanly ways once the "storm" had ended.

Woods attempted to recapture those evanescent Masters-week opportunities when he later posted some of the "right" comments to his website blog. He exclaims that the fans were "absolutely incredible" and that they helped him mentally, expressing that he "did not expect," nor would he forget, the warm reception. Most importantly, he writes, "It's tough when you're in a competitive environment and in the flow of a tournament. I'm not perfect. All I can say is I'm trying to do everything I can without losing my fire and competitive spirit." In this post, Woods relays what he ought to have during the post-round interview. Unfortunately, Tiger's message was too late to be perceived as being genuine, truly springing from him, much less his heart. Instead, it seemed as if the "right" answers arrived only after others told Tiger what he should have said.

An Unsatisfying 2010 Season

Of course, the Masters marked only the beginning of a very long and difficult 2010 season. AP journalist Doug Ferguson notes that the scrutiny would not end with this first event, declaring that "Woods set himself up for failure when he pledged to tone down his temper.... This is the kind of inspection every answer, every act is going to get — maybe for the rest of the year no matter how many autographs he signs." Ferguson was entirely accurate in his predictions.

The media swarmed, reporting everything. In many pieces, discussion of Tiger's game appeared secondary to detailing his behaviors with the galleries and during play. In late April at Quail Hollow, for example, ESPN commentator Bob Harig writes that Woods walked past autograph-seekers during a practice round but stopped a moment later to sign hats and pairing sheets for twenty minutes. Harig also notes that Tiger "went out of his way to make eye contact with the fans" and "even posed for a picture with a kindergarten student." Worthy of note in Harig's comments is the phrase "went out of his way" and the word "even." Both indicate that Woods was changing his norms, but they also point out the apparent extremity of his efforts to accomplish transformation. Most players are not viewed as having performed strenuous exertions to look at the fans or to pose for pictures, but apparently that was the case with Tiger.

Also reporting at Quail Hollow, Drew Shull of *Sports Business Daily* reiterates Tiger's pledge to reform and notes that there were no outbursts on Thursday or Friday, even when his ball went sailing into the water. By early July at Aronimink, Tiger was actively engaging the galleries, according to *Inquirer* staff writer Ray Parrillo, who reports that Woods smiled and waved at children who chanted his name. By November, when Tiger played in an event in China, Peter Stone of the *Sydney Morning Herald* declares that he deserved praise because he was remarkably approachable and "amiable." Again, typical and expected behaviors reaped high praise, at least in part because they had never been part of Tiger's repertoire.

Woods' strides forward were not without struggle, however, argues *Sydney Morning Herald's* Greg Baum in "Conquering the Demons." Tiger's "demons," according to Baum, included keeping his "body language" as neutral as possible despite errant shots. Sensing that Tiger was on the verge of losing the battle as he marked the first anniversary of his last win at the Australian Masters, Baum notes that he "swished his club in self-reproval, let it slip through his hands once, dropped it once in exasperation." When his drive ended up in the rough, "he screwed up his face in anguish." In a final assessment, Baum declares that Woods "escaped with his dignity." This commentary reveals, once again, the extraordinary scrutiny Tiger faced every time he played, but even more importantly, these observations highlight the enormous difficulty of Tiger's mission to modify his actions. Others claim that Woods had outright failed at this effort in 2010. According to Associated Press correspondent Tim Dahlberg, Tiger had made little, if any, progress in keeping his pledge by the August PGA. Tallying bad behaviors of cursing and tossing clubs, Dahlberg argues that "The frustrations of a year's worth of mangled majors seemed ready to erupt all at once." By that point, Tiger was not playing his best and was not even up to playing mediocre golf. With little to celebrate and only negative feelings to control, his frustrations multiplied. As a result, Tiger clearly struggled to keep his behaviors in check, and those exertions doubtlessly interfered with his ability to play well. He seemed to have been sucked into a vicious cycle of intersecting failures.

The 2010 season ended without Tiger winning a tournament, and most of the time he was not even in contention. At the start of the 2011 season, Woods continued to struggle with maintaining proper decorum, as highlighted by the infamous Dubai spitting incident, but his play appeared promising when he again placed fourth at the Masters. Tiger executed some brilliant shots on Sunday, but the late come-from-behind bid was eventually undone by erratic shots and missed putts. Injuries sustained at the Masters then forced Woods' withdrawal from the Players Championship in May, and he did not play for the bulk of the season. When he finally returned, ostensibly fit and ready to contend, his game fell short, and he did not even qualify for the Fed Ex Cup playoffs.

Future Challenges in Altering Nonverbal Behaviors

As early as mid-season 2010, commentators speculated about what had gone wrong with Tiger's game, and those conjectures only increased the following year. Some proclaimed that Tiger had lost his concentration because of guilt and personal problems; others contended that he had lost the intimidation factor as players no longer saw him as unbeatable. The majority, including PGA Tour reporter Craig Dolce, argued that the challenge of making yet another major swing change, this time under the guidance of Sean Foley, had been the source of the decline. As Dolce claims, overhauling the swing "is one of the most difficult tasks they can do in their careers; it's like asking someone to change the way they [*sic*] walk." Unfortunately, Dolce fails to acknowledge, and perhaps even to understand, that Tiger was simultaneously engaged in transforming other nearly instinctive responses. Unlearning and replacing an entire array of complex behaviors obviously posed an enormous challenge.

Since the scandal broke and Tiger was confronted with the necessity of changing his affect during play, he has been at war. Whether he wanted to or not, he has been forced to *try* to control his emotional displays, and he has yet to demonstrate that he has reformed. As a result, several questions have remained unresolved, including Peter Kostis' insightful query after the 2010 Masters. Can Tiger actually control his emotions without eliminating them? In other words, will Tiger be able to maintain his passion for the game while flattening negative displays, behaviors that have clearly not been, and may never be, natural for him?

Kostis proclaims that "if he can lose the cursing and the club throwing, but keep the passion and fire that helps make him great, then all will be well with the golf world" ("Woods Needs Time"). Although Kostis' declaration that "all will be well" is a bit too effusive and reductive, others concur that

Tiger's mission to transform himself is necessary if he is ever to regain his previous stature in the game. Oliver Brown writes that golf is, "at its core, an exercise in self-discipline." If the code of etiquette disappears, Brown argues that Tiger's "unsavoury" "lapses" could become the norm, a horrific prospect. Not everyone judges Tiger so harshly, however. Smiley notes, "The problem for Tiger is that he's an intense guy in love with a gentleman's sport" (57). Appearing in the same sentence, the words "intense," "love," and "gentleman" point to incongruities that may be impossible to reconcile. Whether Tiger Woods can untangle that knot remains uncertain. But he knows he must become a gentleman, no matter the difficulty of that task.

WORKS CITED

Barkow, Al. *The History of the PGA Tour.* New York: Doubleday, 1989. Print.

Baum, Greg. "Conquering the Demons." *Sydney Morning Herald.* 13 Nov. 2010. Web. 15 Nov. 2010.

Bell, Shannon. "Tiger Woods Redemption? Masters Interview Tells a Different Story." *Right Pundits.* 12 Apr. 2010. Web. 18 Aug. 2010.

Birdwhistle, Ray. *Kinesics and Context: Essays in Body Motion Communication.* Philadelphia: University of Pennsylvania Press, 1970. Print.

Brown, Oliver. "Tiger Woods Should Be Spitting Mad Over His Latest Exhibition of Crassness in the Dubai Desert Classic." *The [London] Telegraph.* 16 Feb. 2011. Web. 17 Feb. 2011.

Callahan, Tom. *His Father's Son: Earl and Tiger Woods.* New York: Gotham Books, 2010. Print.

Chaney, Chris. "Add Jim Furyk to the List of Generous Golfers." *Playing from the Wrong Fairway.* 11 Apr. 2011. Web. 5 May 2011.

Cormack, Mike. "Lessons Learned." *Sportsnet.* 13 Apr. 2010. Web. 15 June 2010.

Dahlberg, Tim. "Woods Beyond Frustration as He Curses Way through First Round." *USA Today.* 14 Aug. 2003. Web. 18 Sept. 2010.

Dolce, Craig. "Missing Marquee Event Not the Worst Thing for Woods." *PGA Tour.* 14 Sept. 2010. Web. 20 Sept. 2010.

Donegan, Lawrence. Golf Blog. "Tiger Woods Throws His Club in Frustration During the First Round at Turnberry in the 2009 Open." *The [UK] Guardian.* 27 July 2009. Web. 24 Aug. 2010.

Ekman, Paul, and Wallace V. Friesen. "Head and Body Cues in the Judgment of Emotion: A Reformulation." *Perception and Motor Skills* 24 (1967): 711–24. Print.

Ferguson, Doug. "Former World No. 1 Tiger Woods Gets Attention for All the Wrong Things in Golf." *Canadian Press.* 15 Feb. 2011. Web. 18 Feb. 2011.

Frankb03. Online Posting. *Bettors Chat Forum.* 22 Apr. 2010. Web. 23 Sept. 2010.

Harig, Bob. "Quail Hollow Different for Woods, Lefty." *ESPN.* 28 Apr. 2010. Web. 29 Aug. 2010.

Imrem, Mike. "For Me, It's Still All About Tiger." *Daily Herald.* 9 Aug. 2010. Web. 28 Aug. 2010.

Kawakami, Tim. "Talking Points: After a Long Wait, the Michelson-Woods Era Begins Now." *Mercury News.* 12 Apr. 2010. Web. 18 Aug. 2011.

Kelley, Brent. "Tiger Woods Club Throwing: Tiger Lets His Temper Show." n.d. *About Golf.* Web. 3 Sept. 2011.

Kostis, Peter. "Woods Needs Time to Work Things Out, On and Off the Course." *Golf.com*. 15 Apr. 2010. Web. 10 Sept. 2010.

Leibovitz, Annie. Tiger Woods Photograph. *Vanity Fair*. Feb. 2010: Cover. Print.

Lopresti, Mike. "From the Press Box: Tiger Woods Offers Final Notes from the Masters." *USA Today*. 12 Apr. 2010. Web. 20 Aug. 2010.

Lusetich, Robert. *Unplayable: An Inside Account of Tiger's Most Tumultuous Season*. New York: Atria Books, 2010. Print.

Maxie. Online Posting. *Game On. USA Today*. 13 Apr. 2010. Web. 10 Oct. 2010.

Mehrabian, Albert, and S. R. Ferris. "Inference of Attitudes from Nonverbal Communication in Two Channels." *Journal of Consulting Psychology* 31 (1967): 248–52. Print.

Nantz, Jim. Interview by Mike Francesa. *Mike and the Mad Dog*. WFAN, New York. 12 Apr. 2010. Radio.

Parrillo, Ray. "Tiger Woods Dazzles Them at Aronimink." *The Inquirer*. 1 July 2010. Web. 8 Aug. 2010.

Reilly, Rick. "*Woods* Needs to Clean up His Act: Tiger, Please, Where Are Your Manners?" *ESPN: The Magazine*. 22 July 2009. Web. 10 Sept. 2010.

Rosaforte, Tim. "Jim Furyk at the Ryder Cup." AP Photograph. "Nice Guys Do Finish First." *Golf Digest*. 29 Aug. 2007. Web. 15 Sept. 2010.

Shipnuck, Alan. "Tiger Woods's Mea Culpa Heard Round the World Was a Sad Performance." *Sports Illustrated.com*. 25 Feb. 2010. Web. 24 Mar. 2010.

Shull, Drew. "Tiger Woods Sees Supportive Crowds During First Round at Quail Hollow." *Sports Business Daily*. 29 Apr. 2010. Web. 14 Oct. 2010.

Smiley, Bob. *Follow the Roar: Tailing Tiger for All 604 Holes of His Most Spectacular Season*. New York: HarperCollins, 2008. Print.

Sounes, Howard. *The Wicked Game: Arnold Palmer, Jack Nicklaus, Tiger Woods, and the Story of Modern Golf*. New York: William Morrow, 2004. Print.

Stone, Peter. "Humbled Tiger Looks Like a Man We Can Warm To." *Sydney Morning Herald*. 7 Nov. 2010. Web. 18 Nov. 2010.

Strege, John. *Tiger: A Biography of Tiger Woods*. New York: Broadway Books, 1997. Print.

"Tiger Struggles to Stay on the Straight and Narrow." *Times of India*. 12 Apr. 2010. Web. 21 Aug. 2010.

Tbone5656. Online Posting. *Game On. USA Today*. 13 Apr. 2010. Web. 10 Oct. 2010.

Tirico, Mike. 2010 Masters Tournament Commentary. *ESPN*. 7 Apr. 2010. Television.

Wei, Stephanie. "Should We Cut Tiger Some Slack?" *ESPN Golf*. 17 Apr. 2010. Web. 29 Apr. 2010.

Weir, Tom. "Tiger Woods Gets Ripped by Jim Nantz." *Game On. USA Today*. 13 Apr. 2010. Web. 10 Oct. 2010.

White Shadow. Online Posting. *Game On. USA Today*. 13 Apr. 2010. Web. 10 Oct. 2010.

Whitley, David. "Hello, I'm David and I'm a Tiger-holic." *AOL Sporting News*. 12 Aug. 2010. Web. 20 Aug. 2010.

Woods, Tiger. Apology. Ponte Vedra Beach, FL. 19 Feb. 2010. Press Conference.

_____. Interview with Peter Kostis. Masters Post-Tournament Interview. CBS. 11 Apr. 2010. Television.

_____. Masters Pre-Tournament Press Conference. CBS. 5 Apr. 2010. Television.

_____. "Tiger's Blog: Some Incredible Fan Support." *Tiger Woods Official Website*. 23 Apr. 2010. Web. 5 May 2010.

Ego, Entitlement and Egregious Behavior

Sarah D. Fogle

Q: What is the difference between a Cadillac Escalade and a golf ball?
A: Tiger Woods can drive a golf ball 350 yards.

Q: What is the difference between Santa Claus and Tiger Woods?
A: Santa stopped at three ho's.

One-liners: It turns out Tiger is a lion cheetah!
Crouching Tiger, hidden hydrant!

What brought Tiger Woods to the attention of late-night comedians and made him fodder for jokes for months? In November 2009, a brief, initially somewhat humorous, news flash on central Florida television about a fender-bender car crash outside Woods' home in Orlando soon blossomed into a full-scale scandal of extramarital sex with a virtual parade of partners. The golf superstar whose athletic feats, work ethic, and celebrity status were admired throughout the world found his life rapidly unraveling around him. His fall from superstar grace was nothing short of spectacular.

The man Oprah Winfrey introduced on her television show in 1997 as the person who "transcends golf," who is "magical and ... mesmerizing ... who is just what our world needs now ... [who is] America's son" (qtd. in Cole and Andrews) found himself in the harsh spotlight of disgrace and censure. The man that Gary Whannel described in *Media Sports Stars* as "the perfect hero for the white world ... handsome, well spoken and respectful, with a clear commitment to the puritan work ethic" (177) had become a punch line. The news coverage had revealed anything *but* puritan ethics or morality. A frequent reaction to the increasingly salacious tabloid and mainstream media coverage was astonishment: How could he have done this? Why *would* he have done this? Why would a person who had his record of accomplishments, his beautiful wife and children, his money and status, put at risk his reputation and career, his marriage and family, his own and his wife's health? Adding to the public's astonishment at this most private and controlled superstar's personal behavior was that the scandal had emerged in all its tawdry detail from the largely staid, buttoned-up sport of professional golf, where the most extreme deviance was Jesper Parnevik's or John Daly's pants color or pattern.

In his own words, once he was more or less forced to come forward with a public acknowledgement of his infidelity, Woods attributed his aberrant behavior to his sense of entitlement:

> I stopped living by the core values that I was taught to believe in. I knew my actions were wrong, but I convinced myself that normal rules didn't apply. I never thought about who I was hurting. Instead, I thought only about myself. I ran straight through the boundaries that a married couple should live by. I thought I could get away with whatever I wanted to. I felt that I had worked hard my entire life and deserved to enjoy all the temptations around me. I felt I was entitled. Thanks to money and fame, I didn't have to go far to find them ["Tiger Woods Transcript" 2].

What prompts the elite professional athlete to behave in ways that run counter to expectations, that violate the rules, that transgress generally accepted moral boundaries, and that ultimately may subject him — and it is almost always the *male* athlete — to censure, ridicule, career irrelevance or oblivion, and even criminal penalties? Woods provides the answer to this question in one word: entitlement.

What Tiger Woods did outside his superb athletic exploits and outside his marriage is nothing new — even to the conservative world of professional golf — and although the behaviors are certainly not limited to high-profile star athletes and other celebrities, they are the individuals on whom the media most frequently focuses attention. And while athletes' entitled behavior may take many forms, all too often it involves the objectification of women that leads to risky sexual behavior, infidelity, or the outright abuse of women.

The entitled elite athlete who thinks he is above it all and does not have to follow sporting expectations is a familiar subject for media coverage. Professional basketball player Allen Iverson famously refused to attend the Philadelphia 76ers' mandatory practice sessions: "It's *practice,* man!" Ron Artest of the Indiana Pacers asked his coach for time off from his team obligations so he could promote his rap album. Pro receiver Randy Moss was criticized by his own teammates for not playing hard enough — even slacking off — when he was not the primary receiver on a play. His alleged behavior brings to mind the title of Keyshawn Johnson's book, *Just Give Me the Damn Ball!* John McEnroe was well known for his temper tantrums on the court, typically directed toward line umpires (recall his frequent outbursts of "You *CANNOT* be serious!"), and rising talent Donald Young recently became best known for his profanity-laced "Twitter bomb" against the USTA for being required to compete for a wild card spot in the French Open tournament. He further embarrassed himself by his misspelling in "'Their [*sic*] full of s__t!'" (Price 1). Baseball legend Pete Rose — once a sure bet for the Hall of Fame — was banned from baseball for life for gambling on his own sport. Stars Barry Bonds and Roger Clemens gained notoriety for their steroid use, and Clemens has faced perjury charges for lying in a congressional hearing.

The entitled athlete who crosses social and moral boundaries is also a familiar figure. Star baseball players from Babe Ruth to Alex Rodriguez have had well-deserved reputations for serial marital infidelity, as have a number of professional golfers. Some Minnesota Vikings players created quite a stir with their 2005 "Love Boat" cruise on Lake Minnetonka, during which players engaged in public sex. Although the case was ultimately settled out of court, LA Laker Kobe Bryant was accused of a sexual assault that blemished his otherwise clean reputation. And NFL quarterback Bret Favre became embroiled in scandal after allegations he sexted nude pictures of himself and left voicemails asking for dates to a former New York Jets female employee.

Although they may be denied or settled out of court, some transgressions of elite athletes are criminal, leading to trials and incarceration. The most notorious example, of course, is the O.J. Simpson murder trial and his imprisonment years later for different crimes. While Washington Wizards player Gilbert Arenas served a brief stint in a halfway house and was given probation for bringing guns into the locker room, Plaxico Burress served two years in prison for shooting himself in the leg with a concealed weapon while in a nightclub. NFL quarterback Michael Vick served a longer prison sentence for his brutal dog fighting operation. Pittsburgh Steeler Ben Rothlisberger has developed an ugly reputation for sexual assault against women although charges have not been filed against him. Retired New York Giants player Lawrence Taylor was arrested in 2010 for the rape of a sixteen-year-old girl he met through a pimp. In 2009 former NFL quarterback Steve McNair, married with four children, was murdered by his mistress, who then committed suicide.

Furthermore, entitled behavior is not simply the purview of athletes and sports programs. The media covers, sometimes ad nauseum, such behavior among entertainment celebrities, business leaders, and politicians. One-upping the behavior of Britney Spears and Paris Hilton, actress Lindsay Lohan showed up at her court hearing for a probation violation with a jaunty "f**k you" painted on her fingernail, frequently placed on her cheek in full view of the television cameras, the court, and, more importantly, the judge.

Bernie Madoff cheated investors out of millions with his Ponzi scheme, and International Monetary Fund head Dominique Strauss-Kahn brought his reputation for unwanted sexual advances toward women with him on a visit to New York City and found himself embroiled in an indictment for raping a hotel housekeeper.

Those who hold or run for public office understand they must accept the reality of media scrutiny, but many, nonetheless, inexplicably cross accepted boundaries and subject themselves and their families to exposure and embarrassment. Eliot Spitzer swapped his title of governor of New York for that of "Client Number 9." By going AWOL from his office, South Carolina "luv guv" Mark Stanford created a new euphemism for marital infidelity: "hiking the Appalachian Trail." California governor Arnold Schwarzenegger fathered a child with a household employee, and former presidential candidate John Edwards notoriously lied about fathering a child while carrying on an affair during his wife's battle with terminal breast cancer. With a name stand-up comedians can only dream of, married New York Congressman Anthony Weiner sent sexually graphic texts and Twitter messages, not to mention photos of his private parts, to women, at least one of whom may have been underage. Most famous, of course, were President Bill Clinton's sexual dalliances in the White House that damaged him to the point of impeachment and sullied the office of the presidency, not to mention the Oval Office itself.

Over the past few decades, entitlement has become endemic in American society. Entitlement attitudes and behaviors play out most obviously where celebrity or exceptional accomplishment combines with media coverage and business interests. In this regard, the world of sports and the elite athlete have become the epitome of entitlement. Thanks to media coverage, entitlement arises most often in the behavior of the professional athlete, usually one in a team sport such as football, baseball, or basketball. But a sense of entitlement does not come along as a corollary to a large pay check, although that may certainly have an influence. The problem of entitlement begins much earlier in sports, starting with youth and high school programs and carrying through to college and professional sports. Thanks to the media, there should be no doubt in the public's mind about which universities and colleges have bragging rights for the most elite sports programs, as well as those that have made a name for having — even protecting — disruptive or criminal behavior among players; often these two reputations go hand in hand.

Talented young athletes who progress through various levels of sports programs are also socialized in a very particular way, often leading to objectification and even mistreatment of women. In *Sports Heroes, Fallen Idols,* Stanley Teitelbaum observes that athletes often lack emotional maturity and thus lack empathy and as a result may use people for their own purposes:

"Many of our sports heroes ... have been conditioned from an early age to be self-absorbed. Their sense of entitlement ... has been repeatedly reinforced.... Their distorted self-image may prompt them to relate to others based on how well they fulfill their needs" (23). By no means do all athletes develop a sense of entitlement as they participate in sports at various levels, nor do all athletes become misogynists. But many do, and the public who invest themselves in celebrity culture seem to thrive on the latest salacious "bad boy" sports story or scandal. For every upstanding Kurt Warner the public admires, there is a boundary-breaking Dennis Rodman the public relishes seeing and hearing about.

The term "entitlement" is understood, literally, to mean having an established right to something, for example, benefits from government programs such as Social Security and Medicare. As a matter of company policy, employees in a business might be entitled to a certain number of paid vacation or sick days, and American citizens are entitled to due process under the law. The widespread sense of entitlement that pervades society and its institutions, however, stems not from such earned rights but from a personal belief that one is somehow special.

Entitlement brings with it an increase of an individual's focus on self and concomitant narcissistic behavior. In *The Culture of Narcissism,* Christopher Lasch notes that narcissists outwardly support social rules while harboring the belief that they are exempt; further, they expect gratification on demand and live "in a state of restless, perpetually unsatisfied desire" that suggests an impoverished spirit (xvi). While narcissists may believe they are all powerful, and thus untouchable, they need the admiration of others for validation; they "cannot live without an admiring audience" (10). Jean M. Twenge and W. Keith Campbell attribute this social trend toward entitlement and narcissism, in their opinion an epidemic, to the growing emphasis on self-esteem and self-expression that began in the late 1960s and early 1970s, coupled with a cultural shift away from a strong sense of community (63–64). They also argue that narcissism and entitlement begin at home, analyzing a parenting style they describe as "raising royalty" (73). Children are being raised with an exceptionally strong sense of their individual wonderfulness that, if not carefully managed, can transform high self-regard into an inordinate sense of entitlement.

In terms of the origins of Tiger Woods' well-developed sense of entitlement, one has only to consider Earl and Tida Woods' beliefs about their child golf prodigy expressed in a 1996 interview with Gary Smith of *Sports Illustrated.* Asked a possibly predictable question about Tiger's impact in sports that drew comparisons to Jackie Robinson, Muhammad Ali, and Arthur Ashe, Earl dismissed these stars as also-rans and praised Tiger's superior education, preparation, and charisma. When Gary Smith upped the comparison ante and the sphere of influence to Mandela, Gandhi, and Buddha, Earl quickly concurred. He indicated that Tiger's international presence commanded a world audience and that his multi-ethnic heritage "qualified [him] ... to accomplish miracles" (2). Most remarkably, Earl went on to anoint Tiger as "'the Chosen One ... [with] the power to impact nations. Not people. Nations. The world is just getting a taste of his power'" (2). Earl's further comments suggested that as the father he might be God's conduit to carry out a divine plan: "'This is all destined to be'" (4).

In her conversation with Smith during the same interview, Tiger's mother Tida, not to be outdone, further enhanced the mythology. She told the reporter that Buddhist monks in both Bangkok and Los Angeles had told her that Tiger "possessed wondrous powers" and was destined for greatness — if politics, high office; if the military, top rank. Like her husband, Tida brought up Tiger's ethnicity, claiming that it would "'hold everyone together. He is the Universal Child'" (2). Also like her husband, she felt that she would be carrying out Tiger's divine destiny. One could almost hear the swelling of organ music and see celestial light streaming into the room. Small wonder that John Feinstein titled his book about Tiger *The First Coming*. In his biography of Tiger Woods, John Strege describes the Woods' family living room as originally a "shrine to Tida's Thai heritage that had slowly been transformed into a shrine to her son," with the room an overflowing sea of fourteen-year-old Tiger's golf trophies (31).

But perhaps the seed of entitlement in Tiger Woods may have been planted even earlier, thanks to his well-publicized appearance in 1978 on *The Mike Douglas Show*, just before his third birthday. There he demonstrated his golf skills before adoring studio and national television audiences, as well as the host and celebrities Bob Hope and Jimmy Stewart looking on in admiration. With his cute name and demonstrable skill, Tiger was a pint-sized, immediate phenom; this experience had to be heady stuff for a tyke with a toy-sized golf club.

In *Why Is It Always About You?* Sandy Hotchkiss and James Masterson argue that the emphasis on self-esteem in young children has led to unanticipated consequences, because effort more than accomplishment is the end goal and children should not be made to feel bad about anything. Further, if one does not get what is expected, the blame lies elsewhere, and one is due recourse or compensation. In Hotchkiss and Masterson's view, "A sense of entitlement to 'specialness' and positive outcomes has compromised rather than enhanced genuine self-esteem, which is based on mastery rather than wishful thinking" (94). The relationship between narcissism and entitled behavior is apparent, and both tendencies are likely to be characteristic of high-profile individuals in various arenas, among which sports seems to be fertile ground. Certainly narcissism and entitlement are typical attributes of athletes, particularly at elite levels, but the tendencies begin at a very early age, in organized youth sports. For example, sometimes the decision is made not to keep score, or to give all children a trophy, whether they are on the winning team or not, in order not to damage their self-esteem. In other instances, some young players are singled out for special treatment when their Little League coaches rig their batting orders to give the "better" players more at-bats than average players, and others may "cherry-pick" players for traveling teams. It is adults who do this, and they should know better (Collier 1).

Furthermore, sports at the youth and high school levels more and more are being transformed into professional competition. There are more levels of competition, traveling teams, tournaments, recognition and championships, as well as increasing media — including television — coverage, all of which shine a light on young athletes, as well as their parents. The Little League World Series is a good case in point, with every game televised and drawing a large adult audience; in fact, in 2011, the series broke the attendance record, last set in 1990, with over 40,000 fans at the opening game ("Little League"). As in professional sports, there is an intersection of business and sports. Support systems — a burgeoning business — abound to aid in the skill development of young athletes. Parents who want to make sure their young athlete can compete at higher and higher levels can avail themselves of sports psychologists, private lessons with coaches or even pro athletes, summer sports camps, and private boarding and sports training schools — all for a pretty price, of course. For Earl Woods, training his son for golf success became his mission; Steven Overman reports that he hired a professional coach and "floated five credit cards and two mortgages on their house" to support the effort. He also engaged a sports psychologist to strengthen Tiger's mental focus on golf (12). Tiger was twelve at the time.

While youth- and high school-level sports have increasingly become big business, even toddlers are now being targeted by the business side of sports. Writing about these initiatives in *Until It Hurts*, Mark Hyman describes a company called athleticBaby that, citing the decline of physical activity among American children as a rationale, produces sports DVDs for three-month-old infants with the pitch "Encouraging winners one at a time" (16–17). There are DVDs for golf, soccer, and even basketball, perhaps aiming to transfer dribbling skills from the bib to the hardwood. In a chapter entitled "Tiger Tracks," Hyman asserts that such emphasis on developing winning athletes at a tender age is rooted in Tiger's 1978 appearance on *The Mike Douglas Show*, with the underlying message that any child can be a star athlete if the parent begins training early enough (16–17). He also notes that the age for participating in recreational sports leagues used to be seven or eight but in some areas has been lowered to four and in some instances even eighteen months (17).

Parents can become overly invested in the sports endeavors of their young athletes, whose accomplishments reflect on them as well. Tiger's father was no exception: "No father set out more single-mindedly to groom his son to become a professional athlete than Earl Woods" (Overman 12). But the difference between him and most parents is that he was the father of an athlete with extraordinary ability. Earl Woods' protestations that Tiger could quit the game any time if he tired of it, however, strain credulity (12). The frequent incidents of bad, even violent, behavior of parents at youth and high school sports events suggest a degree of parental involvement that goes far beyond watching their child have a good time and get some exercise. Parents can see such athletic success as the path to a good college or university, to a scholarship, to recognition, even to the professional ranks. Such parents rarely contemplate the reality of just how few athletes make it to the elite level. Sports referee Kevin McNutt says, "Many parents see sports as a lottery ticket to scholarships and wealth. I call it the 'Tiger Woods Syndrome'" (qtd. in Merida 2).

In "Entitlement an Epidemic in Sports," Christine Brennan agrees with McNutt, noting that entitlement begins very early with young athletes and that such behavior is enabled by their parents: "Anyone who has been to a kids' sporting event is familiar with the act of the showboating 12-year-old and his adoring parents. Perhaps this will be known as the Tiger Syndrome, and treated with dread" (2). With even middle school students being recruited by elite programs, small wonder that entitlement begins to take hold early. The University of Kentucky once offered a full-ride basketball scholarship to a fourteen-year-old, and USC offered a Delaware thirteen-year-old a scholarship to play quarterback on the football team (Mills 2). Investment in early training, coaching and lessons, upward mobility in elite sports competitions, and early recruitment to collegiate programs are all ingredients in a potentially toxic recipe for developing a self-absorbed athlete with a strong sense of entitlement.

Because participation in sports, even with the advent of Title IX, is still predominantly a male endeavor and sports are therefore understandably deemed an ultra-masculine environment, an important element in the development of athletes' sense of entitlement is how young males are socialized in gender behavior as they mature and as they develop male identity. The common wisdom is that sports develop good character and teach responsibility, toughness and perseverance, the importance of winning, and leadership — in many respects, how to be a man. But what seems to draw young men to sports is connection with other males. They are taught how to play ball by a father or other male relative, or they join a team of male peers. What may begin as fun, however, can cease to be enjoyable when one's acceptance, status, and identity become linked to the overriding value of winning and being perceived as a winner (Messner, *Out of Play* 50–51). The paradox is that the desired closeness and connection with others are lost when the athlete's identity is inseparable from being successful, a winner; the athlete's performance becomes his identity. His worth is determined by sources of external approval — i.e., coaches, parents, peers, the crowd (Messner, "Boyhood" 328). As a result of the focus on success and winning, his ability to develop meaningful relationships with other people is stunted; he must become extremely focused on the goal, his body, and his objectified enemy rival; and he is unlikely to develop intimacy with other males, much less females (329).

In their article "The Televised Sports Manhood Formula," Messner, Dunbar, and Hunt cite a 1999 study that analyzed television sports programming and commercials over a 23-hour period to determine the dominant themes that emerged for their viewing audience of males aged eight to seventeen years old. The study revealed that this televised sports manhood formula "provides a remarkably stable and concrete view of masculinity as grounded in bravery, risk taking, violence, bodily strength, and heterosexuality" (82). Women, on the other hand, are depicted as "sexy props or prizes for men's successful sport performances or consumption choices" such as beer or automobiles (74). Watching televised football on the weekend bears out this contrast. Male announcers are broadcasting the play-by-play in the booth, and the occasional female sportscaster is doing sideline color, reporting on injuries, or chasing after the college coach trying to get a comment at halftime. Television cameras often zoom in for close-up shots of scantily clad, attractive cheerleaders at football games, and boxing and wrestling matches usually feature even more scantily clothed women parading sexily around the ring between rounds or matches, signaling the next round or event. Commercials during sports programming further reinforce the gender stereotypes depicted in sports programming (75). The authors of the study concluded that the price of playing sports, even being injured, is worth it because the male athletes get all the goodies and privileges: "money, power, glory, and women" (82–84). It is no wonder that the young male viewers, not to mention young male athletes, are socialized to objectify women and to view them as the spoils of sports wars.

The transition of the young athlete into collegiate sports, especially at institutions with top programs, can perpetuate the objectification of women as an available commodity. A common recruiting strategy is use of female campus hostesses. Although Alabama coach Bear Bryant is credited with the idea, with his Bama Babes, the practice predates his reign and continues, archaic though it may be, today. In some cases the names have been changed to be less sexist, as the Miami Hurricane Honeys are now the Cane Connection, and the Bengal Babes at Clemson are now the Tiger PAWS. The University of Florida, however (to this author's dismay), has kept the name Gator Getters. Some schools are somewhat more unisex, opting for such monikers as Baylor Gold, Raider Recruiters at Texas Tech, and Orange Pride at Tennessee, a group comprised of both male and female students.

Although most of these recruiting hostess organizations have rules for proper conduct and are above board in their roles and behaviors, it is clear that sex with potential recruits is not uncommon. Further, using young, attractive women as such hostesses is likely to send ambiguous messages to potential recruits about just what is being offered during the campus visit. A female student at Arizona State generated national attention when she wrote in the campus newspaper that the Sun Devil Recruiters were "hos to attract the bros" (King 1). Recruiting hostesses are used primarily in football recruiting and are often organized under the institution's admissions department "but operated in a shady netherworld as a vital part of any large program, yet detached from the athletic department in an intricate web of plausible deniability" (Bennett 1). In recent years the NCAA has begun to examine the use of hostesses, especially after the events at the University of Colorado in 2005 and during an investigation in 2009 into the University of Tennessee's football recruiting tactics (Low 1).

In addition to these hostess or ambassador groups, some institutions' sports programs have come under fire for hiring strippers for recruiting parties, taking recruits to strip clubs, and even allegedly hiring prostitutes from escort services. Owner of Hardbodies Entertainment Steve Lower breezily explains, "'It's a tradition, like throwing a bachelor party'" (qtd. in "Strippers" 1). In 2005 such questionable practices blew up in a lawsuit against the University of Colorado brought by two female students, who alleged they were raped at a party for football recruits. This was one allegation among many, including that the university had $800,000 in a "slush fund not only to be used to wine, dine, and entertain high school athletes, but to pay victims of assault to remain quiet" (E. Smith 214). Ultimately the allegations involving the athletic department led to multiple resignations, including those of the football coach and the university president. The most recent high-profile scandal, in 2011, involved the University of Miami and booster Nevin Shapiro, who is alleged to have given football players gifts and hired prostitutes for them.

At times the objectification of women and the athlete's sense of entitlement come together with potentially, or very real, tragic consequences. When such acts involve a member of a team, all too often parental excuses and/or

the masculine code of silence intervene against the best interests of the per-
petrator(s) and most certainly of the victim(s). In *Taking the Field*, Messner
asserts that "This culture of silence is built into the spoken and unspoken
codes and rituals. The eroticized dominance bond has already established that
the guys are part of a high-status, privileged in-group" (47). Young athletes
have learned that "they will be rewarded for remaining complicit with the
code of silence and punished for betraying the group" (47). Furthermore,
such punishment can take forms that reinforce the objectification of women,
as vulgar methods are often employed. The most benign would be some sort
of variation on the playground taunt of "You throw like a girl" or "You run
like a girl." But failure to support the code or to exhibit strength and aggression
would be to get tagged a "pussy" or a "wuss" (Robinson 4). In her description
of the sports culture, Laurie Robinson asserts that "anything that resembles
femininity is scorned," and she cites a "high school coach [who] painted a
picture of a vagina on tackling dummies" and others who put "sanitary napkins
in the lockers of players for 'wimpy performance[s]' on the field" (4).

The team locker room supports this code, literally and figuratively, in
that it denotes a physical space as well as a way of thinking and feeling. In
"A Culture of Acceptance," Dean Myers argues that this culture can function
as an enclosed environment that enforces silence and protects the athlete(s)
that misbehave; it is an enclave "where normal societal rules are sometimes
trumped by what has been described as a groupthink culture" (1). In *Living
Out of Bounds*, Overman describes the locker room as a "sanctum sanctorum,"
a "refuge" that separates the athlete from the outside world and its attendant
concerns (28). Further, he notes that the locker room "experience carries
beyond the sensual; the shared space harbors communal dimensions" and "slo-
gans on locker room walls reinforce the tradition of an inner sanctum where
access is denied to all but the elect" (29). Since women journalists were ultimately permitted, albeit under frequently hostile circumstances, to enter locker
rooms in 1970, that space is now somewhat less a "male enclave" (20).
Nonetheless, Overman views the locker room as the athletes' refuge that sym-
bolizes their sense of being an "exclusive fraternity" and isolates them quite
comfortably "from the wider world with its adult responsibilities" (29).

Three cases are noteworthy in regard to the code of silence and the locker
room mentality: the "spur posse" in a Los Angeles high school, the Duke
lacrosse team rape allegations, and the murder of University of Virginia
lacrosse player Yeardley Love. In Lakewood, California, in 1993, a group of
high school athletes formed a "sex gang" called the "spur posse" that engaged
in sex with female classmates, passing them around in turn to each other and
boasting openly about their conquests (E. Smith 76). The athletes' parents
defended their sons and blamed the girls, calling them "loose" and expressing

shock that some even had tattoos! Another attitude was that the boys had done what they did because the girls had tricked them into their behavior (76).

In the well-publicized Duke lacrosse team case in 2006, charges were ultimately dropped and while what actually took place remains a matter of intense dispute, the parents bonded under the position that "their sons were merely behaving like 'young men'"(E. Smith 76). They further rationalized that having a party instead of going out to a club where fake IDs might be used was the more responsible approach. Parents also argued that, because bringing in strippers was common entertainment in the conduct of Wall Street business, having strippers at a college party was routine behavior. These excuses are summed up in the very familiar "boys will be boys" rationale (77), as well as the "specific construction of masculinity" conveyed to boys that "men are supposed to be tough, strong, unfeeling, and most importantly, a 'player'" (84).

In the 2010 case of Yeardley Love and boyfriend George Huguely, both lacrosse players at the University of Virginia, an athlete's violent behavior fueled by sexual jealousy resulted in the young woman's murder. With Huguely's known history of heavy drinking and violent confrontations and assaults, it had to be obvious that he was dangerous, but apparently no one intervened, either to get him help or to protect Love. Sally Jenkins poses what she acknowledges is a difficult question: Is there a culture in sports that encourages male athletes to commit aberrant behavior? While she does not by any means want to indict all athletes, she asks, "Should women fear athletes?" ("George Huguely" 1). She notes that the behaviors of the Virginia male lacrosse team were characterized by "physical swagger, heavy drinking, and fraternal silence" (1). Further, she raises the important question of why male athletes do not treat female athletes, especially in team sports, as their teammates: "*Where* were her brothers?" (1, original emphasis). Athletes who indulge their sexual aggression or commit violence against women are the exception rather than the rule in the larger world of sports, "but an unknown, and certainly larger percentage are complicit by their silence" (Messner, *Out of Play* 109). Why is this the case? Messner argues that male athletes keep silent because of "fear of being humiliated, ostracized, or beaten up" (118).

As young male athletes progress from high school to colleges and universities, they continue to be protected and pampered, even having the rules bent to accommodate or excuse them. Athletes in colleges are provided an array of personal services along with their scholarships: special meals at training tables, athletic residence halls, tutors and special study halls, and, for some, advisement into easy classes or degree programs. Some athletes may have had certain admissions requirements waived for them in order to matric-

ulate. Granted, successful athletic programs and star athletes in these institutions bring in great revenue and other benefits, but that is not at issue here.

It should be no surprise that coddled athletes might find themselves in
suspended adolescence during and after participation in university sports programs. In *Living Out of Bounds*, Overman notes that "This arrangement may
appear benign, but can clearly stifle athletes' self-sufficiency and initiative"
(37). Overman labels the world of sports as Neverland and athletes as inflicted
with "Peter Pan syndrome." He describes athletes as "characterized by their
immaturity. In many ways, they continue to act like lost boys" (30). Earl
Smith calls this environment of arrested development "Sportsworld," in which
young men are largely isolated from women. Their teammates, coaches, and
administrators are male; their primary association with women is within their
families or with those "whose very existence is to serve them"; such isolation
is a contributing factor to male athletes' misogyny as well (165). Overman
further argues that coaching in athletics becomes institutionalized paternalism,
under which athletes are conditioned to yield to autocratic authority. Such
submission enables coaches to control them more readily and leads to their
"'enforced infantilization'" (Meggyesy, qtd. in Overman, 31). Writing about
the athlete's psyche, former MLB player Tom House uses a more crass term —
"'the jock's itch'"— to describe athletes' immaturity and defines it as "'a condition that causes thirty year old men to act the same way they did when they
were thirteen'" (qtd. in Teitelbaum, *Sports Heroes* 19).

In "The Shrinking of Tiger Woods," Alan Shipnuck asserts that Tiger
Woods was infantilized during the period between the infamous Thanksgiving
night car crash and his televised apology by his agent Mark Steinberg. Although
the notion of infantilization might seem unusual, it crops up in several post-
scandal interviews. In reference to allegations Tiger had been using performance-enhancing drugs, Steinberg asked a *New York Times* reporter in an
"instantly infamous plea.... Let's please give the kid a break'" (1). Shipnuck's
acerbic observation immediately following is "Woods is 34 years old" (1).
John Feinstein is even more caustic: "The kid? That would be a 34-year-old
billionaire with two children" ("Disappearance" 2). As corporate sponsors ran
for cover, Gillette's response depicted Tiger as an ill-behaved child being sent
to his room; because he was "taking a 'timeout' from golf, it would take a
'timeout' from promoting him as a sponsor of its products" (Feinstein,
"Unclear" 1). Then there's Tiger's widely reported post-tryst habit of eating
Fruit Loops and watching cartoons.

Athletes who rise to elite status seem to have it all — wealth, privilege,
celebrity — but "continue to function as rebellious adolescents who become
embroiled in antisocial and sometimes dangerous off-the-field activities" (Teitelbaum, *Athletes Who Indulge* 85). Based on her several decades of research

on morality in sports, Sharon K. Stoll has assessed the moral reasoning of thousands of college athletes and found them to have "significantly lower moral-reasoning skills than the general student population — and she says that is a direct result of the competitive sports environment" (qtd. in Bloom 5). Howard Bloom recounts Stoll's description of football players as entitled, unable to think independently, and inclined to believe they are better than everyone else and "can get away with anything" (5).

D. Stanley Eitzen, who has written prolifically about the culture of sports, cites a study of 10th grade to college-age athletes, begun in 1987 and continuing at least until 2009, whose "research reveals consistently that sport stifles moral reasoning and moral development" (169). Three major findings regarding moral development are that "athletes score lower than their non-athlete peers ... male athletes score lower than female athletes ... [and] scores for all athlete populations steadily decline from 9th grade through university age, whereas scores for non-athletes tend to increase" (169). Eitzen points out that these research findings do not bear out the popular belief that participation in sports instills values and builds character; to the contrary, he finds it ironic that sports as "presently conducted in youth leagues, schools, and at the professional level [do] not enhance positive character traits" (169).

When the elite athlete who is good enough to make it into the professional ranks is signed to a team, or when an athlete emerges from a college sports team into professional individual competition — Tiger Woods, for example — he often arrives with a well-developed sense of entitlement and perhaps a narcissistic self-concept. Add to these traits the inevitable media attention and corporate endorsements, and the athlete may soon become a commodity, a brand, a celebrity whose stardom exceeds his mere athletic prowess. In many instances, the elite celebrity athlete is headed for some type of headline-making boundary transgression, whether it be using illegal drugs, running up gambling debts, engaging in infidelity or other risky sexual behavior, committing crimes, or simply exhibiting arrogant, presumptuous behavior. As former pro baseball player Jim Bouton has sharply observed, "Athletes are not special people, they are people with special skills" (qtd. in Teitelbaum, *Sports Heroes* 9).

When Tiger announced his entrance onto the international stage with his "Hello World" Nike commercial that challenged viewers with the question "Are you ready for me?" what would have been seen as entitlement in a lesser athlete may have been interpreted merely as confidence. Tiger's challenge was acceptable because his talent was so spectacular for one so young. In his mind, and in his father's mind, however, he was beginning to fulfill his destiny as the Chosen One. In *The First Coming*, John Feinstein writes that Tiger's first year on the professional tour, eagerly embraced by the sport, the media, and corporate sponsors, was "an amazing one" (33). But he notes as well that rocky times lie ahead, not with his golf but with the man himself: "Is there anyone out there willing to tell Tiger Woods he's *not* the Messiah?" (34). In Feinstein's opinion, Tiger's selection by *Sports Illustrated* as Sportsman of the Year in 1996 was puzzling, but it also began the "Tiger as Messiah" idea, which was reinforced in Gary Smith's interview with Earl and Tida Woods (35–36). In Mike Lupica's words, Tiger's selection was "the first time they've given someone Sportsman of the Year based on spec" (qtd. in Feinstein 35).

A key element in Gary Smith's interview for *Sports Illustrated* is his personal observation while listening to Earl Woods speaking about his son at the Fred Haskins dinner honoring Tiger for his college golf exploits. Smith asks the reader to listen, to hear a grinding sound:

> That's the relentless chewing mechanism of fame, girding to grind the purity and the promise to dust. Not the promise of talent but the bigger promise, the father's promise, the one that stakes everything on the boy's not becoming separated from his own humanity and from all the humanity crowding around him [1].

Smith was somehow prescient of what ultimately lay ahead of Tiger as his career in professional golf progressed and especially as he acted upon his sense of entitlement.

What usually happens to the highly accomplished, charismatic elite athlete who transforms his sport is that he becomes the focus of media coverage and an endorser of corporate products. In *Sport in a Changing World,* Howard Nixon argues that the athlete is consumed by what he calls the "Golden Triangle": "a dominant network of powerful and intertwined people and organizations in highly commercialized sports, the media, and the corporate world" (2). A symbiotic relationship develops that increases the sport's wealth and power, and athletes chosen for endorsements become celebrities who further enrich their sport. Nixon writes that social class is a dominant influence — and he cites golf as a good example — in that the Golden Triangle is often "more strongly influenced by the tastes of and purchasing power of more affluent members of society ... [because they] can buy more, and more expensive, consumer goods" (74–76). Further, Nixon describes Tiger Woods, along with Michael Jordan, as mediated products rather than human beings. They are depicted favorably "because their images are carefully constructed by the Golden Triangle to take advantage of their superstar status and maximize their potential as commercial commodities" (77). Jonathan Mahler notes that Tiger was so influential in his sport, his sponsorships and manufacturing, and his golf course development projects that he created a "classic economic bubble, the Tiger Bubble" (32).

The combination of athletic accomplishment, product endorsements, and media coverage makes the elite athlete famous and grants him celebrity status that may increasingly distance him from the sense of self that Gary Smith noted. As well, entitlement is an obvious corollary to fame and celebrity and may result in what Teitelbaum calls the "toxic athlete profile":

> Fame is routinely accompanied by the development of an inflated self-image, a sense of invincibility, and in some cases an outrageous sense of being entitled to act beyond the customary boundaries established by our culture. Grandiosity, a sense of entitlement, poor judgment, a denial of vulnerability, and impulsiveness characterize the behaviors of many heroes [*Sports Heroes* 102].

Fame and celebrity bring godly comparisons; the term "celebrity worship" applies to athletes as well as other notables in society. For example, following the NBA playoffs between Chicago and Boston in 1986, Larry Bird said about Michael Jordan, "'I think he's God disguised as Michael Jordan'" (qtd. in Rhoden 201). During an Olympics press conference in 1992, a Japanese reporter asked MJ, "'How does it feel to be God?'" (qtd. in Rhoden 202). Be like Mike, be like God; be Mike, be God. Rhoden writes that the public shapes the star/celebrity athlete into what it wants him to be "according to [its] own values, dreams, and biases"; the public assigns specific attributes of greatness "even though — or rather because — [it knows] so little about him" (202). Roger Abrams sounds the cautionary note that "we see these men and women as larger than life," adding that the Greeks afforded their gods vices to enjoy on Olympus (2).

Tiger Woods was elevated to deity status — or at least to that of Jesus — while still in college when his father anointed him the "Chosen One." John Feinstein's book title, *The First Coming*, and his discussion of Tiger as Messiah reinforce this image. While Tiger may never have been directly called God, he has behaved in ways that engendered god-like responses from fans. Feinstein describes Tiger on the first day of the 1997 U.S. Open, drawing the attention of thousands. On the driving range, he tells a nearby friend, "'Watch this.'" With a phalanx of security falling into immediate formation and the media in slavish pursuit, Tiger walks through the crowd seamlessly, like parting the Red Sea; when he moves, everyone else moves, and then he returns to his original spot on the range: "It was a remarkable display of absolute power" (3). In *Follow the Roar*, Bob Smiley describes fan behavior during the 2008 U.S. Open after Tiger completed his round. As he approaches the officiating area, "two fans on the ground literally fall to their knees and bow down in homage" (247); Smiley points out that Tiger is all the more impressive because "he's *not* a god" (247), but the fans kneel to his greatness nonetheless. Objects of celebrity worship perhaps allow the "weekend warrior" amateur or casual athlete to see himself as he wishes he could be; celebrity athletes can "arouse the religious passions of followers ... who find spiritual meaning, personal fulfillment, and awe-inspiring motivation in the presence of these idols" (Laderman 64–65). Such an effect is testimony to the power of celebrity on the common folk.

Celebrity worship has become prevalent in part because the notion of what constitutes a hero has changed. Past heroes might have been revered for an outstanding accomplishment or feat, from which their fame would derive. Today, asking young persons what they want to be when they grow up might elicit the response "Famous." The notion that fame is something that accompanies heroic action has been replaced by achieving fame as the end goal: "We have forsaken our traditional heroes and replaced them with actors and athletes ... where once we admired people who do great things, now we admire people who play people who do great things" (Len Sherman, qtd. in Cashmore 50). Furthermore, celebrities do not have to acquire the hero's responsibilities, and they often break the rules that govern most of society; these new heroes may or may not accomplish anything, but they are ubiquitous (Cashmore 50–51). In celebrity culture, religious terms abound: superstars are idols and icons; fans are devoted and adoring; heroes' bad behaviors are falls from grace; and second chances and comebacks are redemptions — witness Michael Vick's recent return to star quarterback status with the Philadelphia Eagles.

In *Gods Behaving Badly*, Pete Ward asserts that celebrity culture is a "virus infecting all cultural life" (2) and that its inauthenticity "invokes a knowing adoration of what are openly labeled as false gods" (7). Celebrity gods are not gods at all but very human in both their accomplishments and failures. According to Ward, "the subplot of celebrity discourse is (im)morality" (2). The public celebrates the ascension of the hero/star as well as "the seeming inevitability that these figures will fail" (7). Failure makes the hero more human, but the public wants its heroes not to be fallible; "We may enjoy the prurient, but we are actually desperate for everyone to stick together. This is why we abhor the love rat and despise the person who has it all and just seems to throw it all away" (7). Ward is insistent that the public's greatest interest is focused on the heroes' private lives and their fidelity (115), and that celebrity worship "is focused on the celebration of their perfect form" (121) — performing perfectly, being in perfect shape, having a perfect physique. "The perfect body is more than an aesthetic appreciation. This is about sex. Celebrities are the objectification of desire" (121). Ward specifically names Tiger Woods as combining sin and bad acts, as well as his public acknowledgment of his behavior, in his celebrity narrative (122).

As an athlete celebrity god, Tiger Woods' fall from grace was precipitated by his serial infidelity with, if his admissions are true, scores of women. One would assume that his embarrassment must be further exacerbated by accounts of his sexual proclivities, reported graphic text messages, and countless televised statements of his partners. One might also assume that his behavior was an open secret among his closest handlers, who maintained the male athlete's code of silence and protected him from wider exposure until the night he wrecked his Escalade. Perhaps the VIP lounges in clubs and hotels that Tiger visited on his pro tour trips became an elite version of the locker room refuge. The story of the unfaithful athlete husband is anything but new in the world of sports. What has changed over time is the degree of media coverage devoted to these scandals, whereas in a previous time "the darker side of our heroes' behavior was hidden by a gentlemen's agreement among sportswriters, who colluded to preserve their pure image and shield the public" (Teitelbaum, *Sports Heroes* 246).

In the world of professional sports, the prevalence of women who make themselves available or outright throw themselves at male athletes at home and on the road is a well-documented phenomenon. Wilt Chamberlain once boasted that he had slept with 20,000 women — a feat some calculated as virtually humanly impossible. The 20th anniversary in November 2011 of Magic Johnson's announcement that he had contracted AIDS is, among other more positive things, a stark reminder of the possible consequences of casual sex while traveling with the team. Sally Jenkins reported that, when asked about his infidelity, Johnson phrased his answer in terms of trying to "accommodate" women, as though he would have somehow been impolite to have refused their advances or availability ("Where's the Magic?" 1). Magic Johnson has repeated a joke about the NBA which illustrates the practice of infidelity in professional sports. "'Question: What's the hardest thing about going on the road? Answer: Trying not to smile as you kiss your wife goodbye'" (qtd. in Ortiz, "Using Power" 546).

Having conducted longitudinal research on marriages in professional sports, Steven M. Ortiz describes the "spoiled athlete syndrome" that provides athletes with a center of power from which to control their marriages in a way that also permits them to engage in infidelity on the road ("Using Power" 532). Like others, Ortiz cites the origin of this entitled behavior in youth sports and argues that it socializes males in both "gender work and control work" (533). He further notes the male athlete's tendency to objectify women and see women on the road as fulfilling for sex but not for love, which resides in the relationship with a wife and family at home. Ortiz describes this as the "virgin-prostitute syndrome" that assigns the wife the role of mother and the woman on the road as sex object (545). In fact, being a mother and being sexual may be incompatible in the husband's mind (546). Anxiety about infidelity on the road may make the wife more sexually available at home; such compliance only increases the power of the husband at home and away (547).

Frequently heard comments after the Tiger scandal broke were expressions of disbelief that he would stray from his beautiful Swedish wife to cheat with the women he chose. With the power, celebrity, and wealth of the professional athlete, a beautiful wife simply becomes one beautiful woman amid many others; her physical attractiveness gives her no power in the marriage when the husband has access to hordes of pretty women (548–9). Finally, Ortiz describes the prevalence of sports groupies and cheating as "institutionalized adultery" or an "adultery culture" supported and protected by both single and married teammates in a climate of masculine privilege. In fact, sometimes wives who travel with their husbands are complicit in maintaining this culture of adultery ("Traveling" 227). It is also doubtful that Tiger's scandal and other more sobering cautionary tales involving elite athletes will end the practice of cheating while married. An Atlanta lawyer who represents athletes advises his clients to prepare themselves for potential human failings: his advice is to include a "bad-boy clause" in pre-nuptial agreements so the athlete can avoid financial penalty if a divorce results from infidelity. Athletes know about such a clause and will ask for it (Merrill and Nelson 2).

What led the supremely successful athlete-like-no-other Tiger Woods to implode his athletic career, his marriage, his image, his vaunted expectations for privacy? Was it his role-model father Earl's philandering and how he treated Tida? Was he, as John Callahan's book title suggests, his father's son? Was it hanging out with celebrity athlete high-roller buddies Charles Barkley and Michael Jordan in Las Vegas clubs? Was it the absence of the controlling factor in his life represented by his father after Earl's death? Was it the inability to resist temptation? Was he afflicted with "toxic athlete syndrome"? The answer lies in Tiger's own words, in his public apology: He didn't think he had to follow the rules others live by. He was thinking about himself first and foremost. He crossed boundaries in his marriage. He thought he could get away with anything. He deserved to enjoy all the temptations he encountered. He felt *entitled*. What the revelations about Tiger's secret life managed to do was to render what the public thought was an extraordinary individual down to a very ordinary human being.

Perhaps, as some have suggested, the public needs to reconsider its notion of the hero and heroic acts, and to view elite athletes as more human than celebrity god. Perhaps there is a need to return to the idea of sport as a healthy recreational outlet to be enjoyed. And it would undoubtedly be healthy to separate the reality from the hype; star athletes are not "masters of the universe" (Abrams 1). Blogger Reasonable Robinson, following Tiger's public apology for cheating, referred to him as a "fallen Angel [who] ... has lost his status in Brand Heaven" (qtd. in Ward 88). In *Gods Behaving Badly*, Ward asserts that celebrities are not divinities but "false gods ... idols," that "Tiger

Woods is called a fallen angel with a knowing sense that he was never really an angel at all" (88–89). In terms of entitlement, and why those who feel entitled behave the way they often do, former President Bill Clinton gave the most incisive answer in an interview when Dan Rather asked, regarding Monica Lewinsky, why? "Just because I could" (Hancock 1).

WORKS CITED

Abrams, Roger I. "Sports Entitlement." *Huffington Post.* 26 Mar. 2010. Web. 27 July 2011.

Bennett, Dashiell. "A Brief History of Campus Recruiting Hostesses." *Deadspin.com.* 9 Dec. 2010. Web. 27 Aug. 2011.

Bloom, Howard. "Football Players — Their Complete Sense of Entitlement (and Lack of Morality)." *Sports Business News.* 5 Sept. 2006. Web. 15 Feb. 2011.

Brennan, Christine. "Entitlement an Epidemic in Sports." *USA Today.* 1 Apr. 2010. Web. 15 June 2011.

Cashmore, Ellis. *Celebrity Culture.* New York: Routledge, 2006. Print.

Cole, C. L., and David L. Andrews. "America's New Son: Tiger Woods and America's New Multiculturalism." *Commodified and Criminalized: New Racism and African Americans in Contemporary Sports.* Eds. David J. Leonard and G. Richard King. Lanham, MD: Rowman & Littlefield, 2011. 23–40. Print.

Collier, Gene. "Athletes Aren't Special." *[Pittsburgh] Post-Gazette.* 20 June 2010. Web. 1 Feb. 2011.

Eitzen, D. Stanley. "Ethical Dilemmas in American Sport: The Dark Side of Competition." *Sport in Contemporary Society: An Anthology.* Ed. D. Stanley Eitzen. Boulder, CO: Paradigm, 2009. 161–170. Print.

Feinstein, John. "The Disappearance of Tiger Woods." *The Observer.* 6 Feb. 2010. Web. 4 May 2011.

_____. *The First Coming: Tiger Woods: Master or Martyr?* New York: Ballantine, 1998. Print.

_____. "Unclear Exactly Where Tiger, Tour Are Headed." *The Washington Post.* 14 Dec. 2009. Web. 4 May 2011.

Hancock, David. "Clinton Cheated 'Because I Could.'" CBS News. 11 Feb. 2009. Web. 30 Aug. 2011.

Hotchkiss, Sandy, and James Masterson. *Why Is It Always About You? The Seven Deadly Sins of Narcissism.* New York: Free Press, 2003. Print.

Hyman, Mark. *Until It Hurts: America's Obsession with Youth Sports and How It Harms Our Kids.* Boston: Beacon Press, 2009. Print.

Jenkins, Sally. "George Huguely, Ben Rothlisberger, Lawrence Taylor: Male Athletes Encouraged to Do the Wrong Thing." *The Washington Post.* 8 May 2010. Web. 26 Aug. 2011.

_____. "Where's the Magic?" *SIVault.com. Sports Illustrated.* 25 Nov. 1991. Web. 9 Nov. 2011.

King, Kelley. "Doing the Legwork." *SI.com Scorecard. Sports Illustrated,* 22 Jan. 2003. Web. 27 Aug. 2011.

Laderman, Gary. *Sacred Matters: Celebrity Worship, Sexual Ecstasies, the Living Dead, and Other Sins of Religious Life in the United States.* New York: New Press, 2009. Print.

Lasch, Christopher. *The Culture of Narcissism: American Life in An Age of Diminishing Expectations.* New York: W. W. Norton, 1979. Print.

"Little League Sets Attandance Record." *ESPN.* 19 Aug. 2011. Web. 13 Nov. 2011.

Low, Chris. "NCAA Eyes Use of Hostesses." *ESPN: College Football.* 9 Dec. 2009. Web. 27 Aug. 2011.

Mahler, Jonathan. "The Tiger Bubble." *New York Times Magazine.* 28 Mar. 2010. Web. 3 Nov. 2011.

Merida, Kevin. "Spoiled Sports: When the Problem with Youth Athletics Is Grown-Ups." *The Washington Post.* 6 Apr. 2003. Web. 19 July 2011.

Merrill, Elizabeth, and Amy K. Nelson. "The Sports Infidelity Equation." *ESPN.* 25 Nov. 2010. Web. 16 Aug. 2011.

Messner, Michael A. "Boyhood, Organized Sports, and the Construction of Masculinities." *Sport in Contemporary Society: An Anthology.* Ed. D. Stanley Eitzen. Boulder, CO: Paradigm, 2009. 50–66. Print.

_____. *Out of Play: Critical Essays on Gender and Sport.* Albany: State University of New York Press, 2007. Print.

_____. *Taking the Field: Women, Men, and Sports.* Minneapolis: University of Minnesota Press, 2002. Print.

_____, Michele Dunbar, and Darnell Hunt. "The Televised Sports Manhood Formula." *Sport in Contemporary Society: An Anthology.* Ed. D. Stanley Eitzen. Boulder, CO: Paradigm, 2009, 71–84. Print.

Mills, Keith. "Athlete Entitlement Reaches New Heights at NFL Draft." *PressBox.com.* 25 Apr. 2010. Web. 15 Feb. 2011.

Myers, Dean. "A Culture of Acceptance." *ColumbiaSportsJournalism.com.* 2011. Web. 30 Aug. 2011.

Nixon, Howard L. II. *Sport in a Changing World.* Boulder, CO: Paradigm, 2008. Print.

Ortiz, Steven M. "Traveling with the Ball Club: A Code of Conduct for Wives Only." *Symbolic Interaction* 20.3 (1997): 225–249. Print.

_____. "Using Power: An Exploration of Control Work in the Sport Marriage." *Sociological Perspectives* 49.4 (2006): 527–557. Print.

Overman, Steven J. *Living Out of Bounds: The Male Athlete and Everyday Life.* Lincoln: University of Nebraska Press, 2010. Print.

Price, S. L. "Inside Tennis." *SI.com. Sports Illustrated,* 7 Sept. 2011. Web. 7 Sept. 2011.

Rhoden, William C. *$40 Million Slaves: The Rise, Fall, and Redemption of the Black Athlete.* New York: Crown, 2006. Print.

Robinson, Laurie Nicole. "Professional Athletes — Held to a Higher Standard and Above the Law: A Comment on High-Profile Criminal Defendants and the Need for States to Establish High-Profile Courts." *Indiana Law Journal* 73.4 (2008): 1–34. Web. 11 Apr. 2011.

Shipnuck, Alan. "The Shrinking of Tiger Woods." *IVault.com. Sports Illustrated,* 1 Mar. 2010. Web. 13 Nov. 2011.

Smiley, Bob. *Follow the Roar: Tailing Tiger for All 604 Holes of His Most Spectacular Season.* New York: HarperCollins, 2008. Print.

Smith, Earl. *Race, Sport, and the American Dream.* 2nd ed. Durham: Carolina Academic Press, 2009. Print.

Smith, Gary. "The Chosen One." *CNNSI.com.* CNN. 23 Dec. 1996. Web. 26 Oct. 2011.

Strege, John. *A Biography of Tiger Woods.* New York: Broadway Books, 1997.

"Strippers Said to Be Commonplace at Football Recruitment Parties." *Fox News.* 10 Feb. 2004. Web. 27 Aug. 2011.

Teitelbaum, Stanley. *Athletes Who Indulge Their Dark Side: Sex, Drugs, and Cover-Ups.* Santa Barbara, CA: Praeger, 2010. Print.

_____. *Sports Heroes, Fallen Idols.* Lincoln: University of Nebraska Press, 2005. Print.

"Tiger Woods Transcript: Apology Statement Full Text." *Huffington Post.* 19 Feb. 2010. Web. 31 Oct. 2011.

Twenge, Jean M., and W. Keith Campbell. *The Narcissism Epidemic: Living in the Age of Entitlement.* New York: Free Press, 2009. Print.

Ward, Pete. *Gods Behaving Badly: Media, Religion, and Celebrity Culture.* Waco: Baylor University Press, 2011. Print.

Whannel, Gary. *Media Sports Stars: Masculinities and Moralities.* London: Routledge, 2001. Print.

PART II: EVERYMAN TIGER

Reluctantly Playing the Race Game

Linda H. Straubel
and Donna J. Barbie

Golf has a "shameful racial history," asserts CBS sports writer Steve Elling. Few people seem to have felt shame when the game was first played in America, however, as wealthy Caucasian men joined exclusive clubs, not only to hone and display their skills, but also to interact with their own kind and to seal important business deals. These clubs very often employed black men as waiters, busboys, and caddies. They could not become members. Not surprisingly, long-standing and long-accepted racial discrimination was codified by country clubs and even by the Professional Golfers' Association. According to the Tour's official rules, 1934–61, "Professional golfers of the Caucasian Race, over the age of eighteen (18) years ... who can qualify under the terms and conditions hereinafter specified, shall be eligible" for membership (Jones 383, 391). As these rules verify, the professional circuit banned black players for more than three decades.

Broaching the issue of racial exclusion, founder of Shoal Creek Country Club Hall W. Thompson stated, "'We have the right to associate with or not to associate with whomever we choose. The country club is our home.... [We don't exclude anyone] except the blacks [since including them is] just not done in Birmingham, Al.'" (qtd. in Sounes 146). Clearly, Thompson felt no shame. Although his declaration might not seem particularly noteworthy, given the tradition of racism that has enveloped golf in America, it might be surprising to learn that he delivered this statement in 1990 (Sounes 146–7). That was a depressing twenty-seven years after Martin Luther King, Jr.'s, famous Birmingham protests, thirty-six years after the Supreme Court struck down the "separate but equal" credo, and an astonishing forty-two years after Truman ended official discrimination in the military.

Some might argue that Tiger Woods' success on the links indicates that golf has outgrown its racist past, and others might even extend that assertion to American culture in general. Contentions about a post-racial America would be simplistic, however. Woods, a person of color, has indeed become the most renowned golfer in the past half-century, but he has also embodied, in many ways, America's ambiguous preoccupation with race. For instance, Earl Woods, Tiger's father and his earliest and most ferocious publicist, saw an advantage in highlighting Tiger's racial heritage. Framing his son's story as the American Dream finally coming to fruition for "others," Earl emphasized that Tiger overcame racial obstacles in order to play golf. Even though Earl's narratives resonated with companies that marketed the young golfer so successfully, as well as with the culture at large, Tiger has tried to dodge issues of race. He has stressed his aspiration to be the best golfer ever, without racial qualifier. As a result, many perceive that Tiger has "disidentified" himself as black and repudiated any obligations to the African American community. Despite Tiger's efforts to distance himself from racial matters, he has never been able to extricate himself from the morass. Sometimes prompting the controversies himself but most often thrust into the cultural conversation by the actions and words of others, Tiger Woods has found himself at the center of America's obsession with race.

Earl Woods: Stories of Racial Obstacles

In the mid–1970s, Tiger's father and mother, Earl Woods and his second wife Kultida, settled in a very modest neighborhood in Cypress, California, near the Navy golf course. As part of the Seal Beach U.S. Naval Station, the course came replete with fluttering American flags, a surface-to-air missile beside the putting green, and a pond with a scale model of the *USS Los Angeles*. Earl, a slightly burly ex–Green Beret with two Vietnam tours to his credit, frequently walked past all these symbols of America with his tiny, golfing son, Tiger (Sounes 123). On the face of it, this is an image of democracy and racial harmony in action: Earl is retired from quite a successful military career in a fully integrated U.S. military, thanks in large part to Truman's 1948 executive order. That change, like the entire history of race relations in America, was not as simple as it sounds. Similarly, Earl's relationship with those in charge of the military golf course was not all that harmonious, as he frequently reported to the media.

Earl, for example, told the story of Tiger being forbidden to play on the course anywhere but the putting green. He attributed the prohibition to racism. Earl asserted that conflict arose because those who played on and managed the course primarily comprised

> retired naval personnel who knew blacks only as cooks and servers, and along comes me, a retired lieutenant colonel outranking 99 percent of them, and I have the nerve to take up golf at 42 and immediately become a low handicap and beat them, and then I have the *audacity* to have this kid [qtd. in Smith].

Earl asserts that course authorities, out of spite and racism, "took away Tiger's playing privileges twice, said he was too young, even though there were other kids too young who they let play." Even though Tiger proved himself worthy at the age of three by beating seasoned veterans, including one of the course pros, Earl states that Tiger was kicked off the course again. "That's when we switched him to another course," Earl concludes (qtd. in Smith). This story, as well as many others Earl narrated, might not have been exactly accurate. Howard Sounes, in his authoritative *The Wicked Game*, argues that there really was a rule against children younger than ten playing anywhere but the putting green (124). In light of this evidence, it is difficult to know if Earl's perceptions about racism were accurate.

Ascertaining the veracity of Earl's claim actually matters little. It is more important to understand that this anecdote fits into a pattern, indicating how alert Earl was to potential racism because he had been subjected to discrimination when he was growing up. Earl's awareness of the sting of racism was not unfounded, even after he and Kultida settled into the quiet California neighborhood. As he told his Thai wife, "Look, forget being Thai, because in the United States there are only two colors, white and nonwhite. Everybody else is lumped in the same boat." This sad wisdom is partly borne out by the family's early experiences in the mixed, but light-skinned neighborhood. They were subjected to jeering racial epithets and kids throwing limes at them (Sounes 120). Clearly, California was not a model of harmony and equality.

Possibly because of Earl's experiences, he often featured Tiger as the victim of racism. Whether Tiger was actually subjected to racism as a child is debatable, however. The most renowned of the narratives features Tiger's first day of school, where he was tied to a tree and pelted with rocks. There are various accounts of this incident in Smith's article, in John Strege's *Tiger: A Biography of Tiger Woods* (18), and Robert Lusetich's book *Unplayable*. Lusetich quotes Tiger himself telling the sad and appalling tale. According to Tiger, he is called "monkey" and even has the "n-word" written across his chest (45). Earl told and retold this story, and most listeners have apparently found it believable. To his credit, Sounes interviewed school personnel who would have been involved. Without exception, they all claim none of this ever happened (127–8). Additional information supports the possibility of this narrative's inaccuracy. Many of Tiger's kindergarten classmates were also children of color, and yet they were never subjected to racial tormenting.

Sounes questions why Tiger would have been singled out and expresses skepticism about the story (128). Is it to be believed? What would cause Earl and Tiger to make such claims, and why would school officials deny them? Certainly, teachers and the principal would have a vested interest in denying the story, especially if they did nothing to stop the torment, as both Earl and Tiger have asserted. On the other hand, the Woodses may, in fact, have benefited because the narrative so aptly illustrates the American Dream with all its mythic power of achievement in the face of adversity. Regardless, the very fact that the episode has been so widely believed tells its own tale. True or not, the story makes sense in a divided culture that insists on seeing people through the lens of race and where such incidents are commonplace.

Racial Identity

The first time I [Linda] had ever heard of Tiger Woods was in 1995 when a friend asked, "You've heard of Tiger Woods, the golfer, right? Black ... handsome to die for?" I nodded vaguely; his casual assumption that I had heard of the man made me feel as if to do otherwise would be akin to admitting I had been living under a rock for who knows how long. Although I was impressed that my friend, a middle-aged, heterosexual male, was secure enough in his manhood to refer to another man as "handsome to die for," and while I did have a vague picture of the smiling young golfer he was talking about, it never occurred to me to question his other descriptor of Woods as "black." Apparently, we were not alone in this, and that speaks volumes about the dichotomous racial divisions in our country.

America and Tiger, especially as represented by the media, were in conflict about his racial identity from the beginning of his emergence as a golfing star. In *Tiger: The Real Story*, Steve Helling explains that, even during his college years, long before his turning pro, Tiger disliked "racial" attention: "He wasn't there to make a social statement or to break down barriers; he was there to play golf. Frequently annoyed with the media who featured him as the "first African American to play somewhere," Tiger was not "striving to be the first or the youngest or even the greatest. He just wanted to win at golf" (102). Although Tiger did indeed win many tournaments, there was no "just" in his future. Race has continued to be a significant element of his story.

As he was about to turn pro, Tiger attempted to clarify his racial identity in a one-page handout for the press: "The purpose of this statement is to explain my heritage for [those] who may be seeing me play for the first time. It is the final and only comment I will make regarding the issue," he vows. After spelling out his heritage, he affirms that he feels "very fortunate" and "*EQUALLY PROUD* to be both African American and Asian."Hoping to settle the issue once and for all, he concludes, "The critical and fundamental point is that ethnic background and/or composition should *not* make a difference. It does *not* make a difference to me. The bottom line is that I am an American ... and proud of it!" (Woods, original emphasis). At this point, Tiger clearly has faith in his ability to define himself. Responding to the media's expressed wish to see him as representative of African Americans, Tiger closes his statement with the hope that he "can just be a golfer and a human being" (Woods). Despite Tiger's hopes, he could hardly have believed that the world would let him forget his race altogether. He had plenty of reminders, including a letter he received as a college freshman after one of his U.S. Amateur victories. "You can take the nigger out of the jungle, but you can't take the jungle out of the nigger," it read. Tiger showed it to a teammate, then taped it to his wall as a reminder. He also reminded himself to let his clubs talk for him (Strege 85). Woods would strive to put racial issues aside and to prevail by winning tournaments.

Despite Tiger's proclamations that the media statement would serve as his final word on race, he addressed the issue again in 1997 during an interview with Oprah Winfrey. As a child, Woods incorporated parts of his father's and mother's heritages, including Caucasian, Black, Indian and Asian, to come up with the term "Cablinasian," and he informed Oprah's massive audience that "Cablinasian" was his preferred ethnic designator. As UCLA History professor Henry Yu points out, Tiger's term "achieved no currency nor usage.... the power of racial categories comes from their work of tying a number of people together under a single description" (12). No matter how often Tiger repeated his disavowal of race as a compelling force in his life, he has continued to be classified as black.

Although a great many people presume Tiger's black heritage, a considerable number of others perceive that he has "disidentified" with African Americans. Sports correspondent for *The Telegraph* Oliver Brown, for example, asserts that Woods responded to "a black constituency desperate to celebrate him as an idol ... not by embracing the black dimension of his heritage, but by erasing it." Stanford professor Eamonn Callan analyzes Tiger Woods' situation, comparing voluntary assimilation to "assimilationism." He defines the latter as "forced assimilation," wherein citizens are compelled to abandon their own heritage before they can be accepted as "real Americans." Callan argues that Tiger faced no coercion but made a choice to voluntarily assimilate. "Whatever gratitude Woods might owe to those whose struggle against racism in America made his professional success possible," Callan concludes, "it creates no obligation for him to identify himself as African American" (490).

Success and Racial Obligation

As Callan's article indicates, scholars have long debated the link between race and obligation. Taking up both issues in his play *Radio Golf,* African American playwright August Wilson clearly identifies Woods as a phenomenally successful black man. Tiger appears as a giant poster on the set, his image commenting on black aspirations and upward mobility. Middle Tennessee State University professor Ronald Kates tackles the connection between race and success, claiming that the symbolic poster reveals that "Woods has had to continually fight the expectation that his blackness somehow requires him to address problems in an urban America of which he had never been a part" (29). In support of his argument, Kates quotes William Rhoden, *New York Times* columnist and author of *Forty Million Dollar Slaves.* According to Rhoden, America's black athletes have traditionally considered themselves to be "part of a larger cause," but adds "'today, when so many black athletes have little or no sense of who or what came before, there is no sense of the athlete as part of a larger community, as a foot soldier in a larger struggle'" (qtd. in Kates 29).

Kates asserts that like the play's African American characters, Woods "faces a similar dichotomy" (29). Although one of the characters re-discovers his "roots" and a dedication to preserving his African American neighborhood, the other succumbs to his ambitions to develop the area. He self-servingly convinces himself that "a re-developed neighborhood featuring Whole Foods, Starbucks, and Barnes & Noble will undoubtedly benefit" the surrounding emerging African American middle class in the '90s (Kates 27). The play nonetheless warns that they are still "on shaky ground and ever-ripe for corruption" (Weiss). In the end, the poster is symbolically torn off the wall, suggesting Tiger's uncertain role in the dilemma of profiting through assimilation and embracing a specifically African American identity.

Perhaps those claiming that Tiger Woods has "disidentified" with African Americans and blacks who take offense at his "rebuff" are voicing a far from settled controversy over the "talented tenth" begun by eminent African American scholar W. E. B. DuBois over a hundred years ago. As DuBois asserts, "The Negro race, like all races, is going to be saved by its exceptional men.... it is the problem of developing the Best of this race that they may guide the Mass away from the contamination and death of the Worst, in their own and other races." DuBois then asks, "Was there ever a nation on God's fair earth civilized from the bottom upward? Never; it is, ever was and ever will be from the top downward that culture filters. The Talented Tenth rises and pulls all that are worth the saving up to their vantage ground."

Although the "exceptional men" that DuBois references are primarily literary, educational, and political leaders, might one not count the extremely successful, such as America's sports heroes, among today's Talented Tenth? What might be expected of them? How are they to contribute? Tiger felt the pressure, like it or not. As Strege reports, Tiger "had been burdened with a cause he had not chosen. He was talented and he was black, and, as a result, he was no longer playing only for himself. He was playing for an entire race" (45). *New York Times* writer Larry Dorman also points to that implicit obligation, asserting that Jim Thorpe, the only African American golfer on the PGA Tour in 1994, and Tiger Woods constituted the "present and future" of minority players on the Tour. In an article published immediately after Tiger's first Masters victory in 1997, Dorman notes that the accomplishment was "remarkable," at least in part, because of its "social significance," comparing the win to Jackie Robinson's accomplishment in baseball a half-century before. As Dorman argues, Tiger bore "additional weight of expectations and hopes" as he walked the Augusta National ("Woods Tears Up Augusta").

Although Woods may not have always embraced other people's expectations that he should be the "Great Black Hope," he *has* "given back," most typically through his Foundation. Strege notes that the Foundation recently celebrated Earl Woods Scholars becoming seniors in 2010, added two Tiger Woods Learning Centers (1), and extended its reach to include scholarships to students in Korea, Thailand, and China, as well as the United States (13). The Foundation's 2010 report includes an impressive list of donors including Nike, Gatorade, and AT&T (17). Yet, for some, these efforts are still not be enough. A harsh exchange between Tiger Woods and ESPN reporter Mark Schwarz illustrates the problem. At a 2008 Bay Hill press conference, Schwarz states, "When you were a year old, there were twelve African Americans on the Tour. Today, depending on how you define the demographics, there's one. From a racial diversity standpoint, the Tour seems to have gone backwards. What does that mean to you?" Given Woods' history of deflecting racial questions, this is not a good start. Woods nonetheless states that "it's become harder to play out here." He also notes that many courses mandate golf carts, significantly reducing the number of caddies, and thus hampering, if not eliminating, many blacks' avenue to playing the game (qtd. in Lusetich 44). Unsatisfied, Schwarz launches into his last question. He asks what Woods would say to people who might claim that Tiger "'could do so much more for this cause. He could be more accessible ... he could use his resources and be there and reach out to people'" (qtd. in Lusetich 44–45). Schwarz seems to have hit a nerve. Defending himself, Tiger points to the work of his Foundation, affirming that his most important contribution is helping children to find their way, but not necessarily through golf. Here, Woods and his critics were again at cross-purposes. People who are concerned about racial diversity on America's golf courses and the professional tour point to Tiger's obligation to help redress the golfing world's racial imbalance. Tiger assumed that giving back did not necessarily involve race or the game.

In 2006, another critic, Gary ("the G-Man") Toms chastises Woods. Asserting that Tiger "has chosen to ignore an aspect of golf that is so painfully obvious for many inside and outside of the sport," Toms urges him to be a "true hero and leader" by openly addressing the issue of racial discrimination in golf. "Imagine the impact it would have on society," Toms continues, "if he spoke out explicitly on behalf of those still excluded." Toms wants Tiger to "work to ensure that this [exclusion] is halted."

As Tiger became extraordinarily famous, the divide between his wish to be treated simply as an American and a golfer and everyone else's expectations that he serve as the "Great Black Hope" (Dorman "A Way Out") was growing. As Yu writes, "Whether it was Jackie Robinson, Michael Jordan, Tiger Woods, or Woods' contemporary Colin Powell, Americans had learned by the end of the twentieth century to fantasize that a single person would save them from racial problems which were endemic and built into the structure of U.S. society" (14). Yu's argument seems oversimplified and reductive, however. Those wanting to see Tiger as a positive symbol may never have considered him a savior but instead viewed him as proof that America was already saved, that the country had "turned the corner" and that more progress would result. He was then, perhaps, a mile marker of a culture's progress, not so much the cause of the progress already made or still to come, but a good sign. His place as a shining star on the predominantly white golf courses might mean "See how far we've come," not "Oh, Tiger, save us."

Racial Controversies Haunt Him, Anyway

A considerable number of sensational incidents that have entangled Tiger Woods would appear to negate such claims of a post-racial America, however. In some cases, ironically enough, Tiger played an active role in linking himself to race, and at other times, he was simply thrust into the fray. Several of these situations remained more or less contained firestorms, but others exploded furiously and threatened to burn out of control.

The first controversy occurred just as Tiger entered professional golf in 1996. Tiger was trying to thread his way through the maze of racial classification and his own urges to ignore race when Nike offered him one of the most lucrative endorsement deals of any sports figure in history. Once Woods signed, Nike unveiled the "Hello World" campaign, including a giant mural on the side of a building in Portland, Oregon. Sounes' *The Wicked Game* includes a picture of this enormous mural of Tiger wearing a baseball cap emblazoned with Nike's iconic swoosh. Woods gazes serenely expressionless into some resplendent future that only he can see. According to Sounes, Tiger's multi-ethnic look attracted and excited Nike more than his successful golf game (180). As part of the campaign, Nike ran a television ad that presents a series of video clips of Tiger at various ages, each portion displaying a print declaration of his achievement at a particular age. One caption reads, "I am the only man to win three consecutive U.S. Amateur titles." At the end, another caption asks, "I'm told I'm not ready for you. Are you ready for me?" These positive images of Tiger's past success and promise of future achievements are disrupted by an inflammatory claim, however. That statement reads: "There are still golf courses in the United States that I cannot play because of the color of my skin." Instead of simply relaying a "feel good" vision of racial acceptance and harmony, the ad brings racial conflict to the fore.

The American media responded immediately, focusing on the last statement. *New York Times* writer Richard Sandomir, for example, points to the irony that the "brash Nike empire" was using Tiger's African American roots to gain market share despite the player's emphatic assertions of his mixed ethnicity. Dorman also notes that "race was never a big issue with him [Tiger]," adding that "Madison Avenue has changed all that" by presenting him as "some avenging angel crashing the great white gates of golf" ("We'll Be"). *Washington Post* columnist James Glassman reacted by contacting Nike to request a list of discriminatory courses, and Nike's spokesman eventually had to admit no such list existed. As the representative told Glassman, Tiger's celebrity meant he could play on any course he wished and that the message was not meant to be taken literally (Strege 194–5). Glassman describes the ad as "discordant, dishonest, and vile," based on the false image of a victimized Tiger. All of these commentaries focus on the hypocrisy of the campaign. On the one hand, Tiger was asking the media to leave his race out of it, yet when it was convenient or lucrative, he allowed himself, or allowed Nike through him, to "play the race card." Although this controversy burned hot, it burned out quickly as media turned its attention to Tiger's performances on the links.

Woods seems to have invited the "Hello World" debate, at least to a certain extent, but firestorms of racial controversy simply enveloped him at other times. A prime example is the infamous Fuzzy Zoeller incident. Zoeller was an elite player in the 1970s and '80s who, according to his official website, is "one of the great characters" of golf. Many commentators have noted that his "character" includes a sometimes unfortunate sense of humor. Tiger was the butt of Fuzzy's "humor" during the 1997 Masters tournament, and those comments created a spate of racial accusations that has never died out entirely.

During a post-round interview, Zoeller is clearly irked by reporters' questions about Tiger's spectacular performance. It probably didn't help that Zoeller had scored a pathetic 78 that day ("Golfer Says"). Wearing sunglasses, holding a drink, and talking very fast, Fuzzy states that Tiger is "doing quite well," mentioning that he is "pretty impressive." Then Zoeller refers to Woods as "that little boy." If the "boy" reference were not enough to raise hackles, Fuzzy exhorts the reporters to tell Tiger "not to serve fried chicken next year" because Woods would have the privilege of choosing the Champions Dinner menu the following year. Almost immediately after the fried chicken comment, Zoeller says, "Got it," and snaps his fingers. He abruptly turns and walks away, but only a few paces. This would have been quite enough, with the racial implications of "fried chicken" heaped on top of "boy," but Zoeller is not finished. He swivels suddenly and calls out loudly, "or collard greens or whatever the hell they serve." In less than eighteen seconds, not only does he employ familiar stereotypes associated with African Americans, but he also uses the word "they" with unmistakable purpose. Zoeller pegged Tiger into a category of "otherness," someone to be resented and even disparaged because of his race.

Of course, when the interview aired on CNN's *Golf Weekly* a week later, the world rose up in righteous indignation to defend the new darling of the golfing world, and Zoeller had to apologize. As he writes in the carefully scripted statement, "My comments were not intended to be racially derogatory, and I apologize for the fact that they were misconstrued in that fashion." Unfortunately, this portion of the statement is essentially a non-apology, emphasizing that he held no racist intent and then pointing to others who obviously misinterpreted his jokes. He continues,

> Anybody who knows me knows that I am a jokester.... It's too bad that something I said in jest was turned into something it's not. But I didn't mean anything by it and I'm sorry if I offended anybody. If Tiger is offended by it, I apologize to him, too. I have nothing but the utmost respect for Tiger as a person and an athlete ["Golfer Says"].

Here, Zoeller only hints at the reason the apology was necessary by stating that he is sorry for having "offended" people. He fails to mention who those "anybodies" might be or why they might be offended. Clearly, he does not even want to mention race. Like so many before and after him, Zoeller relies on the "no intent" defense. If he did not intend to be racist, he cannot be perceived as a racist. Asserting that he was attempting to be funny, Zoeller implies that racial slurs delivered as humor cannot be taken seriously and therefore do not count. His use of "if" in the final two sentences is very telling. Zoeller is sorry for the incident, but both "ifs" indicate that easily offended people are responsible for misinterpreting his remarks.

Although Tiger likely hoped for the firestorm to die out quickly, his response only added to the controversy. Instead of commenting quickly and personally, Tiger Woods left it to his representatives at IMG to pen a brief statement several days after the story broke. On Tiger's behalf, IMG notes, "At first I was shocked to hear that Fuzzy Zoeller had made these unfortunate remarks. His attempt at humor was out of bounds, and I was disappointed by it. But having played golf with Fuzzy, I know he is a jokester; and I have concluded that no personal animosity toward me was intended." The statement concludes, "I know he feels badly about his remarks. We all make mistakes, and it is time to move on. I accept Fuzzy's apology and hope everyone can now put this behind us" (qtd. in Wilner). Capitalizing on omissions in Zoeller's apology, the IMG statement also fails to note, with any specificity, the reasons Zoeller's remarks were "unfortunate." In fact, the statement remains even more nebulous than the apology, as it mentions no one other than Tiger as a potential victim of Zoeller's humor. Capturing Tiger's attempts to avoid issues of race, the IMG statement focuses on Tiger's individual disappointment, reinforces the "no ill intent" defense, accepts the apology, and announces that the episode is over. In that way, everyone can move on.

The firestorm did not die out, however, even after the release of IMG's statement. Following the story closely for nearly a month, the press wanted the two players to meet face to face. As *New York Times* sports writer Joe Drape writes, Woods "cleared up one major off-course distraction" when he had lunch with Zoeller and again declared the incident to be "over." Even then, the "conversation" still did not wane. AP sports journalist Barry Wilner, for example, offers a statement by Kweisi Mfume, president of the N.A.A.C.P. Mfume calls Zoeller's remarks "vicious and demeaning," adding that they show a "lack of respect not only for Mr. Woods but for people of color everywhere." *Washington Post* columnist William Raspberry concurs that all is not well in America, offering a litany of recent racial incidents, including Zoeller's remarks. However, Raspberry insists that Zoeller's comments were "not the same thing — not even close" to the racism that is enacted by many American businesses. Although he agrees that Zoeller's comments were racist, Raspberry argues that African American attention cannot be distracted from responding to systemically injurious discrimination.

Even after more than a decade, people still express opinions about Zoeller's eighteen-second mistake. Some focus on Zoeller's role in the fiasco. Nearly all of the YouTube posts in response to a clip of the original interview, for example, give Zoeller the "thumbs down." Assemblyguy, for example, labels Zoeller "a dumb redneck douche." Other people, nonetheless, criticize Tiger. Despite Woods' unqualified acceptance of Zoeller's apology, some people wanted the exoneration to come a lot sooner, claiming that Tiger left Fuzzy "twisting" in the wind. Expressing completely opposing views, others assert that Woods let Zoeller off the hook far too easily, never calling him out for his racist remarks. As these commentaries indicate, some firestorms die down after a time, but they continue to smolder.

One of the "racial" controversies enveloping Tiger, the Martha Burk/ Augusta National debate, did not even seem to be about race. In July 2002, Chair of the National Council of Women's Organizations, Martha Burk wrote a letter to William "Hootie" Johnson, Chair of the Augusta National Golf Club, asking the board to allow women to become members. Johnson responded stridently, stating that the club would not be "bullied, threatened ... or coerced at the point of a bayonet.' Taken aback by Johnson's rhetoric, Burk declared that she would "communicate with others" to achieve her goals (qtd. in Litsky). One might ask, and rightfully so, how Tiger Woods came to be sucked into this volatile "conversation." He is not a member of Augusta National, nor has he expressed interest in women's issues. Despite those realities, the media would not allow him to stay out of the fray, because he was the world's top-ranked golfer and the reigning Masters Champion, but most especially because of Tiger's ethnicity. Burk and her followers believed that Tiger, a person of color, would certainly understand and rise up in righteous indignation in defense of others who had been subjected to discriminatory practices. How wrong they were.

According to Jere Longman and Clifton Brown, Woods was "caught off guard" when asked about his position on the "incendiary issue" in mid-year. His response was classic vacuous fence-sitting: "It would be nice to see everyone have an equal chance to participate, but there is nothing you can do about it" (qtd. in Longman and Brown). Clearly, Woods did not accept the role as firebrand. He makes this clear by employing impersonal references, "It would be nice" and "you." These expressions serve to separate him from the issue. This is not his mission; someone else needs to work on it. Even after he had a few weeks to rethink his answer, Tiger did little better when he declared, "Do I want to see a female member? ... Yes. But it's our right to have any club set up the way we want to" (qtd. in Longman and Brown). In the first portion of this declaration, he shifts his previous strategy by using "I." The personal pronoun relays his preference for the club to open its membership to women. Although that might indicate he feels some connection to the issue, Woods' later use of "our" and "we" illustrates that he perceives himself to be squarely within the "club" that is under siege. Here he dispels any notion of his "identification" with the women's plight, and he never alters his position even though the media fanned the flames for months.

A series of *New York Times* articles emphasizes Tiger's race as the reason he needed to speak up. Longman and Brown, for example, noted that many people were "enormously" disappointed in Tiger's remarks, writing that they perceived that he was "essentially condoning discrimination and, in the process, turning his back" on black athletes who advocated for civil rights (1). In mid–November, a *Times* editorial suggested that Woods should boycott the Masters to send a strong message against exclusion ("American's All-Male"). The very next day, N.A.A.C.P. Chairman Julian Bond wrote a letter to the *Times* editor, denouncing athletes who play at "discriminatory golf clubs," asserting that they "endorse wrongful exclusion by their presence." Rather than focusing on Woods as the sole player who should take up the cause, however, Bond declares that Tiger "ought not be expected to shoulder this burden alone."

Despite Bonds' attempt to broaden the spotlight, others declared Woods' particular responsibility. Professor of Law at the University of Wisconsin Linda Greene points to the Nike campaign when she writes, "Indeed, it is difficult to reconcile Woods's indifference to exclusion with his public-relations posture as a poster child for racial opportunity." Greene ultimately declares that Woods had "shirked an important opportunity" to stand up for women's equality. Of course, others express opposing positions. *New York Times* sports columnist Dave Anderson proclaims, "Just because Woods is the world's No. 1 golfer, just because he's a mixture of minorities ... he's not obliged to take a sociological stand. It's not his responsibility." Although Tiger was a "featured" player in the early stages of this "conversation," his role faded when he maintained silence. Ultimately, Martha Burk's rhetoric and boycott fizzled in the rain at the Masters.

In 2008, Golf Channel's sports commentator Kelly Tilghman sparked one of the most infamous racial controversies by engaging in some unfortunate banter. Playing off her co-anchor's joke that the only way Tiger's golfing rivals could win was by "beating" him, Tilghman concluded that the players should "lynch" him in a back alley. As Farrell Evans explains, Tilghman started another round "of the stagecraft that passes for racial discourse in this country, with a tragic moment followed by the requisite scenes of accusation, remorse and demands for the protagonist's head, all backed by a chorus of conflicting voices echoing to the rafters" ("Hidden Meaning"). Only touching on the criticism Tilghman received by the press, as well as her two-week suspension, Evans argues that Tiger's response was far more interesting than the scandalous remark itself. Evans explains that "Tiger was quick to forgive and forget." Through his agent, Mark Steinberg, Tiger, attempting once more to rise above the racial fracas, called the incident a "nonissue." His final statement on the matter was, "Regardless of the choice of words used, we know unequivocally that there was no ill intent in her comments" (qtd. in Evans, "Hidden Meaning"). Evans argues, however, that Woods may be more culpable in this incident than Tilghman by ignoring the horrendous implications of the word "lynch" as associated with African Americans. But, Evans asks, "by so blithely dismissing the incident, isn't [Woods] contributing to the offense?" In agreement with people who criticized Tiger for letting Zoeller off too easily, Evans implies that Woods' failure to be insulted reflects his lack of identification with the African American community. His forgiveness ironically constitutes a significant offense ("Hidden Meaning").

Tiger's statement did not end the controversy, however. The magazine *Golfweek* responded to Tilghman's comment and the aftermath by printing a picture of a hanging noose on its cover. Displaying seemingly clever wordplay, the cover story's title, "Caught in a Noose," and sub-title, "Tilghman slips up, and Golf Channel can't wriggle free," compound the damage. According to *Golfweek* editor Dave Seanor, "We knew that image would grab attention, but I didn't anticipate the enormity of it. There's been a huge, negative reaction" (qtd. in "*Golfweek* Editor Fired," *CBS*). PGA Tour Commissioner Tim Finchem called the picture "outrageous and irresponsible." "It smacks of tabloid journalism," he continued, calling it "a naked attempt to inflame and keep alive an incident that was heading to an appropriate conclusion" (qtd. in "*Golfweek* Editor Fired," *CBS*). Although Seanor expressed regret, he was fired. Apparently unmoved by the inflammatory graphic and language on the magazine's cover, *The Daily Skew* labeled the controversy "political correctness run amok." Exonerating Seanor, the writer blames the media, pointing out that Tiger said he wasn't offended ("*Golfweek* Editor Fired," *Daily Skew*).

In a final irony, the same week *Golfweek* displayed a noose on its cover, *Golf World* featured Bill Spiller, marking the 60th anniversary of Spiller's attempt to integrate the U.S. PGA Tour. Starkly contrasting *Golfweek*, the *Golf World* cover featured a black and white photo of a dapper-looking African American in a meditative pose. The text reads: "Making Sense of the Kelly Tilghman Saga," with the subtitle, "The Tragedy of Bill Spiller." Approaching the issue with quiet dignity, *Golf World* offers appropriate discourse on the intersection of race and golf.

An intensely publicized controversy arising in early November 2011 briefly entangled Tiger Woods in another racial firestorm. *New York Times* columnist Richard Sandomir appears to have been prescient about the spark that would set off the controversy when he writes, "Welcome again to the ethnically charged, politically correct battles in the arena of news coverage ... [where]

throwaway lines ... turn into verbal grenades." More than two decades after Sandomir anguishes over the racial discourse, Tiger's former caddie Steve Williams lobbed a "verbal grenade"' at a caddie awards dinner in Shanghai. The lead-up to a "caddies and players only" awards dinner helps to put the remarks in context. Although caddies typically remain "silent partners," Williams, embittered because Tiger had fired him, nonetheless spoke to the media months before the dinner, when Adam Scott, his new boss, won a tournament. Williams declared it the "best win I've ever had in my life" (qtd. in Harig, "Steve"). This assertion was not simply an expression of joyous celebration, however. Williams obviously intended to wound Tiger, because together they had won a great many tournaments as a team. When asked at the Shanghai dinner to explain his previous caustic remarks, Williams replied, "It was my aim to shove it up that black arse —" (qtd. in Harig, "Steve"). The verbal grenade exploded resoundingly. As an unidentified caddie reported, "Never have you been in a room and seen so many jaws drop at the same time" (qtd. in Lawrenson). That night, someone in the room leaked the comments to the media, setting off expressions of shock, followed by accusations and a plethora of apologies, some of them possibly even sincere.

Reporters verbalized no objection to Williams' implicit rage and aggression. Instead, race took center stage. The unnamed caddie remarked, "We knew [Williams] was an idiot but we didn't know he was a racist idiot" (qtd. in Lawrenson). Apparently, everyone in the room immediately realized that the word "black" was very volatile and carried far more baggage than any commonplace profanity. They were absolutely correct. Massive television, radio, and Internet coverage quickly made the incident a global issue. Posts responding to BBC golf correspondent Iain Carter's blog capture the essence of the "conversation." Although a few people, like Elliott and bflex89, assert that the comments were not racist, far more argue the opposite. Hendero, for example, asks, "How much more racist can you get?" VBC1 and scotlandgolfer agree, and David reasons that when "people use these kinds of double-barrelled insults ('stupid git,' etc.) the first word is used to devalue the second one, so yes it is racist, no question."

In the face of widespread outrage, Williams quickly offers an apology on his website: "I apologize for comments I made last night.... I now realize how my comments could be construed as racist. However I assure you that was not my intent. I sincerely apologize to Tiger and anyone else I have offended" (qtd. in Harig, "Steve"). Although Williams actually names racism as the issue, much of this statement eerily echoes Fuzzy Zoeller's apology. Williams uses the word "apologize" twice and even declares himself sincere, but he also pleads the "no intent" defense. Others clearly did not perceive the remarks as humorous, nor did the supposed "humor" apparently give him a free pass, but Williams nonetheless adopts Zoeller's strategy when he declares that the evening was about "joking and fun." Perhaps most significantly, Williams uses the passive voice to affirm that his comments "could be construed" as racist. Again, like Zoeller, Williams essentially points at interpreters, making them responsible for incorrect assumptions. As ESPN's Farrell Evans notes, the apology was actually "scolding" people for being so sensitive ("Stevie").

Even after Williams' apology, the controversy expanded, grenade fragments cutting many people. Adam Scott apologized on behalf of his caddie and confirmed that Williams is not a racist. His best defense was declaring that the event was supposed to have been behind closed doors, and he ultimately was forced to stave off exhortations to fire Williams (Harig, "Tiger Woods"). PGA and European Tours submitted a joint statement condemning racism and chastising Williams, without actually leveling any punishment (Elling). Because the Presidents Cup was scheduled two weeks later, with both Woods and Scott playing in the event, team captains Greg Norman and Fred Couples had to weigh in as well. Euro Captain Norman referred to Williams' comments as "stupid" but then claimed that everyone says stupid things and vouchsafed that the caddie was not a racist ("Woods on Caddie"). Departing from the bland admonishments offered by others, the American captain Couples declared that he would fire a caddie for expressing such toxic anger (Carter).

All of this activity was simply the prologue to Tiger's response. Meeting with his former caddie only four days after the awards dinner, Tiger addressed the issue, stating, "It was a wrong thing to say, something that we both acknowledge.... It was hurtful, certainly, but life goes forward" (qtd. in "Woods on Caddie"). Although he claims that Williams' remarks were "wrong" and "hurtful," Tiger downplays the extent of the wrongdoing. Clearly attempting to avoid the volatile issue, he does not even mention race until a reporter asks him pointedly if Williams is a racist. He answers, "No, Stevie's certainly not a racist, there's no doubt about that" (qtd. in Harig, "Tiger"). Tiger thus exonerates Williams entirely of the most important charge against him. Using his caddie's nickname, Tiger unequivocally proclaims that Williams is absolutely "innocent" of racism. And who would know better than Tiger? Entirely consistent in his approach to such controversies, Woods asserts that it is time to move forward.

Of course, Woods' declarations prompted more commentaries. Several praise Woods for taking the "high road." Harig, for example, argues that Woods could have justifiably "let the situation fester" and applauds him for quelling the uproar ("Tiger"). AOL columnist David Steele offers a comprehensive analysis, first blasting just about everyone involved: Norman, Scott, and the Tours for "circling the wagons" with "the sport's history and reputation on the inside ... and Woods on the outside." Steele then argues that Woods, by accepting Williams' apology, gave golf a gift, a "gesture of generosity to a sport that has not proved" itself worthy (Steele). Others were critical of Tiger. Oliver Brown, for example, bemoaned the lost opportunity to offer a "searing indictment ... of golf's attitude to the race issue." Reminiscent of previous accusations leveled against Tiger, Brown claims that Woods "appears to have rejected any semblance of a black conscience," adding that he was "complicit in preserving the status quo." This well-publicized firestorm lasted five frenzied days and then disappeared, but racial controversies clearly can flare up as a result of any apt spark.

Scandal and Race

A great many racial "conversations" have engulfed Tiger, but none have been so pointed as the commentary that accompanied the spectacular scandal of his multiple extramarital affairs. Most of the earliest stories about the scandal did not mention what Imani Perry, a professor at Princeton's Center for African American Studies, calls the "elephant in the room." Some people responding to online articles nevertheless did just that. Taking the initiative to express outrage that Tiger's sexual partners were white, the writers littered their posts with profanity and racial epithets, all directed at Tiger. Possibly taking a lesson from the controversial "rape" scene in D. W. Griffith's *Birth of a Nation*, they obviously viewed Tiger as the overly sexual black man whose greatest threat is to white women.

Perry declares that journalists' early avoidance of the issue did nothing to quell the potency of Americans' "fear of and fascination" with the "exhausting" tale. As she argues, the story of "black hyper-sexuality and animalistic lust" has a "long and miserable history in the United States." *The Black Side* blogger Elie Mystal agrees that the Woods scandal is fraught with "immense weight of cultural context and stereotypes." He then spells out the problematic stereotype quite frankly: "Media-enhanced history has us predisposed to believe that: (A) White men sit around all day in fear of the black man's penis, and (B) You haven't made it as a rich and successful black man unless you're banging white women, two at a time if possible." As Mystal declares, these issues form the backdrop of the Woods' scandal. Tiger's "blackness has never been so apparent" because of his conquest of white women ("Ten Things").

The sexually voracious black man stereotype was not the only racial issue that arose from the sex scandal. As Mystal points out, the "other side of the racial tension motherboard" also lit up. Chauncey DeVega, editor of the *We Are Respectable Negroes* website, declares that Tiger "walked away from his ancestry and history" long ago. He furthermore argues that Tiger bedded white women "as a means of immunizing himself— or so he thought — from his own blackness." These acts, adds DeVega, constitute "a mode of racial fetishizing and obsession," revealing that Tiger wanted these white women "not because they *happened* to be White. No, he wanted these women *precisely* because they were White" (original emphasis). Yvonne Liu, writer for Color Lines News for Action, sums up the dilemma quite well. Arguing that Tiger has been stereotyped "twice over," she explains that "On the one hand, he's the oversexed beast, with a rapacious appetite for white women. On the other, he's the assimilated, middle class Black or brown man with the animal still raging within, ready to erupt and rupture his career." This is a classic case of the double-edged sword, all ending in the same place.

Post-Racial Tiger?

A growing number of Americans express the desire for the culture to "just get over" race, espousing the belief that America is now enjoying a post-racial harmony. Given the number of stories connecting him to the issue, a post-racial Tiger Woods hardly seems around the corner. Nor does it appear that a post-racial America is in sight. As the "Ten Things" article claims, post-scandal commentator "wolves" have been waiting to pounce on Tiger because he is black. Mystal argues that the media gain nothing by thinking through stereotypes but reap great rewards by reporting on all things racial. Interestingly enough, long before the scandal broke, Toms warns Woods that he could lose the sympathy of whites as quickly as he attained it over the slightest breath of scandal (4). Unfortunately, Toms does not mention that Tiger would not regain sympathies of many blacks that he had lost long ago.

The world has gone quiet on the possibility that Tiger might lead America out of the wilderness of binary race definitions and racial tensions, and the media no longer describe Woods as "The Great Black Hope." Some reporters, like Oliver Brown, acknowledge that Tiger has been uncomfortable at "being pegged as black." Others, including Dermot Gilleece, nonetheless continue to bemoan golf's lack of a "black advocate with the moral strength of Arthur Ashe." Still others believe that Tiger cannot be expected to accept that role. As Dave Anderson exhorts, "PLEASE, let Tiger Woods just play golf.... He's not a social activist. He never has been. And it's unlikely he ever will be. It's not his style" (original emphasis). Despite such pleas, Tiger Woods will likely remain a centerpiece in racial firestorms whether he wishes it or not.

Works Cited

"America's All-Male Golfing Society." *New York Times*. 18 Nov. 2002. Web. 11 Nov. 2011.

Anderson, Dave. "Sports of the Times; Woods Is Not Obliged to Boycott." *New York Times*. 8 Dec. 2002. Web. 12 Nov. 2011.

Bond, Julian. Letter to the Editor. *New York Times*. 19 Nov. 2002. Web. 11 Nov. 2011.

Brown, Oliver. "Why Tiger Woods Refused to Play the Race Card Against His Former Caddie Steve Williams." *The [London] Telegraph*. 9 Nov. 2011. Web. 11 Nov. 2011.

Callan, Eamonn. "The Ethics of Assimilation." *Ethics* 115 (Apr. 2005): 471–500.

Carter, Iain. "Why Golf Should Have Responded Quicker to Williams Slur." *Iain Carter's Blog. BBC Sport*. 6 Nov. 2011. Web. 10 Nov. 2011.

DeVega, Chauncey. "Tiger Woods Is Addicted to White Women or People's Exhibit Number One in the 21st Century Post-Racial Museum of Racial Absurdities." *We Are Respectable Negroes*. 7 Dec. 2009. Web. 30 Oct. 2011.

Dorman, Larry. "A Way Out, if the Right People Lead the Way." *New York Times*. 7 June 1994. Web. 4 Nov. 2011.

_____. "'We'll Be Right Back, After This Hip and Distorted Commercial Break.'" *New York Times*. 1 Sept. 1996. Web. 2 Nov. 2011.

_____. "Woods Tears Up Augusta and Tears Down Barriers." *New York Times*. 14 Apr. 1997. Web. 12 Sept. 2011.

Drape, Joe. "Woods Meets Zoeller for Lunch." *New York Times*. 21 May 1997. Web. 27 Oct. 2011.

DuBois, W.E.B. "The Talented Tenth." *The Negro Problem*. 1903. *Teaching American History*. n.d. Web. 8 Aug. 2011.

Elling, Steve. "Finchem Downright Preachy in 2008 Race Mess." *Steve Elling's Short Game Blog*. 6 Nov. 2011. Web. 10 Nov. 2011.

Evans, Farrell. "Hidden Meaning in Tiger's Reaction to Tilghman's 'Lynch' Remark." *Golf.com*. n.d. Web. 11 Aug. 2011.

_____. "Stevie Williams Shouldn't Get Free Pass." *ESPN*. 6 Nov. 2011. Web. 8 Nov. 2011.

Gilleece, Dermot. "Such a Pity Tiger Hasn't Led Fight Against Racism in Golf." *Independent.ie*. 13 Nov. 2011. Web. 13 Nov. 2011.

Glassman, James. "A Dishonest Ad Campaign." *The Washington Post*. 17 Sept. 1996. A 15. Print.

"Golfer Says Comments About Woods Misconstrued." *CNN*. 21 Apr. 1997. Web. 24 Oct. 2011.

"*Golfweek* Editor Fired for Noose Cover." *CBS Interactive*. 31 Jan. 2008. Web. 29 Oct. 2011.

"*Golfweek* Editor Fired for Noose Cover." *The Daily Skew*. 19 Jan. 2008. Web. 11 Aug. 2011.

Greene, Linda. "BackTalk; At Augusta, It's Symbols That Mean Most." *New York Times*. 4 Aug. 2002. Web. 3 Nov. 2011.

Harig, Bob. "Steve Williams Rips Tiger Woods." *ESPN*. 5 Nov. 2011. Web. 9 Nov. 2011.

_____. "Tiger Woods Takes the High Road." *ESPN*. 8 Nov. 2011. Web. 8 Nov. 2011.

Helling, Steve. *Tiger: The Real Story*. Cambridge, MA: DaCapo Press, 2010. Print.

Hello World. Television Advertisement. 1996. YouTube. 16 June 2006. Web. 28 Oct. 2011.

Jones, Thomas B. "Caucasians Only: Solomon Hughes, the PGA, and the 1948 St. Paul Golf Tournament." *MN History Magazine*. Minnesota Historical Society. 383–393. Winter 2003–4. Web. 18 Oct. 2011.

Kates, Ronald. "Tiger on the Wall: African American Middle-Class Identity in Wilson's *Radio Golf*." *Making Connections* 11.2 (2010): 27–34. *ProQuest*. Web. 11 Sept. 2011.

Lawrenson, Derek. "Woods' Ex-Caddie Williams Stuns Guests at Dinner with Vile Outburst." *[UK] Daily Mail*. 4 Nov. 2011. Web. 5 Nov. 2011.

Litsky, Frank. "Women's Group Vows to Pressure Augusta." *New York Times*. 13 July 2002. Web. 11 Nov. 2011.

Liu, Yvonne. "Tiger Woods Likes White Women, So What?" *Color Lines News for Action.* 14 Dec. 2009. Web. 29 Oct. 2011.

Longman, Jere, and Clifton Brown. "Debate on Women at Augusta Catches Woods Off Balance." *New York Times.* 20 Oct. 2002. Web. 6 Nov. 2011.

Lusetich, Robert. *Unplayable: An Inside Account of Tiger's Most Tumultuous Season.* New York: Atria Books, 2010. Print.

Mystal, Elie. "Tiger Woods and the White Women." *The Black Side.* 9 Dec. 2009. Web. 30 Oct. 2011.

Perry, Imani. "Tiger Woods' Choice of Paramours: 'Catch a Tiger by the...'" *Afro-Netizen.* 11 Dec. 2009. Web. 30 Oct. 2011.

Raspberry, William. "Discrimination Is Measurable, but Racism Is a Fuzzier Target." *The [Eugene] Register Guard.* 26 Apr. 1997. Web. 28 Oct. 2011.

Sandomir, Richard. "Cultural Views: Differing Outlooks." *New York Times.* 6 Sept. 1996. Web. 2 Nov. 2011.

Smith, Gary. "The Chosen One." *SI Vault. Sports Illustrated.* 23 Dec. 1996. Web. 8 Aug. 2011.

Sounes, Howard. *The Wicked Game: Arnold Palmer, Jack Nicklaus, Tiger Woods, and the Business of Modern Golf.* New York: HarperCollins, 2003. Print.

Steele, David. "Tiger Woods Deserves Credit for Taking the High Road." *AOL Fan House.* 8 Nov. 2011 Web. 8 Nov. 2011.

Strege, John. *Tiger: A Biography of Tiger Woods.* New York: Broadway, 1997. Print.

"Ten Things You Could Learn from Tiger Woods." *The Root.* 2 Dec. 2009. Web. 29 Oct. 2011.

Tiger Woods Foundation 2010 Annual Report. Tiger Woods Foundation.Org. 2011. Web. 12 Sept. 2011. pdf.

Toms, "The G-Man" Gary. "Tiger Woods & Golf Course Bigotry: Crouching Tiger, Hidden Racists." *Yahoo! Contributor Network.* Yahoo. 18 July 2006. Web. 18 Aug. 201

Wilner, Barry. "Woods Accepts Apology from Zoeller." *Milwaukee Journal Sentinel.* 25 Apr. 1997. Web. 28 Oct. 2011.

Weiss, Hedy. "'Golf' Is Wilson Par Excellence: Play Drives Home Author's Vision of Black America." *Chicago Sun-Times.* 24 Jan. 2007: 42. *Goodman Theater.* Web. 30 Oct. 2011.

"Woods on Caddie Williams: 'He Did Apologize' for Racial Slur." *CBS Sports.* 8 Nov. 2011. Web. 11 Nov. 2011.

Woods, Tiger. Media Statement. *ReoCities.com.* n.d. Web. 29 Oct. 2011.

Yu, Henry. "Tiger Woods at the Center of History: Looking Back at the Twentieth Century through the Lenses of Race, Sports, and Mass Consumption." Adapted from essay in *Sports Matters: Race, Recreation, and Culture.* Eds. Michael Williard and John Bloom, New York: New York University Press, 2002. n.d. Web. 8 Aug. 2011.

Zoeller, Frank Urban "Fuzzy." Broadcast Interview. *CNN. Golf Weekly.* Hosted by Jim Huber. 20 Apr. 1997. YouTube. 28 Jan. 2008. Web. 25 Oct. 2011.

_____. *Official Home of Fuzzy Zoeller. Fuz.com.* n.d. Web. 24 Oct. 2011.

Painful Pleasures

Jonathan French

I love this game to death. It's like a drug I have to have. I take time off sometimes because of the mental strain it puts on you. But when I'm competing, the will to win overcomes the physical and mental breakdowns (Woods "Media Statement").

In 1997, a huge gallery gathered at the notoriously raucous hole on the PGA Tour, the 16th at the TPC in Scottsdale. As always, the beer-soaked observers had been cheering good shots and booing poor ones. They were ready for the rookie, Tiger Woods. When he walked up to the tee, with senses at full alert, Tiger quickly determined the strike that he would need. This was the critical moment; he was ready. The well-honed swing coiled sharply, as if he had turned on a switch somewhere in his brain, and the explosion of strength and speed powered his back and shoulder, hips and arms, all moving automatically as one. The ball arched high, bounced once, twice, then rolled into the cup. The crowd went crazy, screaming and throwing cups everywhere. Tiger pumped his fist and high-fived his caddie in celebration, beaming with sheer joy. The success and skill of the shot, as well as the roar and adoration of the crowd, were intoxicating. He lived for this excitement. He was hooked.

A moment's reflection on the grace and precision of brain and muscle involved in a great golf swing reveals that every well-trained response is an incredible phenomenon. No creature other than the human works so hard to perfect the small movements needed to accomplish a goal. No other animal has the brain control needed to combine sophisticated sensory and perceptual information with precise motor control to make a difficult movement seemingly automatic. Humans' closest primate relative would be incapable of a good golf swing, even though the species share a considerable genetic history. First, homo sapiens' sense of sight provides distance information to muscle

130

control centers about the target and the effort that must been expended. Unlike most creatures on the earth that rely on the chemical senses of smell and taste, humans depend on vision to navigate and interact with the world. With every stroke, with every step, packets of energy comprising photons of light stream off everything in the scene and into the eyes through the dark hole of the pupil. Some of those packets of energy, smaller than electrons, travel back through the flexible lens, through the viscous fluid that inflates the eye and finally through the morass of neurons and blood vessels, to focus perfectly on the few millimeters of photoreceptors embedded in the retinal wall. The sharpest vision is near the center, in an area called the macula. Perhaps seven out of every one hundred photons make it from the pupil to the photoreceptors. The rest lose energy as they are absorbed by the dark lining of the retinal wall.

The 126 million photoreceptors eventually filter and organize the flashes of light to only a few million ganglion cells that carry the image of the golf ball, the crowd, the grass, everything in sight, streaming continuously through the optic nerve, through the relay station of the geniculate in the brain stem, all the way to the back of the brain. The signals from the eye finally reach the most sophisticated, most complex signal-processing center imaginable, the visual cortex. Within microseconds, the signal is lost in the association areas of the visual cortex, where further processing allows everything in the visual field to be accurately identified and located and included in the response of the nearby motor cortex. The final conditions for the execution of a golf swing are relayed to the cerebellum over the next few microseconds, where the exact commands and muscles are sharpened for the backswing and the strike. Tiger's hole-in-one at the TPC in Scottsdale was not his first, nor his last, but certainly one of his most spectacular shots. His senses, particularly his vision in judging distance and necessary effort, and his well-practiced swing enabled him to achieve the heights of his profession.

Humans have a remarkable flexibility in behavior that few animals can enjoy. Non-humans must focus on survival, a very critical on-the-job training. Although humans do not have the speed of some animals or the strength of others, their brains have enabled them to develop technologies, making them capable of speed and strength that far surpass any animal's abilities. A simple bicycle, for example, magnifies mobility and endurance far beyond that of any other creature. There are over 120 billion neurons in the human brain, more than there are stars in the galaxy, and each can communicate with thousands of its neighbors. The complex coordination of neurons and muscles in a well-coordinated, precision golf swing is quite literally unimaginable.

People take great joy in accomplishments, and some even invest the time to practice and to perfect complex motions, including a golf swing, for the sheer joy of it. Tiger Woods has clearly dedicated himself to golfing perfection, but he has also been subject to the vagaries of the human condition. As such, he offers an excellent opportunity to explore elements that are involved in an expression of a neuromuscular skill, the problems that are caused by repetitive stress injury, the attending effects of drugs that are meant to heal these injuries, and finally the brain's reward system that lies at the base of human motivations, why people often seek pleasures at the expense of their own best interests. An examination of the reward system of the brain might help to explain how the temptation of medication to dilute pain, to forget stress, and to feel joy can lead to dependence and other pursuits of pleasure that become the end in themselves.

The Swing's the Thing

A clever television commercial illustrates the ostensible precision of Tiger's swing, as he hits shot after shot with metronymic regularity. Sent into the misty distance, each ball pings a small buoy off shore. Although the ad is obviously hyperbolic, Tiger Woods' practice regimen is, indeed, legendary. Tiger's website describes his exhausting practice sessions to create perfect "motor memory" and achieve just the right swing. This process relies on the accomplishments of a tiny part of the brain, the cerebellum. The most complex and coordinated psycho motor skills, such as a golf swing, require considerable practice to be reliable, that is, to be ingrained in the cerebellum. Riding a bicycle is easy once basic balance is learned, once the neural components of the balance system understand the necessary control over muscles. This ability seems never to be lost once achieved and honed in the normal brain. People can get on a bicycle without having ridden for decades, and within a few shaky attempts, they can easily ride off as if there had never been a hiatus. As any neuroscientist knows, much of this ability resides in an often unappreciated mass of specialized neurons in the cerebellum, the little brain. Of the 120 billion neurons of the human brain, almost half reside in the cerebellum, and yet it is only a quarter of the size of the rest of the brain.

Nowhere else is the concentration of neural activity so concentrated, a density necessary to produce skilled movement. Nowhere else is the control over skilled motor behavior so automatic, once trained. Yet much of this control is poorly understood. When the golf coach instructs a player to "do that again," neither the coach nor the player would likely be able to explain those discrete actions with any precision. Words would prove ineffectual in capturing the essence of the movements and exertions, but the coach might see when everything is right, and the player can certainly feel it. The player is essentially training the cerebellum. The little brain does not have, nor apparently does it need, language. It only needs the signals from other sensory motor areas to express the skilled, well-honed motion reliably.

The cerebellum excels at smoothing and fine tuning the strength and direction of coordinated movement. A patient with a damaged cerebellum, for example, has spasmodic and grossly coordinated movements. Balance, muscle tone, and posture also are affected. The cerebellum doesn't initiate movement; it refines it to the point of a well-practiced accomplishment. People can't explain how they are able to stay on the bicycle or how they can execute that perfect golf swing. They just know when everything clicks. The cerebellum receives input from the tendons and ligaments in the arms and legs, informing the little brain when and where the limbs are moving and at what speeds. The cerebellum is sent a copy of the information relayed to the muscles just before execution of the movement. The massive Purkinje cells of the cerebellum, often likened to a microscopic sea fan, filter thousands of input neurons, almost 50 million of them, before sending the signals out of the little brain through only 10 million neurons or so. The 5/1 ratio indicates that considerable filtering occurs inside the cerebellum. During the movement, muscle coordination is adjusted immediately, automatically.

The cerebellum is not the switch for skilled behavior. The switch is likely in the more sophisticated and more recently evolved motor cortex, but in the cerebellum, the recording plays out in an automatically executed string of behaviors like a gymnast, diver, or golfer running through a routine, almost unthinkingly. Humans can "remember" a combination to a safe by the way it feels; the movements contain the combination that brains often forget but the hands can speed through. The cerebellum, therefore, is the place that most of the so-called motor memory resides, the training that fine tunes behavior that can't be explained in words, only in deed. Skilled movement from humans arises from unspoken commands deep within the little brain, and it doesn't seem to forget what it records, even decades later.

Pain

The reward of repetition is exactitude, but the price is often inflammation and pain, as plenty of older weekend athletes can attest. Some people have a "natural ability," and coordinated muscle movement comes easily. Tiger Woods is one of those "naturals." In fact, many commentators have argued that Tiger Woods has the best swing in golf history ("Why Tiger"), pointing to the resulting consistency of his ball striking and the accuracy of his approach shots as setting him apart from other talented professionals ("What Makes

Tiger"). Most people, however, must practice a great deal to reach the level where "naturals" begin. Regardless, both groups improve their skills only through many hours of practice. Tiger Woods' practice sessions are focused, intense, and very thorough. About.com guide Brent Kelley indicates that Tiger's typical workouts consist of two hours of range work and on-course swing work in the morning, followed by thirty minutes of putting practice. He then plays nine holes around lunchtime, and in the afternoon, he focuses on his swing and short game. Sometimes he plays another nine holes later in the day. As Woods reports in his official website, "I can spend as much as seven hours on the golf course hitting balls." Many golfers call this kind of practice "pounding" balls, an apt phrase, considering the punishment the body takes in that process. Imagine the repetition injuries that can occur from doing this two or three times a week. Tiger, however, has persisted in this kind of regimen almost daily before a tournament, especially a major. It should come as no surprise that his body has paid dearly for those repetitions.

Muscles attach to bone by a tendon, a fibrous band of tissue that is strong enough to resist tearing when the burden on the muscle pulls against it during movement. Through repetition, the patterns of the exact muscle pull and position are laid down in the cerebellum and motor cortex. Athletes, especially professional athletes, tend to engage in overrepetition, and the tendons sometimes react to the constant pulling with inflammation. The basic, innate inflammatory response, called tendonitis (if the inflammation is around tendons), is meant to protect the tissue from infection. The body's response system cannot easily distinguish between an area that is irritated by extensive movements and one that is afflicted by open wounds.

The inflammation response attracts molecules like histamines that cause capillaries surrounding the injury site to release blood plasma and proteins into the area. This fluid mixture swells the area and gives white blood cells and lymphocytes plenty of space to fight the presumed infection. As the surrounding tissue becomes swollen with fluid, the immediate area becomes tender and hot, providing optimal conditions for infection-fighting cells. Nearly everyone has experienced a painful, burning infection site. More histamine is chemically attracted to the area and keeps the fluid draining from the vessels, as well as maintaining pressure on the area, until back pressure prevents any more fluid release from the blood vessel. This is why people's noses leak fluid from an infection in the nasal passages and why anti-histamines stop the flow by stopping the histamine response.

Because so much occurs around an inflammation site, healthy tissue is often stretched and damaged by the intruders. If the irritated area surrounds a joint where two or more tendons come together, and that is often the case in sports injuries, bone can grind against bone. Tiny lubricant-filled sacs called bursa can prevent grinding injuries in the short term. If the bursa expend all their fluid and become damaged by subsequent rubbing, bursitis occurs, and recovery is very difficult until the bursa sacs are fixed and filled with lubricant again. That can take weeks. Tendonitis, bursitis, and localized tissue damage from swelling and irritation can be extremely painful for many hours after the injury. The body produces a natural substance, cortisol, in response to this kind of stress, aiding in the anti-inflammatory response and promoting healing and pain suppression. A number of synthetic cortisol-like drugs like Prednisone and Cortaid work to bolster the immune reaction. Another means of rallying defenses for inflammation and infection is the use of the Cyclo-oxygenases, or COX enzymes. They also promote swelling and signal more immune responses to the area. Most non-steroidal, anti-inflammatory drugs [NSAID], like aspirin, are COX inhibitors and serve to reduce swelling and pain.

As might be gathered, even the supposedly simple innate inflammatory response can be a very complicated process, and medical treatment has often been controversial. Modern medicine has turned much of its attention to blocking the inflammation rallying cry with anti-inflammatory drugs or by simply masking the pain with painkillers while the body is healing itself. This often leads to a counter-productive cycle, especially for professional athletes, who continuously injure and reinjure their tendons by engaging in compulsive practice. The drugs of choice for prolonged and chronic pain suppression are the opium derivatives like Vicodin and Oxycontin. All opiates (and to a lesser extent anti-histamines) produce biochemical dependence as the body gets used to their help. They also result in tolerance, meaning that, over time, people need more of the drug to produce the same levels of the pain-numbing effect. In addition, a significant side effect of these analgesics makes it difficult to users to know when it is time to quit. That side effect is a profound sense of well-being and euphoria that is activated in the brain's pleasure center.

Such palliatives, therefore, are dangerously seductive. If an athlete, such as Tiger Woods, loses a tournament and is upset by a less-than-stellar performance, despite having worked so hard that his joints ache, drugs might appear to be the solution. Drugs ease woes, mental and physical. Physicians try to be responsive to the needs of their patients and often prescribe powerful opiates, trusting that the patient knows when to stop taking them. At some point, an ethical physician talks with the patient, usually after dependence is manifest, to explain that the drug is creating a bigger danger. Although the physician encourages drug cessation, in many cases the patient is highly dependent on the drug by that point. After the cessation talk, physicians are absolved of further responsibility even though they guided the patients, including professional athletes, to opiate analgesics in the first place. Beginning the process with the best of intentions to reduce suffering, physicians trusted that modern pharmaceuticals are "good for what ails," resulting in another "addicted" patient.

Most pharmacologists prefer to use the term "dependent" rather than addicted because the word "dependent" carries fewer emotionally charged connotations of "addiction," the word typically conjuring images of crazed, desperate people who will do just about anything to get their "fix." "Dependent," on the other hand, describes the problem more accurately, as the patient's immune response and psyche have become dependent on the sense of well-being and pain relief from the drug. Despite the role physicians have played in the problem, society most often blames the patients themselves for the biochemical dependence. Thousands of weekend athletes may be oblivious to their dependency, and no one outside their immediate social circle may realize it, or even care. For sports celebrities, however, drug dependency is big news.

Tiger Woods has long suffered from repetitive stress injuries, as sports commentators have assiduously reported over the years. Woods, for example, was forced to withdraw from the 2010 Players championship from an injury to the joints that rotate the neck. According to Nicole Service of *Health Tree*, Tiger was "expected to make a full recovery from a repetitive stress injury" by following doctors' order of "rest, physical therapy and anti-inflammatory drugs." Typically, the opiate analgesics are prescribed every few hours for a few days to be replaced by the less powerful COX inhibitors, until the patient is pain free, if just until the next re-injury.

Although Woods' neck has not often been in the news, his knee problems have drawn a great deal of attention, for good reason. Tiger suffers from recurrent knee pain as a result of knee surgery in his college days. He has undergone four subsequent surgeries to reduce the pain and inflammation of grating knee joints. The most recent injury resulted from Tiger's exertions during the 2011 Masters tournament, when he hit off some pine straw, twisting his left leg. *Huffington Post* writer Doug Ferguson reports that the injuries included stress fractures and an anterior cruciate ligament [ACL] injury. Ligaments hold bone to bone, and the ACL is one of several that strap the knee in place and one most vulnerable to sharp, twisting movements. Although Ferguson claims that Woods and his agent described the damage as "minor," he also reports that Tiger was injured significantly enough to wear a stabilizing boot and to use crutches for a time. Tiger also stated that he hoped to return to play in a "few weeks" (Ferguson). Those few weeks turned into nearly the entire season as Woods was out of commission from mid–April until early August, nearly two months.

Of course, like all professional athletes and hundreds of thousands of ordinary folks, Tiger is getting older, and the repetitive injuries are taking their toll on less and less resilient bones, tendons and ligaments. How does one cope? Chronic and acute injuries suffered in the course of extreme competition, with an aging body, would lead anyone to seek medical attention. Tiger did just that. It appears that Tiger's medical advisors took the typical route of including prescription drugs to ease the inflammation and pain. The course of drugs starts with NSAID and progresses to the steroids compounds.

Dependence/Addictions

A great many factors doubtlessly contributed to Tiger Woods' deteriorating game in 2010–11, causing a precipitous slide down the world rankings. Although Woods has never discussed his dependencies or addictions with any direct or specific language, avid reporters have pounced on indirect testimonies to declare that he has suffered from both drug and sex addiction. Then, a late-night accident in 2008 simultaneously unveiled Tiger's sexual and drug involvements, quite unexpectedly for most people. The crash, apparently resulting from a domestic dispute because of Woods' extramarital affairs, also revealed that he had been taking a number of drugs for a period of time.

Drugs

Reporter Chris Irvine writes that Elin Woods gave the police two empty prescription bottles of medications that Tiger had been taking sometime prior to his accident. Those bottles purportedly had contained the painkiller Vicodin and the sedative Ambien. According to *Orlando Sentinel* reporters Willoughby Mariano and Henry Pierson Curtis, Woods was unconscious when police arrived at the scene and remained unconscious for about six minutes. He then "faded in and out of consciousness," mumbling incoherently before being transported to the hospital. Although the *Sentinel* article attributes Woods' condition to the accident, a number of other articles speculate that alcohol and one or more drugs might have contributed to the mishap (Silver Fox; Reason; "Cop"). One trooper, who suspected Woods was driving under the influence, sought a subpoena for the results of blood tests, but prosecutors refused to prosecute ("Cop"). Woods ultimately paid the fine for reckless driving, but the issue of possible illicit drug use did not dissipate.

Stories about Tiger Woods' connection to Dr. Anthony Galea have constituted the most potentially damaging allegations of improper drug use. A Canadian physician, Galea pled guilty in July 2011 to bringing unapproved drugs, in particular human growth hormone, into the United States. Long before that court appearance, Tiger reported that Dr. Galea had indeed treated him, but Woods also declared that he had never taken performance-enhancing drugs (Dobbin; Red). Rather, Tiger has always maintained that Galea had treated him with injections of platelet-rich plasma [PRP], an experimental procedure that is not illegal in golf. According to *The Wall Street Journal*'s health columnist Melinda Beck, PRP therapy entails removing a patient's blood, "concentrating the platelets" and then injecting them at the site of an injury to promote healing. Orthopedic surgeon Edward Kalfayan, a doctor for the Seahawks and Mariners, asserts that "blood spinning," a lay term for PRP injections, "does not carry oxygen or have any factors in a concentration that even remotely can aid performance" (qtd. in Beck). PRP is used in the hope of promoting tissue repair, not to bulk up like Sylvester Stallone, and is not perceived as illicit performance-enhancement therapy.

As a result, the only potentially problematical drugs that have been tied to Tiger Woods are Vicodin and Ambien. As has been previously noted, Tiger suffered from repetitive stress injuries and would likely have been prescribed painkillers. Vicodin would certainly help to relieve pain, and Ambien would also serve to keep the pain from injury from intruding too long into his consciousness and to help him sleep. Mariano and Curtis link Tiger's late-night accident in 2008 to the issue of Woods' chronic sleeplessness. Apparently everyone who belongs to Isleworth Country Club knew that Tiger "doesn't always sleep well," according to Lee Janzen, a professional golfer who is also a member of the exclusive club. Janzen adds that "Sometimes he [Woods] gets up really early to work out in the clubhouse" (qtd. in Mariano and Curtis). As these comments suggest, Woods may have used these drugs to relieve and forget about his pain and to help him sleep in a stress-filled world. Most people use them for this purpose.

Are there any other drugs to help with sleep? A quiet revolution occurred in the world of sleep medicine about thirty years ago. Prior to the 1980s, sleep physicians prescribed barbiturates, like Seconal and Amytal. These are heavy-handed anesthetic drugs that force the brain into unconsciousness, resulting in an unnatural sleep. A newer class of drugs, the benzodiazepines, foremost among them diazepam, or Valium, also induce sleep. These drugs, however, result in a more natural sleep in that the brain's electrical activity [EEG] progresses through a more normal cycle than that resulting from the barbiturates. Despite the apparent advantages of Valium, the drug was prescribed less than might be imagined in the early days of sleep medicine. In addition to the cost of the drug, the long-lasting effects of Valium were problematical. A typical dose of Valium could last as long as 15–20 hours, whereas a sleeping dose of Seconal only lasts about 3–4 hours. This phenomenon occurs because the human body manufactures its own sleep-inducing metabolites such as temazepam [Restoril] and oxazepam [Serax], from the Valium. Thus, while the body is breaking down the diazepam, it makes other sedatives, all of them contributing to the long-lasting effect: three for the price of one. Research to identify shorter-acting benzodiazepine derivatives led to the much shorter-acting, better tolerated and more specific compounds like Sonata and Ambien.

Despite the advantages of these benzodiazepine derivatives, they also have drawbacks; most importantly, they are mildly addictive if used more than a few times. The risk of dependence on these drugs might persuade most people to quit them as quickly as possible, but people desperate for good, solid sleep may not heed (or even believe) the warnings of dependence. Like so many other dependence-producing substances, people believe they can just say no at any time, but in reality, it is usually much more difficult. An additional side-effect attends these drugs. They produce amnesia. Ingesting a typical benzodiazepine compound leads very quickly to an astounding inability to remember immediate events for the few hours the drug is active in the bloodstream. Such forgetfulness may be viewed as a distinct advantage if a physician does not want the patient to be alarmed by the person moaning in the next bed at the hospital. The drug helps people to forget the moaning or that leaky faucet or whatever was so stressful it was keeping them awake.

As this commentary indicates, the brain stores memories, and new memories can be stifled in the presence of some drugs like the benzodiazepines. All past memories before the drug onset are still intact, but those surrounding the ingestion of the drug are hazy, at best. The person would have difficulty remembering who was in the room or what was said and may even fail to realize that he/she had just crashed a car in the neighbor's yard. These side-effects make the benzodiazepines dangerous as date rape drugs but a boon to scientists trying to unravel how memories, particularly short-term memories, are stored in neurons. A drug like Ambien serves as a muscle relaxant and results in a slight sense of intoxication and exhilaration, as well as lapses in memory. For all of these reasons, such drugs would appear to be very tempting "cures" for sleeplessness and stress.

Drugs and Sex Enhancement

Apparently, some people employ benzodiazepines like Ambien as a means of enhancing sexual activity. These drugs are easier to obtain than others that might enhance sex, like Ecstasy and other amphetamines, but the price of benzodiazepine-fueled pleasure is not remembering the event very well. Some people might perceive that as an advantage, however, especially if they are seeking to enjoy the sex but to forget it afterwards. Tiger Woods was linked to "recreational" uses of Ambien ("Tiger Woods Scandal") through the testimony of one of his former mistresses, Rachel Uchitel. According to *Daily Mail* reporter David Gardner, Uchitel claimed that she and Woods took Ambien before having sex. As she reported, "You know you have crazier sex on Ambien — you get into that Ambien haze," adding, "We have crazy Ambien sex" (qtd. in Gardner; See also Brown). Although Uchitel notes the "haze" that accompanies the drug, she certainly seems to have remembered those "crazy" sexual experiences.

Another piece of evidence links Woods to Ambien as well. According to the celebrity magazine *U.S. Weekly*, Uchitel bragged to her friends about her affair with Woods and forwarded a private email to the magazine as evidence of their relationship. According to the email, Woods reported a "disturbing" dream of having married Uchitel, holding the lead in a golf tournament, and witnessing Uchitel engaging in sex with two other men. At the end of the email, Woods purportedly asserts, "Now I can't get back to sleep. My body is tired, but my mind is awake. Need an Ambien" (qtd. in "Tiger Dreamt"). Noteworthy in this commentary is Woods' declaration that he cannot get back to sleep, despite physical exhaustion. He also asserts that he "needs" an Ambien, rather than simply wanting it. Although desire for a drug might imply an impetus for its use, "need" could point to physical, and probably emotional, dependence.

Sex

Given revelations about professional athletes in other sports, particularly their astounding sexual escapades, no one should be surprised to learn that professional golfers also find willing sexual partners easily. As *Vanity Fair* documents in "Tiger Woods's Inconvenient Women," gorgeous women find plenty of attention from players who are away from home a good deal of the time. Of course, Tiger Woods was among them. *Daily Mail* reporter Lauren St. John argues that promiscuity is par for the course with professional golfers, noting Nick Faldo and Greg Norman as prime examples. St. John also claims that a number of professional golfers were quite forward with her during interviews, resulting in truncated sessions. As these commentaries indicate, golf is not such a "gentleman's" sport that professional players always forgo the temptations of adoring female fans. The world now knows that Tiger also indulged in extramarital sexual liaisons.

Tiger Woods has never declared that he suffers from sexual addiction, but others have declared just that. After revelations of Tiger's many mistresses created a firestorm of media activity, he disappeared, communicating only through his website. By mid–January 2010, a great many articles claimed that he had been spotted at Pine Grove Behavioral Health and Addiction Services in Hattiesburg, Mississippi. Those reports proved to be accurate, but Woods still did not name his purported problem, even during his televised apology. He alludes to his problems when he states, "It is hard to admit that I need help. But I do. For 45 days, from the end of December to early February, I was in inpatient therapy, receiving guidance for the issues I'm facing" ("Tiger Woods' Apology" 2). Here Woods confirms that he needs "help," has undergone "therapy," has received "guidance" for "issues," but he never mentions sexual addiction. Later in his apology, he pledges to continue in treatment but still remains mum on the nature of that therapy.

Others, however, have proclaimed without restraint that Woods is addicted to sex. *New York Daily News* journalist Jose Martinez, for example, not only declares Woods' addiction, but also asserts the validity of the controversial diagnosis. According to Benoit Denizet-Lewis, author of a book on sexual addiction, the affliction is very real. As he reports, "We mock it or we say it's not a real addiction.... But it's very much the real deal" (qtd. in Martinez). A considerable number of mental health professionals agree with Denizet-Lewis, all earnestly believing that people suffer from the malady. Many others disagree. Some claim that the diagnosis could be a clever ploy to escape culpability for illicit behaviors.

In light of such diverse opinions, the concept of sex addiction deserves further investigation. Currently, Sex Addiction is not listed in the *Diagnostic and Statistical Manual of Mental Disorders* [DSM-IV], the periodical that defines the criteria for conventionally accepted mental illnesses. Aberrant sexual disorders involving inappropriate sexual interest, like pedophilia or having sex with objects, are listed. The course of treatment for these disorders is primarily helping the patient to control acting on urges, as there is no cure. Treatment options range from tranquilizer drugs and abstinence to behavioral conditioning that resembles treatment regimens found in Anthony Burgess' *A Clockwork Orange.*

The controversy about sexual addiction, because the problem does not usually entail any acknowledged sexual disorder, seems to arise from the notion that addiction typically implies conventional physical dependence, like drug addictions. As well, "addiction" usually points to a tolerance that develops over time, as well as physical symptoms associated with withdrawal. These issues do not appear to adhere to "sex addiction." For example, a sex addict, if such a malady exists, would not develop physical symptoms that are associated with withdrawal from an addicting drug. Moreover, with conventional addictions, the cure is usually evidenced by abstinence. For sexual addiction, presumably, the patient would likely be guided towards not abstinence but to engage in sex with an appropriate partner. In addition, no physical symptoms typical of addiction have been demonstrated for sexual behavior, even extreme sexual needs.

Nonetheless, there has been heightened interest in the concept of sexual addiction, perhaps in some measure resulting from publicity about Tiger Woods' treatment. As Martin Kafka proposes in an article for the *Archives of Sexual Behavior*, the term "hypersexual behavior" should be included in the upcoming revision of the DSM-V. *Los Angeles Times* reporter Shari Roan claims this would be an important addition. Although including "hypersexual behavior" in the publication has drawn proponents on either side of the question, plenty of therapists are willing to treat the problem, and rehabilitation clinics offer therapeutic programs, such as Pine Grove's "Gentle Path."

Joy

Given the negative realities of drug dependence and sexual addiction, what causes people to become "hooked"? In other words, why are drugs and sex, especially the pleasures they provide, so compelling that they motivate humans to great heights and to great depths? An attending question is equally compelling. What makes these dependencies so hard to overcome?

To a biologist, there is a neural substrate for happiness and joy, for the rewarding glow humans feel with accomplishment or praise. It is a very small area, the size of a pea in the middle of the stem of the brain called the ventral tegmentum. It sends nerve fibers out to two very powerful clusters of neurons: one in the nucleus accumbens and the other in the frontal lobes. The frontal lobes constitute the center for impulse control. This whole system, called the endogenous rewards system, is arguably one of the most important discoveries in neuroscience. The endogenous rewards system is sometimes called the pleasure center, and the reasons are obvious. When a microscopic wire is put into a rat's brain and the pleasure center is stimulated with a mild jolt, the rat will repeat whatever it was doing to get that stimulation again.

This phenomenon was discovered in the 1950s when James Olds and Peter Milner were trying to teach a rat to avoid a section of a box it was occupying by stimulating an area in the brain that they thought would cause negative reward. Instead of avoiding the taboo section, the rat returned again and again to the place where stimulation had occurred. This phenomenon inspired Olds to make a classic understatement, "I think he likes it." Rats similarly possessed of an electrode in the pleasure area will press a lever to stimulate their own brain to the exclusion of everything else. They will starve if not force fed. They will cross electrified grids and ignore females in heat, just to get to the lever for yet another bar press. They will press the lever to exhaustion, eventually to the point of burning out the area of the brain that produces the stimulation. The concept of "liking" simply does not apply. The animal will crave it. So will humans, dolphins, and every mammal with an endogenous reward system. This pleasure center is the neural substrate for the joy humans experience with every accomplishment, when they are in love, see sunsets, or hear children's laughter.

Research concerning the pleasure center has informed neuroscience about how the brain works, particularly how rewarding motivation works in the brain. It is well known that particular biochemicals activate this structure, including endorphins (endogenous morphine-like substances that reduce pain) and dopamine. But endorphins and dopamine are not the whole story. During daily activity, activation of the pleasure center signifies how much a person enjoys that activity, how much reinforcement that activity offers. Significant studies of brain imaging reveal that areas light up not only during pleasurable activities, but also when humans simply expect to engage in pleasurable activity. In other words, humans experience pleasure by anticipating pleasure. Even more astounding, the pleasure effect is greatest when the reward is not certain. Imagine a closely contested golf tournament. The anticipation of ultimate victory, mixed with anxieties of potential loss, would make the joy of the pursuit of victory and the joy of the victory itself all the more intense and sweeter. This phenomenon causes gamblers to persevere in sometimes lost causes, for just one more roll of the die, despite the odds and regardless of sometimes dire financial consequences.

Very Human Tiger

No one can verify that Tiger Woods has been dependent upon Ambien or Vicodin, nor can anyone certify that he suffers from hypersexual disorder, but evidence does indicate that he sought the relief, and even the joys, that drugs and sex could provide. Might the drugs and the sex have replaced the pleasures of golf for a time? Might neural stimulation of his reward center, previously reaped from the cheer of the crowd and especially when a hard-fought victory had not been certain, been reached more easily and more directly by pain-blocking drugs and hazily remembered sex? The pursuit of drugs and sex would certainly provide immediate reinforcement with less effort. Nearly anyone would be tempted to be chemically at peace, relaxed, and unconcerned.

Tiger Woods has been one of the most accomplished athletes in the world. In all probability, the roar of the crowd and the attending neural stimulation that arises from the sounds and sight of that adoration helped to make him an extraordinary athlete. But Woods has also shown that he is a mere mortal, subject to the same temptations and weakness of ordinary people. It is entirely possible that he will enjoy more successes on the golf course because he is still young enough to make a comeback. All those motor memories are still intact. Tiger has also demonstrated, over and over, that he has the drive to persevere and practice hard. Despite recent poor performance on the links, he is still out there trying to show people that he is great. How impressive would it be, however, if Tiger, the ordinary man, did extraordinary things because of new-found inner strength and belief in himself rather than in the roar of adoring fans? That may be where true recovery lies.

WORKS CITED

Beck, Melinda. "Why 'Blood Spinning' Is Legal." *Health Mailbox: The Wall Street Journal.* 6 Apr. 2010. Web. 21 Nov. 2011.

Brown, Andrew M. "Tiger Woods 'Took Ambien to Spice Up Sex.' But Did He Raid the Fridge Afterwards?" *The [London] Telegraph.* 5 Dec. 2009. Web. 22 Nov. 2011.

"Cop Suspected Tiger of Driving Under the Influence." *NBC Sports.* 7 Dec. 2009. Web. 21 Nov. 2011.

Diagnostic and Statistical Manual of Mental Disorders. American Psychiatric Association. *Psychiatry OnLine.com.* n.d. Web. 20 Nov. 2011.

Dobbin, Ben. "Dr. Anthony Galea Pleads Guilty: Tiger Woods, A-Rod Doctor Admits to Smuggling Drugs into US." *Huffington Post.* 6 July 2011. Web. 22 Nov. 2011.

Ferguson, Doug. "Tiger Woods Injury: Left Knee Injured, Will Miss a Few Weeks." *Huffington Post.* 26 Apr. 2011. Web. 18 Oct. 2011.

Gardner, David. "Tiger Woods 'Took Sleeping Pills to Spice up Sex with Mistress.'" *Daily Mail.* 5 Dec. 2009. Web. 22 Nov. 2011.

Irvine, Chris. "What Drugs Did Tiger Woods' Wife Hand over to Paramedics?" *Independent Woman.* 8 Dec. 2009. Web. 20 Nov. 2011.

Kelley, Brent. "How Much Does Tiger Woods Practice Golf?" About.com: Golf. n.d. Web.

Kafka, Martin P. "Hypersexual Disorder: A Proposed Diagnosis for DSM-V." *Archives of Sexual Behavior* 39.2 (Apr. 2010): 377–400. Print.

Mariano, Willoughby, and Henry Pierson Curtis. "Tiger Woods Accident: Tiger Woods' Wife Used Golf Club to Free Him from SUV." *Orlando Sentinel.* 29 Nov. 2009. Web. 21 Nov. 2011.

Martinez, Jose. "Tiger Woods Sex Scandal: Golfer Being Treated for Sex Addiction at Mississippi Rehab, Says Author." *New York Daily News.* 19 Jan. 2010. Web. 17 Oct. 2011.

Reason, Mark. "Tiger Woods Continues his Descent with Drug Overdose Suspicions." *The [London] Telegraph.* 9 Dec. 2009. Web. 18 Sept. 2011.

Red, Christian. "Tiger Woods Never Received Performance-Enhancing Drugs from Dr. Anthony Galea: Attorney." *New York Daily News.* 11 July 2011. Web. 22 Nov. 2011.

Roan, Shari. "'Hypersexual Disorder' Might Make DSM-5." *Los Angeles Times.* 23 May 2011. Web. 20 Nov. 2011.

St. John, Lauren. "I Know Pro Golfers ALL Play Around — They've Tried to Score with Me." *Daily Mail.* 14 Dec. 2009. Web. 14 Oct. 2011.

Service, Nicole. "Tiger Woods Expected to Make Full Recovery from Neck Injury." *Health Tree.* 21 May 2011. Web. 2 Nov. 2011.

Silver Fox. "Dr. Galea and Vicodin May Spell T-R-O-U-B-L-E for Tiger Woods." *Bleacher Report.* 15 Dec. 2009. Web. 22 Nov. 2011.

"Tiger Dreamt of Mistress, Derek Jeter, David Boreanaz Having Sex." *U.S. Weekly.* 4 Dec. 2009. Web. 20 Nov. 2011.

"Tiger Woods' Apology: Full Transcript." *CNN.* 19 Feb. 2009. Web. 3 Nov. 2011.

"Tiger Woods Scandal: From Mistresses to Ambien Use." 5 Dec. 2009. *Home Testing Blog.* 20 Nov. 2011.

"Tiger Woods's Inconvenient Women." *Vanity Fair.* 31 Mar. 2010. Web. 15 Nov. 2011.

"What Makes Tiger So Good?" *Ruthless Golf.* 23 June 2011. Web. 19 Oct. 2011.

"Why Tiger Woods Is So Good." *Golf Swing Feeling.* n.d. Web. 21 Oct. 2011.

Woods, Tiger. "Fitness: Workout Regimen." *TigerWoods.com.* Web. 14 Oct. 2011.

_____. Media Statement. *ReoCities.com.* n.d. Web. 29 Oct. 2011.

Responsible Adults in
the Toy Department

Steve Master

On April 5, 2010, *Sports Illustrated*'s Joe Posnanski, one of the most respected and widely read sports journalists in the United States, devoted his popular blog to Tiger Woods' press conference in Augusta, Georgia, just a few days before the start of the 2010 Masters. This represented the second time Woods would speak publically about the serial infidelity that soiled his public image and ultimately destroyed his marriage. His first appearance was a professionally staged and awkward apology in front of family, friends, and a few wire service reporters who were denied the opportunity to ask questions. This time, Tiger would take questions from sports writers, many of whom had spent their careers writing about Woods, arguably the greatest athlete of their generation. Interestingly, Posnanski devotes very little of his blog to Tiger's "performance" during the press conference. He insists that he has no interest in "judging the guy" and admits that distinguishing between genuine and scripted expressions of contrition is certainly difficult. Nonetheless, Posnanski remains intensely intrigued by the press conference — not in anticipation of what Tiger might *say*, but what his fellow sports writers might *ask*. He writes:

> I never really saw this press conference as being about Tiger Woods. In a larger sense, it was about the media. It was about the audience. Tiger isn't the only one on trial here. We are on trial too, right? We are on trial because for the first time the media — both mainstream and non-mainstream — has taken down a truly dominant athlete and shattered him. Not because he's a criminal. Not because he's someone who played the game unfairly or endangered people's lives or illegally recruited athletes or messed with the sport's integrity. No. Instead, Tiger Woods was exposed as a man who led a wild life and cheated on his wife.

Posnanski's suggestion that this event represented a "trial" not only for Woods, but also for journalists, was characteristically intuitive. It reflected the growing notion that this scandal, for all the problems it caused Woods, had become equally damaging to the image of 21st century journalism. Yet for all the obvious ironies illuminated by Posnanski's alternative take on these proceedings, one wonders whether the wrong journalists, that is sports writers, were being "tried" on this bizarre spring afternoon at Augusta National. To be sure, Posnanski showed commendable awareness in writing that "we are on trial." Although a veteran sports journalist, he rightly considers himself a member of the profession at large and, as such, feels sullied by coverage of the Woods "affair." This is only natural. Members of any profession are elevated by their best and diminished by their worst. And yet this proverbial "verdict" should, and ultimately will, render a far more favorable judgment towards Posnanski and his sports-writing colleagues who were invited to participate in this Augusta press conference than the mainstream media at large.

The truth is that sports writers — the men and women working in what was once dubbed the "toy department" of newspapers — often came across as the only adults in the room during the round-the-clock body count of Tiger's mistresses. With few exceptions, they routinely shied away from the more sordid aspects of the story and wrote about it in ways relevant to their beats and within the confines of ethical journalistic standards. Most, like Posnanski, rejected the invitation to "judge the guy." Many were sharply critical of the mainstream media coverage and were quite clear with their readers about what they considered and did not consider newsworthy. By contrast, much of the mainstream media showed no such concerns. Many quickly embraced the tabloid-style coverage; others, bowing to competitive pressures and a sense of inevitability, went along, leaving their journalistic integrity at the door.

Posnanski's notion that the media frenzy had become a story within the Tiger Woods story was not a novel one. As the saga swelled into a runaway train of sensationalism, everyone from independent bloggers to media watchdogs to academics began weighing in on the appropriateness of the coverage. Thomas Cooper, a professor of media ethics at Emerson College, dubbed it "smotherage" (qtd. in Wharton), a notion wholly supported by a rising tide of self-examination by various media outlets. Michael Fitzpatrick of *Bleacher Report*, an online sports blog, explored the issue under the deadly accurate headline "Tiger Woods Blurring the Lines between Mainstream and Tabloid Journalism." An *Orlando Sentinel* headline wondered: "Tiger Woods and the TMZ Effect: Can Mainstream Media Compete?" (Boedeker). *American Journalism Review* examined the controversy in a story headlined: "Lost in the Woods: How the Mainstream Media too often Dropped Sourcing Standards and Blindly Followed the Lead of Tabloid and Entertainment Web Sites during the Tiger Woods Extravaganza" (Farhi). And a *New York Magazine* article, written by Will Leitch, asked this telling question: "Will Tiger Change Sports Journalism?"

Such hand-wringing could not have been more appropriate. The volume and breadth of coverage was on par with a war or international disaster. During the week of November 30 to December 6, 2009, as details about the Thanksgiving eve car accident that triggered the scandal began to emerge, the drama was the third most reported story in the United States mainstream media, behind the war in Afghanistan and the economic crisis, according to the weekly news index monitored by the Pew Research Center's Project for Excellence in Journalism [PEJ]. PEJ weekly data reveal that Tiger was the second biggest newsmaker (behind President Obama in all cases) for five one-week periods between November 30, 2009, and April 11, 2010 ("Afghanistan," "Economy," "Health," "In a Diverse Week," "Mine"). And he was the No. 4 newsmaker the week of August 23–29, 2010, when his divorce became final ("Elections").

Simply put, Tiger Woods' coverage saturated American popular culture with such force that few media outlets felt they could get away with ignoring it. NBC broadcast journalist Chris Matthews dedicated a segment of his political show, *Hardball,* to the story. It was covered almost daily by the NBC's popular *Today* morning show and made the front page of the *New York Post* ten consecutive days, according to *Sports Illustrated* writer Rick Lipsey (SI Golf Group). To many news consumers and media watchdogs alike, this "smotherage" seemed particularly distasteful at a time of two wars, a sagging economy, and almost ten percent unemployment. It certainly raised valid questions about the values and priorities being reflected by a national media bent clearly on chasing ratings at the expense of traditional journalistic standards and ethics.

Even more disconcerting than the volume of coverage, however, was the voyeuristic nature of those stories, as well as the shocking collapse of journalistic sourcing standards. Common components of the Woods stories — on networks, in major metro dailies, in mainstream consumer magazines — included interviews with and images of Tiger's alleged mistresses; reports about Woods' sexual and other personal habits; speculation of domestic dispute that set the scandal in motion; conjecture regarding possible causes for Tiger's infidelity; questions about Woods' relationship with his wife; rumors that he was addicted to painkillers and/or had used performance-enhancing drugs; and far too many images of his children. Also widely reported was what appears to be a false narrative about his wife, Elin, attacking him with a golf club upon learning of his infidelity. This story became so pervasive it was spoofed on *Saturday Night Live.* Ironically, the skit featured a Woods public statement being aired as "breaking news" on CNN's *The Situation Room*, yet another illustration of the "laughable" amount of media coverage being devoted to the scandal.

Will Leitch, a contributing editor at *New York Magazine*, found it beyond laughable. He indicated the coverage was perhaps transformational, a sudden and dangerous plunge on that proverbial slippery slope. Leitch claims, "It certainly feels like something's shifted, hasn't it? The idea that a new mistress made the crawl on [ESPN's] SportsCenter is amazing." And Tim McGuire, a former editor of the *Minneapolis Star Tribune* who now teaches journalism at Arizona State University, wrote poignantly about a collapse of ethical standards on his blog. "When I teach ethics," McGuire asserts, "I hammer home to students the distinction between three levels of information: right to know, need to know and want to know." McGuire notes that "right to know" is legally mandated by statute, such as public records, and "need to know" covers information vital in helping readers understand issues and perform civic duties. "Then there is the want to know," McGuire continues, striking at the heart of journalists' ethical failures in their Woods coverage:

> People want to know some really kinky stuff, so reputable news organizations have traditionally developed some standards that say, "hey, that stuff is none of our business. It is prurient. There is no need for us to know that stuff." That quaint concept may have died this week because of an unrestrained media's desire to cover Tiger Woods, his car accident and perhaps every single sexual misadventure in his life.

Some were quick to contest McGuire's critique, arguing that Tiger's status as a "public figure" exposed him to this type of invasive coverage. This is patently false, from both ethical and moral standpoints. Even those in public office are entitled to some degree of privacy. As Anita L. Allen, who teaches law and philosophy at the University of Pennsylvania School of Law, writes in the *New York Times*: "Woods owes the public full legal accountability for the injurious consequences of the mysterious 2:00 A.M. car crash: he broke the traffic laws and he committed property torts. But he doesn't owe the public explanations, justifications, or transparency with respect to his extramarital relationships." And yet a new and alarming journalistic principle appeared to be emerging, an odd combination of gang mentality and capitalism run amok. Reputable news organizations seemed to defend their actions with a rationalization that, if it persists, will be transformational indeed: "If the other guy is doing it, *we* can — and (for competitive purposes) must."

A closely related cause for concern — one sure to have a tangible impact on credibility within the profession — was the shabby manner in which the stories were sourced, often with no substantiating evidence. A simple report in a publication — any publication — about a new mistress spread like fire into the mainstream media, as though that bold line separating legitimate news sources from less credible ones had disappeared. *American Journalism Review* explored this collapse of sourcing standards by examining a December 6 issue of the British tabloid *News of the World*. In an article titled "Tiger Had Me in the Rough," a woman named Mindy Lawton describes her alleged affair with Tiger and some intimate details about his personal preferences. According to the *AJR* story:

> Most suspicious were some of Lawton's direct quotes; she referred to Woods as a "sportsman" and a parking lot as a "car park," British locutions unlikely to have been uttered by a Florida restaurant manager. It didn't help the story's credibility that it was published by the *News of the World*, one of Britain's racier tabloids, which often pays sources for stories. Yet none of it seemed to matter. Within hours of publication, Lawton's name was flying around the Internet, landing not just on blogs and gossip sites that have never made any claim to journalistic integrity but in mainstream media outlets that do. The *Orlando Sentinel*, the *Miami Herald* and the *Chicago Sun-Times*, among others, eagerly picked up the *News*' account, as did NBC's *Today* show. Dozens more publications cited no source at all in recounting what Lawton had to say. None of the outlets that picked up the story appears to have spent much effort asking a fundamental question about it: *Was it true?* [Farhi, original emphasis].

Professor McGuire addresses this issue, writing, "I pray I did not miss the memo that said speculation about rumors is what really matters.... Things don't become news just because some irresponsible fool asserts something. In journalism, we VERIFY facts in an attempt to show they are true." But verification takes time — a dilemma traditional media are still grappling with in today's Twitter-driven 24-hour news cycle, which includes more and more outlets dedicated to tabloid-style coverage of celebrities. Roy Peter Clark of the Poynter Institute, a prestigious journalism think tank in St. Petersburg, Florida, writes eloquently about this tremendous challenge facing mainstream outlets:

> With social networks and blogs sending their alerts, with supermarket tabloids shining a spotlight, and with cable news programs hungry for extended soap opera narratives, the traditional press often feels pressured into a level and style of coverage in disproportion to a story's true significance. Such stories, like Tiger's, are always interesting, but are they important? Editors at traditional news organizations may feel as if they face an impossible choice: Follow the coverage of the tabloids, or turn their backs on all aspects of a sleazy story, making their news organizations vulnerable to less scrupulous competitors.

Certainly, these are tough calls for editors. And during the Woods scandal, social media provided a unique window into the editorial angst being felt in newsrooms. The message board of one website in particular, Sports journalists.com, offered an especially revealing glimpse on January 15, 2010. Working the sports desk at an undisclosed daily in Mississippi, HejiraHenry grappled with an unsubstantiated report that Tiger had checked into a Mississippi clinic to receive treatment for sex addiction. As HejiraHenry asserts, "AP says they're watching the Tiger in rehab story but have no plans to file anything. We feel compelled to do something, as the clinic is in our state. Do we run a brief with the credit to (celebrity news and gossip web site) *RadarOnline?*" Fourteen minutes later, user Ryan Sonner responds: "You're really going to run something you pulled from *Radaronline.com?*" The ensuing twelve pages of comments provided some lively debate, but the overwhelming majority opinion was reflected in this brief but telling response: "Let whoever's in charge of the celebrity gossip roundup deal with it. This part of the story isn't a *sports* story." Most revealing about Sonner's response was his rejection of this rumor as a "sports story," giving cover to his sports colleague, Hejira-Henry, who was working in a newsroom obviously pressured to report on *RadarOnline*'s report. Sonner clearly *meant* that this isn't a story, period, based on the lack of reliability in the reporting, that it's *not* acceptable for a "reputable web site to report what a semi-reputable web site is reporting" (Wright) without independent verification. However, he sardonically adds that if HejiraHenry's co-workers insist, they should publish the report in a section of the newspaper where rumor, innuendo, and invasion of privacy are more common and accepted — the celebrity gossip snippets.

This, of course, was a fair and familiar refrain among sports journalists amid the scandal. Yet, despite obvious efforts by most sports writers to remain above the fray, media critics unfairly included the sports writers with the sinners. This is ironic on several levels. For many years, members of the "toy department" fought to earn the respect given to the responsible "adults" covering news in the mainstream media. Now sports writers are suffering guilt by association with the so-called adults. This was, of course, inevitable. Tiger, after all, is a sports figure, so surely sports journalists must be driving the story, right? In addition, sports writers have certainly participated in "taking down" star athletes and athletic institutions before. In fact, these types of investigative pieces are what ultimately led to sports writers' ultimate acceptance in newsrooms as "serious" journalists.

Investigations by sports writers have exposed steroid and drug abuse, gambling, violent crime, recruiting and academic scandals, and numerous other ills within the industry. Yet in these cases, crimes were committed. Rules were broken. Innocents were victimized. Health and safety were compromised. The integrity of a sport was undercut. Adultery? Not so much. Personal foibles — and heaven knows athletes have their share — have long been considered out of bounds, provided they do not have an impact on the athlete or team's performance. *Washington Post* sports columnist Michael Wilbon, noting the multitude of sports figures rumored to have had extramarital affairs, claims: "Whispers and innuendo followed (Babe) Ruth and (Joe) Louis. *TMZ* and *US Magazine* stalk Tiger Woods."

This is not to suggest sports writers ignored the Woods scandal. They did not. But for the most part, they covered the components that affected the sport, not the sordid between-the-sheets narratives. Many stories focused on how the scandal might have an impact on golf history, given Tiger's proximity to breaking Jack Nicklaus' record for major championships. A number of others documented how it might change the sport financially, given Tiger's status as a sponsor and fan magnet, as the most significant figure in the sport's history. Still others explored how it might affect Tiger's vast arsenal of personal sponsorship deals.

Some have wondered whether, before the scandal broke, sports writers were asleep at the wheel. Why didn't a sports writer break this story? The answer here reflects not a failure, but a firm sense of boundaries — a conviction that it is *not* professionally appropriate to peek behind the curtain of an athlete's private life. Not that sports writers are immune to gossip. They are human, after all. And the good ones are especially sensitive to the "noise" on their beats, as *Sports Illustrated* golf writer Alan Shipnuck revealed soon after the scandal went public. Sure enough, such noise concerning Tiger's "alleged" infidelities emerged after he missed the cut at the 2009 British Open. Shipnuck writes, "A month (after the British Open), at the PGA Championship, I had lunch with two veteran scribes. We all compared notes on what we'd been hearing lately and decided, yep, he's fooling around." Notice the casual, ho-hum tone here — more water cooler chatter than hushed tones prefacing a Watergate-style investigation. Shipnuck continues:

> What's a responsible reporter supposed to do with such a hunch? Even if *SI*'s lawyers signed off on it, I'm not inclined to trash a guy's reputation based solely on innuendo and third-hand gossip.... Let's suppose that, pre–Thanksgiving, *SI* had obtained some sort of smoking gun — pictures of a parking lot tryst, or R-rated text messages — I still don't know if that's a story we should break. Prior to his mysterious car accident, Woods' private life was still private. Is it the responsibility of a sports writer to reveal the details of an athlete's sex life? The answer is yes, if it's affecting his game. When two NBA teammates are courting the same pop singer and thus disrupting team chemistry, that's clearly a story. What's happening behind closed doors at the Island Hotel between consenting adults? I don't think so.

The circumstances for sports writers changed, of course, when Tiger wrecked his car. A possible injury was newsworthy. The appearance of a domestic dispute was certainly newsworthy. Tiger's actions and damage control after the accident were newsworthy, largely because they would affect the sport so deeply. And — though this is the most contentious part of the debate over Tiger coverage — the obvious gap between the revelations and his carefully managed public image was newsworthy. Ultimately, the many stories and opinion columns that sprung up from these issues demonstrated sports journalists at their best rather than their worst.

This is even true of the writers who had the harshest things to say about Woods, such as *Washington Post* sports columnist Sally Jenkins. Shortly after the car accident, Jenkins claims: "We aren't entitled to know everything about him, and certainly aren't entitled to know everything about his family.... whatever is happening in Woods' private life at the moment, he is certainly entitled to his privacy and may well deserve some sympathy." Yet, in the same column, Jenkins sharply criticizes Woods for refusing to talk to police after the car accident, arguing that he had a "responsibility to talk to police because of the nature of his job. He's a public figure, and the message he sent is that traffic cops are beneath him" ("Sally Jenkins Discusses"). Here, within a single column, Jenkins distinguishes between parts of the Woods story appropriate for reporters to pursue and the areas that should be off-limits. In subsequent columns, both Jenkins and her *Washington Post* sports colleague, John Feinstein, reiterate Woods' right to privacy while differentiating privacy from secrecy. The argument here centered on what Jenkins called the "sheer size of the gap between Woods' public image, crafted so shrewdly by his handlers, and his *secret* conduct" ("Tiger Woods"). Jenkins continues:

> A violation of privacy is merely embarrassing. It's the violation of his secrecy that's destroyed his public persona. Big difference.... Woods' puerile foibles wouldn't be any of our business if his sole entry into the public sphere were on the golf course. But Woods — and the huge corporate entities around him — spent the past decade specifically creating an image that goes far beyond his performance in golf, and profited hugely from it. He sold himself as a principled, self-disciplined and buttoned up family man.... He created an iconic image ... and now cries privacy when reality assails it.... there's a lot of salaciousness in the Woods saga, but there's also a valuable vetting of a powerful public brand ["Tiger Woods"].

It's fair to ask, of course, how one might determine the actual "value" of this vetting. There is little doubt that Tiger's fans — and, more so, golf's bean-counters — would have preferred to remain, indefinitely, in a state of blissful ignorance. Moreover, sports writers are likely more sensitive than the public to this branding issue because they, to a large degree, are seen as "dupes" who transmitted this false public image to the masses. And yet here is a sports writer, a journalist, engaging in an honest substantive debate stemming from the Tiger Woods saga. A contentious issue, perhaps, but fair and newsworthy, worlds removed from the salacious, gratuitous gossip found elsewhere in the media. Despite appearances to the contrary, there was plenty of outstanding journalism produced during the Tiger Woods scandal. Sports writers, as Jenkins' work illustrates, provided the bulk of it.

This "valuable vetting" of Woods reached a crescendo on April 5, 2010, when Tiger entered the Augusta National press room for his first post-scandal press conference. Bowing to a habit ingrained in all sports writers, Posnanski kept score by breaking the questions into twelve general categories. Most were related to how Tiger was able to "live that life." This is a perfectly suitable question that sports writers, especially, would ask because it pertains more to Tiger's legendary abilities to compete at the highest levels than his shortcomings. As Posnanski writes, "with his life a steady stream of heated texts and secret rendezvous and lies, how did he continue to win golf tournaments through it all?" There were also multiple questions about his relationship to the doctor implicated in steroids scandals, about rehab, about how he's handling things, and about why he didn't talk sooner.

All told, Posnanski summarizes: "I don't think anyone hit below the belt, or came across as absurdly judgmental. I suspect some will say it should have been harder hitting and others will think it was absurdly moralistic to start with. I thought the questions were pretty sound." Of course, a few questions towed the line, about family, whether wife Elin would attend the Masters, etc. Posnanski rightly described these as "touchy." Yet, from a sports perspective, the question about his wife attending the Masters was more appropriate than it sounds. Tiger's emotional state — and how it might affect his performance — was a major storyline entering the tournament. Given his reported attempts to rebuild his family, Elin's attendance or absence could well offer clues as to how heavily his family situation might weigh his golf. Touchy, yes, but relevant to the tournament.

Some, of course, were disappointed the questions weren't at least a little more hard-hitting. But James Frank, former editor at *Golf Magazine,* explains that Tiger chose this time and place for the press conference because, given Augusta's long-standing tradition of civility and good manners, asking a question about "sexting would be like farting in church." Frank continues, emphasizing that, well, these were sports writers. As opposed to other media types — ones not admitted to this press conference — they were doing their jobs in the traditional sense of the word. He writes,

> While I think the golf press corps could have done a better job chipping away at Tiger — read the transcript and you'll see they asked some pretty good questions — I understand why they didn't do more. We aren't investigative reporters, unless you consider asking a player what club he hit into

15 an investigation. Most of what we do is reactive, reacting to the ebb and flow of a tournament, analyzing revisions to a golf course, profiling a hot player. One of the reasons we love golf is that we haven't had to be proactive. The game has always been relatively trouble-free: No steroids (well, not much), no cheating (well, very little), with a strong connection to real people, like ourselves, who play the game. Everything that made the Tiger story so shocking and so riveting to the outside world the last five months — scandal, sex, drugs — are things golf writers don't usually write about. A fact Team Tiger, Augusta National, and anyone else who had a hand in planning yesterday's press conference was counting on. The story of Tiger's fall from grace was broken and reported by a completely different media.

Years ago, Frank's critique might have offended the guys in the "toy department." To say that sports writers don't usually write about "scandal, sex and drugs" might have implied that they aren't serious reporters. But, despite Frank's precise description of the *appeal* of writing about sports, and particularly about golf, sports writers have spent the last several decades showing they can, when necessary, report extremely effectively on the most serious of issues. And this is vital, as sports in so many ways reflect community and culture. Within this beat, sports writers cover crime, labor strikes, health, education, human interest, war, politics, and more. And, yes, within this modern-day model of the sports writer, they have "taken down" athletes. Joe Posnanski asserts that the media "took down" Tiger Woods for "leading a wild life and cheating on his wife." Perhaps. But those seeking a ray of professionalism amid this dark episode in American media must start with the sports writers, Posnanski and his colleagues, who showed the most restraint, the most professionalism, the most maturity. True, holding his initial post-scandal press conference in front of sports writers was the best thing for Tiger Woods. But, given the sports writers' performance, it was also the best thing for journalism.

WORKS CITED

"Afghanistan Dominates While Two Scandals Fascinate." *Project for Excellence in Journalism News Coverage Index.* Pew Research Center. 7 Dec. 2009. Web. 19 June 2010.

Allen, Anita. "Does Tiger Woods Have a Right to Privacy?" *New York Times.* 3 Dec. 2009. Web. 13 Oct. 2011.

Boedeker, Hal. "Tiger Woods and the TMZ Effect: Can Mainstream Media Compete?" *Orlando Sentinel.* 10 Jan. 2010. Web. 16 July 2010.

Clark, Roy Peter. "When Scandals Strike Celebrities Like Tiger Woods, Try Practicing 'Collateral Journalism.'" Poynter.org. 18 Feb. 2010. Web. 25 June 2010.

"Economy and Health Lead but Economy Gains Attention." *Project for Excellence in Journalism News Coverage Index.* Pew Research Center. 14 Dec. 2009. Web. 19 June 2010.

"Elections, Katrina and Economy Split the News Agenda." *Project for Excellence in Journalism News Coverage Index.* Pew Research Center. 30 Aug. 2010. Web. 9 Sept. 2010.

Farhi, Paul. "Lost in the Woods." *American Journalism Review.* Mar. 2010. Web. 21 July 2010.

Feinstein, John. "Tiger Woods's Half-Apology." *Washington Post.* 20 Feb. 2010. Web. 25 June 2010.

Fitzpatrick, Michael. "Tiger Woods Blurring the Line between Mainstream and Tabloid Journalism." *Bleacher Report.* 14 Mar. 2010. Web. 11 June 2010.

Frank, James. "Tiger and 'Friends': Working the Media at Augusta." *MEDIAITE.* 6 Apr. 2010. Web. 26 July 2010.

"Health Care Generates Its Biggest Week of Coverage." *Project for Excellence in Journalism News Coverage Index.* Pew Research Center. 22 Mar. 2010. Web. 19 June 2010.

HejiraHenry. "With the AP AWOL, How Will You Handle the Tiger Sex Rehab Story?" Sportsjournalists.com. 15 Jan. 2010. Web. 18 July 2010.

"In a Diverse Week, A Stimulus Debate Drives the News." *Project for Excellence in Journalism News Coverage Index.* Pew Research Center. 22 Feb. 2010. Web. 19 June 2010.

Jenkins, Sally. "Sally Jenkins Discusses Tiger Woods's Evasive Maneuvers." *Washington Post.* 1 Dec. 2009. Web. 22 June 2009.

_____. "Tiger Woods Should Take This Opportunity to Grow Up." *Washington Post.* 24 Dec. 2009. Web. 26 June 2009.

Leitch, Will. "Will Tiger Change Sports Journalism?" *New York Magazine.* 9 Dec. 2009. Web. 17 June 2010.

McGuire, Tim. "This Want to Know and Need to Know Distinction Matters in Tiger Woods Case." Arizona State University Walter Cronkite School of Journalism and Mass Communication. 2 Dec. 2009. Web. 23 June 2010.

"Mine Accident Captivates Media." *Project for Excellence in Journalism News Coverage Index.* Pew Research Center. 12 Apr. 2010. Web. 19 June 2010.

Posnanski, Joe. "The Tiger Press Conference." *SportsIllustrated.com.* 5 Apr. 2010. Web. 6 June 2010.

Shipnuck, Alan. "Alan Shipnuck's Mailbag: Tiger Woods, New Groove Rules and More." Golf.com. 7 Jan. 2010. Web. 12 June 2010.

SI Golf Group. "PGA Tour Confidential. The Tiger Woods Scandal." Golf.com. 6 Dec. 2009. Web. 19 June 2010.

Sonner, Ryan. "With the AP AWOL, How Will You Handle the Tiger Sex Rehab Story?" Sportsjournalists.com. 15 Jan. 2010. Web. 18 July 2010.

Wharton, David. "Tiger Woods Regrets 'Transgressions.'" *Los Angeles Times.* 3 Dec. 2009. Web. 17 June 2010.

Wilbon, Michael. "Some Context on Tiger and His 'Transgressions' Is Needed." *Washington Post.* 3 Dec. 2009. Web. 11 Oct. 2011.

Wright, Robert. "Sex and the Digital City." *New York Times.* 19 Jan. 2010. Web. 11 Oct. 2011.

Public Apology and Acts of Contrition

James G. Shoopman

Between Thanksgiving and Christmas 2009, millions of people around the world suddenly knew his most embarrassing secret. He had betrayed his family, his coworkers, and his fans, not with a single "mistake" but by repeatedly violating a nearly universal moral norm. He committed adultery with large numbers of women, including porn stars, night club hostesses, waitresses, and perhaps, quite literally, the girl next door. Now everyone knew that he was not the person he had pretended to be, and his behavior put everyone he worked with at great risk of serious financial loss. More importantly, he stood to lose his fanbase, the support of friends, and his wife and children. Because he was a public figure, he appeared on television to apologize, with his mother in the room and the whole world watching.

That was the situation Tiger Woods faced on February 19, 2010. As many public figures have done before and since, Woods performed a now familiar ritual of public contrition, hoping to save his family life, his career, and what might be left of his reputation. This act prompts questions that warrant further investigation as they "played out" in the Tiger Woods case. What is the nature of apology, and what are the motivations and inherent risks of expressing contrition? Why was Tiger compelled to offer a public apology even though his "crimes" concerned his private life? What was Tiger trying to achieve with this vitally important act of mass communication? What are the necessary elements of a potentially effective public apology, and did Tiger adhere to that model, developing the elements satisfactorily? Was Tiger's apology ultimately successful?

Nature of Apology

Apology is a special form of communication that has become an important object of formal study for psychologists, business and political consultants, and communication scholars, all of them producing an increasingly large body of literature on this subject. One of the most extensive modern studies, *On Apology,* was authored by Aaron Lazar, Dean and Professor of Psychiatry at the University of Massachusetts Medical School. In this work, Lazar defines apology as "an encounter between two parties in which one party, the offender, acknowledges responsibility for an offense or grievance and expresses regret or remorse to a second party, the aggrieved" (23). Such encounters are typically initiated because people recognize that offended persons actually need an apology in order to get past the anger and pain of being harmed. Certainly, restoration of any damaged relationship may require apology as a first step.

Apologies are often proffered not only because offended persons need to receive an apology, but also because offenders need to express regret. According to Lazar, offenders must first develop two related psychological capabilities to feel contrition: "The first is empathy, a person's ability to be aware of and understand how another person thinks and feels. The second concept is guilt, the capacity to apply standards of right and wrong to our behavior toward others and to punish ourselves emotionally when we hurt others" (135). Most psychologically normal people experience both mental states in varying measures, and the subsequent emotional pain motivates them to apologize to people they have offended, especially if they wish to remain in an ongoing relationship with that person or group of persons.

Despite the potential healing that can result from apology, Lazar lists several risks of apology, including (1) being viewed as the original instigator of the offense, because the person at fault is normally expected to be the first to apologize; (2) risking ridicule for misbehavior; (3) risking perceptions of weakness, because of the willingness to apologize; and (4) risking rejection and humiliation if the apology is not accepted. Because of these emotional risks, Lazar considers any apology, genuine or not it would seem, to be an act of courage (142). If an apology occurs at all, it is because the drive to restore the damaged relationship overcomes the offender's fears.

Alongside, or sometimes instead of, intrinsic emotional motivations for apology, many offenders are also trying to alter external circumstances that might lead to harm for themselves or others. Lazar suggests two such drives. An offender may be "using the apology to avoid abandonment, stigmatization, damage to reputation, retaliation or punishment of any kind" (145). On the other hand, offenders may also be trying to "keep their relationships intact or enhance their social stature" (Lazar 157). Because it is clear that Tiger was trying to regain the trust and support of a great many people, including his wife, coworkers, and fans, he was obviously trying to avoid a great many negative ramifications for his bad behaviors.

Private Harm on Public Display

Renowned public figures need to apologize in public for transgressions in private life under particular circumstances. Because their livelihoods depend, in some measure, on the trust of an adoring public, celebrities certainly must deal with what Lazar has called "external circumstances that might lead to harm" (145) if they cannot keep misbehavior entirely private. Prior to his public apology, Tiger's misbehavior had been on public display for weeks. The public aspect of Tiger's fall began when the *National Inquirer* published allegations of Tiger's marital infidelity. Even though the woman involved denied these claims and the *National Inquirer* has a reputation for exaggeration and falsehood, the story soon spread to mainstream media. Tiger's neighborhood automobile accident aroused further inquiry, and within a short period of time, it was clear that Tiger Woods had betrayed his wife on multiple occasions with multiple women. At least a dozen women were no longer keeping his secret, and Tiger faced the reality that he could no longer credibly deny the string of infidelities.

If Tiger had not been a married family man, there probably would have been little or no scandal. Although few may actually say so, people are rarely surprised or even very offended by promiscuous behavior among young, unmarried athletes. In some corners, sexual conquests are privately cheered as proof of the virile manhood that makes an athlete a powerful competitor. But Tiger was married, and he had clearly erred. Because his transgressions were revealed in a most public way, his acts of contrition necessitated an equally public display of remorse.

In the immediate aftermath of all this scrutiny, Tiger issued two public apologies on his website. The first, posted on December 2, was roundly criticized as deficient. The second was issued on December 11. Much of the first letter entailed a plea for privacy, but the second letter more directly refers to "my infidelity," stating, "I am profoundly sorry and ... [I] ask forgiveness," as well as announcing a hiatus from professional golf ("Tiger Woods Taking Hiatus"). It seemed to express a genuine sense of remorse but was still short of the apology most people expected. A very long period of silence did nothing to satisfy people's expectations. Weeks later, just prior to Tiger's final televised apology, John Kador, a business consultant who wrote the popular work, *Effective Apology*, speculated on what Woods should say in a public act of contrition. As Kador declares, "I fear Tiger Woods still doesn't get the meaning of accountability and effective apology" ("What Tiger Woods Should Say"). Many others doubtlessly concurred with Kador. Tiger's televised apology on February 19, 2010, was the last public effort in what scholar Keith Michael Hearit calls an apologetic "campaign," wherein public offenders keep apologizing until they finally hit the right note in the right way. Only then do demands for a convincing apology subside (206).

Public Apology: Risky Business

If private apology is fraught with risks, public apology is much more complex, requiring even greater courage. According to a variety of scholars, public apology is primal, its power derived from the basic qualities of verbalized contrition, but it is also professionally sophisticated and psychologically complex. Virtually every major publication on the subject acknowledges that public apology, despite its complexity, is far more common than it was in the middle of the 20th century. Dr. Lazar says that he attributes

> the increase in national and even international apologies, in part to the fact that formerly powerless groups are now demanding respect and denouncing behaviors that devalue them. But we can also understand this phenomenon as the expression of an evolving social contract that expands to include the rights and needs of these groups [55].

Lazar argues that apology is essentially an exchange of power: the offender atones for his offense by giving power over to the offended, particularly the power to restore the offender's place in the life of the offended (52, 167).

This theory of transferred power may suggest that the growing motivation of the powerful to hand over power arises because society views authority differently than it did in the mid-twentieth century. "Question authority!" is not simply a popular bumper sticker; the idea has become a norm, requiring everyone from Popes to Presidents to apologize for offenses and abuses. At one time, a man as powerful as Tiger Woods would not have been vulnerable to exposure of his sexual transgressions at all. If a scandal arose, a celebrity would either simply disappear forever from public life or go away for a season, only to return after all the anger settled. Public figures are no longer allowed such latitude. In his book *Crisis Management by Apology: Corporate Response to Allegations of Wrongdoing,* Hearit writes

> Parties as diverse as politicians, sports figures, entertainers, businesses, not-for-profit organizations, institutions and governments now face daily criticism to which they must defend their actions or face damage to their carefully constructed images and the loss of consumer confidence and patronage [3].

As a result of this change, leaders in the public sphere often rely on public apology to save their institutions and personal careers.

Because Tiger's apology addressed a broad audience, including the world of professional golf and his sponsors, it is useful to note how the business world, in particular, seeks to manage crisis by public apology. As with any major corporate scandal, a lot of money has been at stake in Tiger's rehabilitation. This makes apology financially, as well as psychologically, risky business. Reiterating and expanding on Lazar's disempowerment theory, business world apology-guru John Kador warns,

> The main impediment to apologizing is that we can't control how our apology will be received. Apology, at its core, is really an exchange of shame and power between the offender and the victim. Apology involves a role reversal. Apologizers relinquish power and put themselves at the mercy of their victims, who may or may not accept the apology ... apology derives its moral authority from this fundamental uncertainty. There are no guarantees [43]

Due to this uncertainty, the corporate and political worlds have always been leery of admissions of guilt and how this might affect the financial bottom-line. This bottom-line focus might seem inherently selfish but need not always be so. Protecting shareholders from financial loss due to employee transgressions is a reasonably fair and ethical consideration. No one can know for sure how concerned Tiger was about his stakeholders in the midst of the scandal, but they were doubtlessly worried about how he would handle the problem.

It is important to note, however, that even in an anti-authoritarian zeitgeist that holds institutional giants responsible to make up for public wrongs, not every person or organization chooses to apologize. Some public leaders follow the philosophy of John Wayne's character in *She Wore a Yellow Ribbon*, who warned, "Never apologize; it's a sign of weakness." Hearit notes that these people might employ a number of other strategies to deal with public scandal, including outright denial, counter-attack, differentiation and legal negotiation (15, 124). Many corporate entities have protected themselves from legal liability by directing spokespersons to say they are "sorry" for some sad state of affairs but without actually admitting any kind of guilt. Lazar refers to this as using the word "sorry" in the "empathic" sense, suggesting the speaker empathizes with pain of those suffering but does not take responsibility for that pain (96–97).

All this implies that public apology is full of inherent risks. A growing number of the wealthy and powerful nonetheless opt to engage in what has by now become a predictable ritual of self-mortification. Hearit refers to this as a "secular remediation ritual." As he indicates, the ritual in the corporate realm is not so much about gaining forgiveness as "the exacting of a proportional humiliation by which to propitiate the wrongdoing. Socially, such acts function to restore faith in the social hierarchy by a discourse that praises the very values individuals and organizations are accused of having broken" (205). As Tiger's connection to his stakeholders is far more personal than that of some large corporation, seeking public forgiveness may still have been an important motivator, but the corporate nature of Tiger Woods as an institution is also a reality. With that in mind, Tiger initiated and endured the "secular remediation ritual" that Hearit, Kador, and Lazar note is enacted quite predictably.

Hearit posits several common characteristics for this ritual, including professional scripting (3). No one knows if Tiger wrote his own apology, but most commentators point out that the media event was "carefully controlled" and that Woods read from a manuscript that was subsequently released to his website. The voluntary self-mortification was also presented in what Hearit calls "a heightened mode of communication," live television broadcast (33, 35). In addition, Tiger delivered the public apology at an appropriate time, neither too soon, which might suggest a lack of appropriate reflection and suffering, nor too late, which might suggest the apologizer is simply caving in to public demand (Kador 131; Lazar 176–177).

Elements of an Effective Apology

Hearit emphasizes that an important goal of public apology is creating the impression that the apology is truthful, sincere, and voluntary as it addresses all stakeholders (64). In *Effective Apology*, John Kador provides a recipe, of sorts, for public acts of contrition that mend fences, build bridges, and restore trust. He lists five elements of an effective apology, public or private: acknowledging fault, accepting responsibility and blame, expressing remorse, offering restitution, and assuring the offense will not be repeated. Although Kador asserts these five elements are normally sufficient to ensure an effective apology, Lazar argues that other elements may appear in an effective apology, including asking for forgiveness.

Acknowledging Fault

In order to clearly acknowledge fault, the offender must unequivocally state the actual offense. Supposedly a devoted husband and father, Tiger's actions belied that carefully crafted image. He broke the rules of the culture: monogamy and loyalty. Tiger unequivocally declares "The issue involved here is my repeated irresponsible behavior. I was unfaithful. I had affairs. I cheated"

("Tiger Woods' Apology" 1). There is no smoothing-over or blaming anyone else in these very direct and terse sentences. He defines his behavior as "irresponsible" and verbalizes three words that are most commonly used to define adultery: "unfaithful," "affairs" and "cheated."

With those words, Tiger clearly admits that he was at fault and names exactly what he has done. For the fault to be fully acknowledged, an offender must also identify and acknowledge the victims of his actions. In this case there were multiple offended parties, and Tiger alludes to some of them at the start of the event. As he states, "Many of you cheered for me, or worked with me, or supported me" ("Tiger Woods' Apology" 1). Employing more precise language, he then admits that he has "let down" his fans. Although he mentions his fans specifically only once, he clearly understands that they had an emotional attachment to him and that he has disappointed them. He also confesses that his friends, whom he refers to four times, have valid reasons to be critical of his actions. In addition to acknowledging that he victimized his family, Tiger admits he hurt "kids all around the world who admired me," offering a very "special apology" to parents who "used to point to me as a role model for their kids" ("Tiger Woods' Apology" 2). Clearly, Tiger understood that some constituents had significant emotional investments in this situation.

In one fairly substantial portion of the statement, Tiger offers assurances to the people involved with the Tiger Woods Foundation that he remains dedicated to their mission. He also verbalizes regret that he has hurt his business partners by causing them "considerable worry" ("Tiger Woods' Apology" 1). All of these may be referred to as "stakeholders"— people who were financially invested in Tiger Woods' public reputation. This would include his many sponsors, the professional golf community, and various business interests who used Tiger as a spokesperson. The financial implications of Tiger's fall were enormous for the business of professional golf and for everyone who depended on Tiger's reputation to sell everything from telephones to razors to sports shoes. Tiger's use of the word "worry" would seem to understate the depth of their concern, as well as the gravity of the situation, but he does attempt to signal to them that he understands their stake in him.

Very early in his statement, Tiger moves from a list of general victims to the person he most obviously and most profoundly hurt, his wife Elin. She is the first person Tiger acknowledges by name. In fact, Elin is the only person Tiger mentions by name other than PGA Commissioner Tim Finchem, whom he thanks near the end of the statement. Not only does Tiger use Elin's name eight times, but he also refers to her as his "wife" seven times, clearly signaling that she is the primary focus of his contrition. Most people would agree that Elin ought to have been the centerpiece of the statement. Not only did Tiger betray his marriage vows, but his affairs resulted in even greater humiliation than most wives suffer in these situations because his infidelities fueled a veritable feeding frenzy of media stories and public commentary. Public humiliation warranted public contrition. As can be discerned by close analysis, Tiger's apology is an excellent example of Lazar's concept that apology is an exchange of power. In the 1,545-word statement, commentary about and apologies to Elin and the children, whom he never mentions by name, take up nearly 33 percent of the words he utters. By making Elin the specific focus of the apology, Tiger seems to be seeking atonement by turning power over to his victim.

Although one might argue that Elin's humiliation only increased as a result of the public apology, Tiger confirms the extent of his powerlessness in the fate of their relationship. He reports that Elin had actually pointed out to him: "My real apology to her will not come in the form of words; it will come from my behavior over time" ("Tiger Woods' Apology" 1). Not only does Tiger confirm that a few words of public contrition will certainly not automatically restore his marriage, but he also admits that Elin made him aware of that reality. She clearly has the power to accept or reject his private and public apologies.

Accepting Responsibility and Blame

To accept responsibility also entails accepting appropriate blame for the offense. Immediately after acknowledging fault, Tiger says, "What I did is not acceptable and I am the only person to blame" ("Tiger Woods' Apology" 1). Tiger does not even remotely suggest that he was sexually seduced or that he was dissatisfied at home. He does, however, flirt a little with blaming the seductions of money and fame. He says, "I felt that I had worked hard my entire life and deserved to enjoy all the temptations around me. I felt I was entitled. Thanks to money and fame I didn't have to go far to find them." But then he immediately says, "I was wrong. I was foolish. I don't get to play by different rules. The same boundaries that apply to everyone apply to me. I brought this shame on myself" ("Tiger Woods' Apology" 2).

In essence, Woods takes full responsibility for his own behavior and blames no one else. Significantly, he also goes to great lengths to defend his wife from charges that she tried to physically harm him on the night of the accident that launched subsequent inquiries. As he reports, "It angers me that people would fabricate a story like that," adding, "She never hit me that night or any other night. There has never been an episode of domestic violence in our marriage. Ever" ("Tiger Woods' Apology" 1). This comment has nothing to do with his own transgressions and is done purely to restore Elin's innocence and dignity.

Expressing Remorse

True remorse implies at least a certain level of emotion. Properly expressed, remorse communicates genuine sorrow for harm done as a result of the offense. Lazar writes that remorse itself "serves as a form of self-punishment" (108), serving to help the offended understand that the offender has suffered because of hurtful actions. Kador says that offenders must focus on the consequences of their behavior, without trying to minimize the offense by insisting they never intended for such painful things to occur (189). The "I did not intend to hurt" approach would certainly fail to signal remorse. In his apology, Tiger says, "I am also aware of the pain my behavior has caused to those of you in this room ... my failures have made me look at myself in a way I never wanted to before ... for all that I have done, I am so sorry" ("Tiger Woods' Apology" 1). Eschewing the "lack of intentionality" defense, Tiger directly addresses the harm he has done and his sorrow and remorse for the pain he caused.

Offering Restitution

Restitution involves offering tangible or symbolic loss to atone for the offense. Of course, in cases where something has been taken away, that thing must be in some sense returned. Sometimes, however, the nature of many offenses precludes actually returning what was taken, such as causing a death or depriving someone of dignity. Lazar suggests offended parties need

> restoration of respect and dignity, assurances that they and the offender have shared values, assurances they were not at fault [for their own pain], assurances they are safe from further harm from the offender, knowledge that the offender has suffered as a result of the offense, a promise of adequate reparations, and an opportunity to communicate their suffering and other feelings about the offense [34–35; cf. Kador 32–33].

Tiger's loss of reputation probably deprived many in his circle of future income, and Tiger's ability to offer reparations of "future" income is speculative at this point.

In addition, Tiger undoubtedly took, among other things, some people's pleasure of identifying with his achievements and enjoying his victories. Lazar warns that "when ... reparations are available but not acted upon, the apology fails," but "when the offense is intangible, such as insults or humiliations, reparations may be symbolic in nature" (Lazar 127, 129). In Tiger's case, a respectful absence from the game, in order to pursue therapy, was a form of symbolic restitution. In some ways, the public apology itself constituted symbolic restitution. A famous, wealthy, and powerful man humiliated himself and admitted to great transgression before family, friends, and co-workers. The suffering emanating from this act served as a form of reparation for the pain he had caused his public. It was "symbolic" restitution, but the suffering was very real.

Assuring Offense Will Not Be Repeated

One extremely important element of apology is the offender's reassurance that the offended party is safe from further harm. This is especially true if the goal involves restoration of a relationship. In several places, Tiger offers reassurances. He admits, "I owe it to my family to become a better person. I owe it to those closest to me to become a better man ... when I do return [to professional golf] I need to make my behavior more respectful of the game" ("Tiger Woods' Apology" 3). Although the "better man" and "better person" references are very vague, Woods attempts to provide necessary assurances. Oftentimes, such promises additionally require some indication that the apologizer respects the social order and commonly held values in the culture (Hearit 36, 70). In his apology, Tiger directly states, "I stopped living by the core values that I was taught to believe in ... I don't get to play by different rules" ("Tiger Woods' Apology" 2). Here, Woods signals that becoming a "better man" and "better person" requires returning to "core values" by recommitting himself to his Buddhist upbringing. Although the vast majority of the audience was certainly not Buddhist, Tiger doubtlessly trusts that they understand, and even identify with, the benefits of living within a belief system.

In conjunction with declarations about returning to Buddhism, Tiger refers to rehabilitative therapy he received prior to the public apology, as well as his need for further help. These passages constitute Woods' most important assurances that he will not repeat his offenses. Alluding to his problem with sexual addiction, Tiger says, "It's hard to admit that I need help but I do. For 45 days from the end of December to early February, I was in inpatient therapy receiving guidance for the issues I'm facing. I have a long way to go, but I've taken my first steps in the right direction" ("Tiger Woods' Apology" 2). Tiger refers here to time spent as an inpatient at Pine Grove Health and Addiction Services, an extension of Forest General Hospital in Hattiesburg, Mississippi. Pine Grove, in existence since 1984, and the hospital to which it is attached, in existence since 1952, are longstanding and reputable institutions, not the typical habitat of celebrities in temporary rehab (*Forest General; Pine Grove*).

Like many similar institutions around the country, Pine Grove incorporates a Twelve Step addiction recovery process, built on the relatively successful process used in Alcoholics Anonymous. Confessional apology is a vital component to that therapy, and Tiger clearly employs language common to recovery communities, saying that "I've taken my *first steps* in the right direction" ("Tiger Woods' Apology" 2, emphasis added). Even more revealing, Woods reports, "I've had a lot of time to think about what I've done. My failures have made me look at myself in a way I never wanted to before. It's now up to me to *make amends*" ("Tiger Woods' Apology" 2, emphasis added). All Twelve Step groups essentially regard addictions as substitutes for healthy connections with people. Sometimes utilizing slightly modified therapies originally crafted in Alcoholics Anonymous, these programs guide their patients to establish and maintain healthy relationships. In keeping with the literature on apology, two steps are particularly relevant to indicate Tiger's motivation for the televised apology. According Dr. Patrick Carnes, Executive Director of the Gentle Path program at Pine Grove and author of several books on sexual addiction, including *Out of the Shadows: Understanding Sexual Addiction*, step eight requires sufferers to create a list of people who have been harmed and to make amends to them all. Step nine mandates that amends are "direct wherever possible, except when to do so would injure them or others" (137). Woods' public apology would clearly seem to address those steps.

Tiger's unusual reference to a faith commitment is also consistent with a Twelve Step model of recovery from addiction, requiring a commitment to a "higher power" without necessarily defining "God" in any conventional way. According to Carnes, step two requires followers to declare that a "power greater than ourselves could restore us to sanity," and step three necessitates "a decision to turn our will and our lives over to the care of God as we understood him" (137). In seeming fulfillment of these requirements, Woods asserts, "I have a lot of work to do, and I intend to dedicate myself to doing it. Part of following this path for me is Buddhism, which my mother taught me at a young age" ("Tiger Woods' Apology" 3). Of course, Tiger's use of "path" is noteworthy here. In addition, his mother's presence in the immediate physical audience would seem to underscore the seriousness of his effort at rehabilitation.

Some people have suggested that Tiger's reference to Buddhism was a rebuke to Fox News analyst Brit Hume, who asserted Tiger should turn to Christianity for a good model of repentance and contrition ("Tiger Woods Returns"). Such an interpretation is remarkably narrow and skeptical, however, and Tiger is more likely referring to the higher power at the center of his recovery effort. Describing Buddhism in ways quite relevant to addiction recovery, Woods asserts, "Buddhism teaches that a craving for things outside ourselves causes an unhappy and pointless search for security. It teaches me to stop following every impulse and to learn restraint" ("Tiger Woods' Apology" 3). Here Woods conjoins a Twelve Step requirement with a pledge to adhere to the tenets of his faith in an effort to assure he will not err again.

Because so many celebrity offenders are "doing rehab" these days, this sort of reassurance is often mocked. In reference to the Congressman Weiner sexting scandal, *Washington Post* columnist E. J. Dionne cynically argues,

> What's amazing is that the Scandal Management Handbook, 36th edition, offered him [Weiner] the perfect way out. When caught, fess up immediately, declare right from the start you are a victim of a terrible addiction, go into treatment and disappear for a while. You are rarely challenged these days when you take a loss of virtue and turn it into a medical condition.

People often assume that identifying oneself as an "addict" means the subject is blaming the addiction and not accepting responsibility for his/her actions. On the contrary, serious recovery therapy actually requires taking personal responsibility for the harm done "under the influence" of the addiction. Making amends, often in the form of public apology and contrition, is usually an essential aspect of accepting that responsibility.

It is certainly possible that Tiger only went into "therapy" in order to regain the public's confidence, but people are too often contemptuous about "rehab" and addiction therapy because they do not actually understand it. Only time will tell if Tiger sincerely believes he has a dangerous addiction. Although Elin finally decided to divorce Woods, thus removing the constraints of marital commitments, genuine Twelve Step recovery from sexual addiction will require Tiger to develop a "good abstinence." In harmony with that concept, Buddhism mandates abstinence from harmful sexual activities. Tiger Woods has obviously been a phenomenal athlete, and all successful athletes understand the need for discipline. If Tiger is serious about maintaining a program of recovery from addiction, public apology was a vital and necessary step toward emotional health, as well restoration to the world of professional golf.

Asking for Forgiveness

With all that in mind, Tiger engaged in a ritual act of confession and repentance, in the hope of receiving forgiveness. The pattern of this communication is deeply rooted in the American psyche. Nearly universal in religious life, especially throughout the American Christian tradition, the pattern is specifically laid out as a communicative ceremony in the standards of the Catholic confessional: contrition, confession, absolution and penance. Tiger echoes some of the religious roots of apology by saying "I have a lot to *atone* for" ("Tiger Woods' Apology" 1, emphasis added). Sometimes, in seeking such atonement, apologies include additional elements not mentioned by Kador, such as asking for forgiveness.

Lazar believes that directly asking for forgiveness can be an appropriate step in some cases (228–50), and many religious communities might concur. Kador nonetheless argues that forgiving someone is a different matter from accepting an apology, suggesting that asking for forgiveness makes the exchange more about the offender's need to be forgiven than about the offended person's need to receive an apology (181–182). Tiger does not put his audience in the position to fulfill that need because he never uses the word "forgive" or "forgiveness." He does, however, conclude his apology by saying, "I ask you to find room in your heart to one day believe in me again" ("Tiger Woods' Apology" 3). Although "find room in your heart" and "believe in me" stop just short of a forthright appeal, Tiger's request is not for immediate forgiveness, but for eventual reconciliation in the proper time. He does not put anyone in the position of having to give *him* immediate comfort. Instead he expresses hope of a future restoration.

Judging the Success of Tiger's Apology

Given the criteria listed by Kador, can Tiger's televised apology be viewed as effective? Did it indeed mend fences, build bridges, or restore trust? The text of the apology certainly meets the criteria laid out by Kador and Lazar. Tiger doesn't mince words about his offense. He takes full responsibility, blaming nothing and no one else. He seems to show remorse, offers symbolic restitution, and reassures everyone, his wife included, that he is intent on changing his behavior. In a clear effort to convince listeners of his sincerity, Tiger acknowledges the dissonance between his previous image and his behaviors: "I have made you question who I am" ("Tiger Woods' Apology" 1). In a sense, this statement acknowledges that the audience has a perfect right, in addition to good reasons, to be skeptical. It is understandable for people to question: if he was lying then, what is to say that he is not lying now? Although celebrities such as Tiger Woods deliver public acts of contrition for a variety of reasons, some of them sincere, and some of them cynical, the parties they have offended cannot accept apologies that they suspect are disingenuous. Because Tiger's apology came only after the discovery of his misdeeds, it is not possible to declare conclusively that his apology was truthful, sincere, and purely voluntary. Portions of the text of the apology do suggest a high probability of sincerity, and many people listened sympathetically, perhaps convinced that he was truthful and earnest.

Although Woods' statement fits the mold of an appropriate apology, some still remain skeptical about why Woods apologized publically, as well as the sincerity of his remorse and promise of reformation. It is entirely possible, of course, that Tiger's decision to publicly apologize was prompted by the industry that depended on the rehabilitation of his image. Hearit notes that "encouragement for individuals and organizations to apologize is likely to come from the economic interests that individuals and institutions represent" (207). Perhaps partly for this reason, not everyone "bought" the televised performance. Focusing not on the script but on Tiger's delivery of the apology, David Hinckley of the *New York Daily News* writes that "Woods was a man saying the right things out loud while everything about his demeanor was silently screaming, 'I don't want to be here.'" Summarizing Tiger's performance with a pun, Hinckley declares that Tiger looked as if he had been caught in a "bear trap." *Sports Illustrated* writer Alan Shipnuck also comments on Woods' demeanor, noting how "diminished" Tiger looked and labeling the "mea culpa" a "sad performance."

Other commentaries nevertheless argue that the apology was effective. In an article for the *Huffington Post*, Rabbi Shmuley Boteach interprets Tiger's obvious discomfort as a display of appropriate suffering. Boteach writes that Tiger "looked the entire time like he meant it. It was that rarest of things, a sincere and unconditional statement of contrition and responsibility from a public figure for cheating on his wife." Taking a different tack, Thomas Boswell, *Washington Post* sports columnist, pronounces the apology "strong and believable," based upon Tiger's clear "voice" in particular portions of the script (1). Noting that many people probably expected Tiger to ask for forgiveness, Boswell homes in on Tiger's actual request at the end of the statement. Boswell writes, "I doubt I've ever heard an athlete ask the public to 'believe in me'" (2), asserting that the phrase signals Tiger's apparent need for fans to have a faith in him that is typically reserved for religious figures. Although Boswell's commentary resonates with several of Earl Woods' public proclamations about Tiger's being the "Chosen One," Tiger's utterance may instead indicate his hopes to once again be a hero.

Clearly, Tiger sought to offer an apology that would be received well by his public. The repeated attempts at a successful expression of contrition are evidence of this, as is the significant step of finally appearing on television to deliver the last apology. Even so, many disbelieve that the apology was motivated by any measure of empathy or genuine guilt. Tiger's clearly stated concern for his wife's reputation, an issue apart from his own standing, may nevertheless point to his sincerity. It must have surely been painful to mention the embarrassing incident that launched the whole media frenzy, his after-midnight auto accident and the rumors that Elin had tried to physically assault him with a golf club. Yet he broached those events for his wife's sake. Tiger declares, "Elin has shown enormous grace and poise throughout this ordeal. Elin deserves praise, not blame" ("Tiger Woods' Apology" 2). In that portion of his carefully scripted apology, Woods attempts to restore the dignity of the most offended person in the whole situation, an effort that certainly suggests empathy and guilt.

Some commentators were especially critical of Tiger for the extensive time he took, during the televised apology, to chastise the media for their unwanted scrutiny of his family. Rick Cerrona, Media Relations director for the New York Yankees, called his anger a "PR disaster," and Midwin Charles, a legal contributor to a television court program, "thought it was a misstep to attack the media.... He brought this attention on himself by going out there and having those affairs. Get over it" (qtd. in Buschschluter). Tiger freely admits his own complicity in the media firestorm when he says, "Some have written things about my family. Despite the damage I have done, I still believe it is right to shield my family from the public spotlight. They did not do these things. I did" ("Tiger Woods' Apology" 1). He explains that he has always maintained a strict zone of privacy around his wife and especially his children. His anger regarding the violation of their privacy is clearly real when he says, "However, my behavior doesn't make it right for the media to follow my 2½-year-old daughter to school and report the school's location. They staked out my wife and pursued my mom. Whatever my wrongdoings, for the sake of my family, please leave my wife and kids alone" ("Tiger Woods' Apology" 1).

Although some might claim that Tiger's outrage is misplaced in an apology, especially since his own behaviors prompted the media to stalk his family, it is entirely possible that this anger at a serious breach of civility resonated perfectly with the ethos of golf. There is no other sport more intensely concerned with appropriate courtesy and gracious good manners. As a result, this portion of the apology is especially potent, because Tiger momentarily lays aside the apologizers' role of surrendering power in order to fiercely defend his family. For a moment, he becomes their strong protector, showing everyone that despite what he has done to his family, he does care about them and will fight to protect them from media exploitation. With these words, he is reasserting his legitimate role as protective husband and father.

Some media pundits were offended by this rebuke, but those people in the typically polite and respectful world of professional golf may have heard this as an appropriate demand for everyone to play by a civil set of rules. On reflection, this section of the apology communicated to the entire world that Woods is not entirely different from his carefully crafted image as a caring husband and father. Although some commentators may have felt that this portion diluted the apologetic character of the event, on the contrary, these words may have actually lent credibility to the entire statement.

Despite his husbandly and fatherly protectiveness, as well as his efforts to reaffirm Elin's dignity, Tiger did not ultimately save his marriage. Moreover, he did not convince everyone of his rehabilitation and fitness to rejoin the exclusive club of professional golf. Nonetheless, his televised apology, as an act of mass communication and as a personal act of atonement, can be provisionally regarded as "effective." Certainly it was not a "failed" apology. Because he did make an unequivocal confession of fault, took full responsibility, showed some measure of remorse, and gave assurances he would not repeat the misbehavior, Tiger Woods, at least to a certain extent, mended some fences, built some bridges, and restored some trust. By doing all of this in a publicly humiliating reversal of power, he was able to convince some people that his contrition was genuine. No one can be certain, but it may be possible that, in time, he will be fully granted the absolution he seeks.

WORKS CITED

Boswell, Thomas. "Tiger Woods Apology: What's Real? What Do We Believe?" *Washington Post.* 20 Feb. 2010. Web. 4 Nov. 2011.

Boteach, Shmuley. "Tiger's Courageous Confession." *Huffington Post Sports.* 20 Feb. 2010. Web. 4 Nov. 2011.

Buschschluter, Vanessa. "U.S. Media on Tiger Woods Statement." *BBC News.* 19 Feb. 2010. Web. 4 Nov. 2011.

Carnes, Patrick. *Out of the Shadows: Understanding Sexual Addiction.* Minneapolis: Compcare Publications, 1983. Print.

Dionne, E. J. "Scandal Obsession Obscures Issues." *The Daytona Beach News-Journal.* 10 June 2011. Web. 4 Nov. 2011.

Forrest General Hospital. Forrest General. n.d. Web. 4. Nov. 2011.

Hearit, Keith Michael. *Crisis Management by Apology: Corporate Responses to Allegations of Wrongdoing.* Mahwah, NJ: Lawrence Erlbaum, 2006. Print.

Hinckley, David. "Tiger Woods Apology: Golfer's Mouth Said 'I'm Sorry,' Demeanor Said 'I Don't Want to Be Here.'" *New York Daily News.* 19 Feb. 2010. Web. 4 Nov. 2011.

Hume, Brit. "Tiger Woods Must Become a Christian to Be Forgiven." *Fox News Sunday.* 3 Jan. 2010. YouTube. 3 Jan. 2010. Web. 4 Nov. 2011.

Kador, John. *Effective Apology: Mending Fences, Building Bridges, and Restoring Trust.* San Francisco: Berrett-Kohler, 2009. Print.

_____. "What Tiger Woods Should Say." *CNN Opinion.* 19 Feb. 2010. Web. 12 Sept. 2011.

Lazar, Aaron. *On Apology.* New York: Oxford University Press, 2004. Print.

Pine Grove Behavioral Health & Addiction Services. Pine Grove. n.d. Web. 4 Nov. 2011.

Shipnuck, Alan. "Tiger Woods's Mea Culpa Heard Round the World Was a Sad Performance." *Sports Illustrated.* 25 Feb. 2010. Web. 24 Mar. 2011.

"Tiger Woods' Apology: Full Transcript." *CNN.* 19 Feb. 2009. Web. 3 Nov. 2011.

"Tiger Woods Returns to Buddhism." *ISKCON News.* 24 Feb. 2010. Web. 4 Nov. 2011.

"Tiger Woods Taking Hiatus from Golf." *TigerWoods.com.* 11 Nov. 2009. Web. 30 Sept. 2011.

Par for the Course:
The "Bimbo Tally"

Libbie Searcy

When Tiger Woods crashed, the media dished out details in abundance, and the public ate them up. As the news broke, and kept breaking, of how Tiger — the family man who represented the realization of the American Dream — had over a dozen extramarital affairs, the scandal dominated web searches. *The Independent* reported that Google and Yahoo searches about the scandal swelled; in fact, in the thirty days after the news of his affairs broke, searches for Tiger's name on Yahoo increased 3,900 percent (Bernstein). Millions of Americans rely on the Internet to locate desired information, so stories appearing on mainstream news and gossip websites helped to shape how average Americans perceived the people involved in the Tiger Woods scandal, as well as how they viewed gender and sexuality. Media often provided offensive and reductive coverage by portraying Tiger as a victim of sexually aggressive women and of his purported sex addiction; failing to educate the public about sex addiction while simultaneously applauding Tiger for coming forward about his alleged addiction; simplistically classifying and objectifying women who had affairs with Tiger based on their physicality and professions; neglecting to explore the nature of those relationships; and/or offering dismissive coverage of scandal-related products that encouraged violence against women.

Much media coverage suggested that all of these women were, by definition, "bad girls," and a "bad girl" faces more brutal criticism and harsher judgment than a "bad boy" ever does. Although the sexual revolution that began in the 1960s challenged traditional values and allowed people to engage in sexual activity for its own sake, America remains a nation with both Puritanical roots and great fascination with sexual matters. All forms of media bombard the public with sexual content because it sells, feeding the cultural obsession, yet many people remain quick to judge others for the choices they make regarding sexual behavior. People use terms like "promiscuous" as though everyone agrees on what that means, and perhaps the TV show *Queer as Folk* offered the most useful definition: "Promiscuous is anyone having more sex than you." Although many people now feel free to explore their sexuality, an old double standard persists: "promiscuous" women tend to be labeled "sluts" while "promiscuous" men are "players"— the latter term often having a positive connotation lacking in the former. In fact, the origin of the word "slut" (slutte) had no sexual connotation, referring only to a literally dirty woman; this cloud of "dirtiness" came to surround "promiscuous" women *exclusively*. One need not be versed in feminist theory to know that America is a patriarchal culture in which women still struggle to be perceived — even to exist — as sexual subjects (the empowered "do-er") rather than as sexual objects (the powerless "done-to"). Furthermore, the line between sexual subject and sexual object is often hard to discern. For women, sexuality can be a source of power and also a source of powerlessness — a double-edged sword. Media afford real and fictional women a great deal of attention based upon their sexual behavior or sexy appearance. At what point does that attention become negative rather than positive? What distinguishes a sexually empowered woman (a sexual *subject*) from a girl with low self-esteem who defines empowerment as merely pleasing a man (a sexual *object*)? Of course, no universal answers to these questions exist, so the public must remain skeptical about media portrayals and assessments of women.

Victim of Temptation

One element of the Tiger Woods "story" after the "fall" was defining him as a victim of temptation. Posting an apology on his website, he writes, "I regret those transgressions with all of my heart." The same day, Eleanor Hong reported on the NBC News website, "Now, we're hanging on a single word in his explanation, it seems." Hong notes that the single word "transgressions" was the most popular item in Google Trends' list of search terms. Although some Americans may not have known the definition, many web surfers may well have felt that the term merited questioning, especially given its association with sin — a fact noted by much of the media. What did *not* get media attention, however, was Tiger's repeated reference to his "behavior"— a rhetorical maneuver that placed the focus on his actions rather than on his character, including the fundamental ways he might view women.

Immediately following this statement came the disturbing message from

Good Morning, America that wealthy and powerful men (poor things) who cheat just cannot help it. As Juju Chang reports, on the *Good Morning, America* broadcast and website, "Relationship experts suggest that men may be hard-wired to stray." The online version of this report, co-written by Sarah Netter, is entitled "Tiger Woods Sex Scandal: Why Powerful Men Can't Resist Temptation" and subtitled "Men Who Seem to Have It All Are Vulnerable to Aggressive Admirers, Experts Say." This title and subtitle relay several distinct messages. Using the word "can't" instead of "don't" in association with "resist" suggests that these men have no choice. In addition, "temptation" and "aggressive" conjure images of ruthless seductresses who menace "vulnerable" men. Finally, despite the authors' attempt to add "authority" by referring to experts, the lack of the qualifying term "some" is pathetically reductive.

One of the experts cited is "renowned sex anthropologist Helen Fisher." Chang and Netter summarize Fisher's argument: "it's no coincidence that powerful men get caught in headline-grabbing scandals." The word "caught" calls to mind an innocent creature trapped in an inescapable net — an image the authors reinforce by noting that sex scandals have "ensnared" powerful men throughout the ages. Fisher claims, "The opposite sex is very attracted to someone who is powerful. Particularly women are attracted to men who are powerful." Fisher offers nothing about men exploiting their power to "ensnare" women. In the same article, male family therapist Terry Real advises female readers, "If you want your husband to not have a lover, then you'd better act like a lover. That means that you have to be passionate." Chang and Netter might have challenged Real's implication that wives across America should take a trip to Victoria's Secret if they expect their husbands not to stray. After the story aired, Chang continues the commentary with *Good Morning, America* anchor Robin Roberts. When Chang summarizes one "relationship expert's" claim that married mothers sometimes neglect their husbands and cause them to cheat, Roberts interrupts her by saying, "Don't do that" to indicate she does not agree that wives are to blame. Ultimately, Chang and Netter send sexist messages, signaling that one need not have a penis to reinforce patriarchal values.

Much media coverage portrayed Tiger as a victim not only of temptresses but also of sex addiction. In fact, the media, not Woods, first speculated that he might be a sex addict. Following Tiger's website apology, which included no reference to addiction, Russell Goldman, who authored many articles about the scandal, notes that reports of Tiger's affairs "were quickly followed this week by headlines and talk-show guests wondering aloud if the world's No. 1 golfer, Tiger Woods, is a 'sex addict.'" The title of the article, "Tiger Woods a Sex Addict? Only If He's Lucky," suggests that Tiger would be "lucky" if the public believed he suffers from an addiction and, thus, deserves compassion. Goldman includes statements from Judy Kuriansky, Columbia University psychologist and sex expert, who cautions people against making premature assumptions: "There are a lot of people out there calling him a sex addict." She adds, "[S]omeone can hold up that diagnosis and say, 'I can't control my behavior.' Then he goes into rehab and the public gives him a pass." As this expert indicates, media, and by extension the public, sought some justification for Tiger's behaviors. Goldman insightfully includes Kuriansky's warning against assuming that poor choices necessarily equate to sexual addiction: "But you have to ask is this really the behavior of an addict, or is this the behavior of a very rich, powerful, celebrity, [*sic*] man, who has been given lots of opportunities?" However, Goldman undermines Kuriansky's appropriate question when he provides commentary by Richard Lustberg, a sports psychologist. Lustberg asserts that "Woods' affairs are not that unusual for any man, but particularly not that unusual for a professional athlete" and adds, "Men will be men." His belief that "men will be men" and that Tiger's affairs are not uncommon for "any man" surely merited some kind of counter-argument. Goldman's article might have included other credible experts who would note that most men do not have affairs — much less more than a dozen. He also might have acknowledged that the "men will be men" mentality harms both genders by implying that women should expect less from men and that men are either too weak to be faithful or too animalistic to resist sex. Articles like Goldman's would have readers believe that, even if Tiger were not the victim of temptresses and/or sexual addiction, he was a victim of his own innate male urges — a message that harms both genders.

Sexual Addiction's Poster-Child

Although Tiger Woods may, indeed, be a sex addict, the media should have made it clear that sexual addiction goes far beyond mere promiscuity or cheating on a spouse and getting caught. If the American public associates infidelity and/or promiscuity as the sole measure of addiction, then sex might be perceived as a dangerous drug. In a culture that is, in many ways, sexually obsessed and sexually repressed at the same time, demonizing sex only makes it easier for people to pass judgment on others based on how they choose to explore their sexuality. Furthermore, someone who has been led to believe that an unfaithful spouse is a sex addict simply because that spouse has a pattern of cheating may be less likely to hold that spouse accountable for his/her choices.

Well before Tiger himself alluded to sexual addiction, the media praised Tiger for serving as its potential poster-child. For example, Dan Childs' article entitled "Tiger Woods May Be Role Model for Battling Sex Addiction" appeared on ABC's health page — the *health* page. Childs quotes Dr. David Greenfield, sexuality expert and clinical director of The Healing Center, as saying that the Tiger Woods scandal might "push sex addiction over the top in terms of public recognition, understanding and accessibility, which is a good thing." Not only had Tiger yet to come forward, but neither the expert nor the journalist seemed to realize that admitting to a problem does not necessarily equate to genuinely educating the public about that problem. Celebrities do, indeed, have a virtually guaranteed platform, but a celebrity should actually stand on that platform and say something of value before the media applaud.

Some journalists believed they got exactly what they needed to help Tiger redeem himself after he stood on a platform to deliver his public apology. For example, Elise Nersesian's article, written for *Women's Health* and appearing on the *Today* website, explores sex addiction in relation to the Tiger Woods scandal. Referring to his public apology and his entrance into rehab, she writes, "So far, the star appears to be on the road to redemption." Nersesian interviewed Maureen Canning, a licensed marriage and family therapist. According to Canning, Tiger had "given comfort to spouses who have long suspected their partners are incapable of fidelity" and "created a dialogue among couples, giving them a definition for a serious problem that's plagued relationships." Nersesian does not question Canning's implication that people now have Tiger to thank for gaining new knowledge.

In addition to crediting Tiger with improving other people's relationships, Nersesian reinforces sexist assumptions. She includes commentary by Ian Kerner, Ph.D., who claims that "women have a hard time believing that sexual compulsion exists because in part, they can't relate to it." After Kerner discusses how, for biological reasons, sex is more an "emotional" act for women than it is for men, Nersesian then validates his assertions by concluding that women experience a "physiological response" that functions like "a hormonal safeguard from developing an obsession." Nersesian does not discuss several significant issues: the existence of female sex addicts, the fact that so many men do not suffer from sex addiction, or the fact that women do, in fact, have a libido. The author and those she interviewed fail to address debilitating gender constructs, including how sexually permissive women tend to be perceived as dirty to a far greater degree than men do. Such an omission reinforces patriarchal attitudes about gender and sexuality. Nersesian compounds her failings in the conclusion:

> Despite the shock and betrayal many women feel when they discover their partner is an addict (usually the way Elin found out: by going through her husband's text messages), Canning says women play a significant role in the

problem. "It's almost impossible to not know, on some level, that your man is cheating," she says. "Women often pick people who they subconsciously don't trust, knowing he has the capacity to cheat."

Undermining accurate information provided earlier in the article, Nersesian presumes that most women snoop through their husband's text messages and that someone can be diagnosed as a sex addict based on text messages alone. Furthermore, she fails to question Canning's preposterous assertion that women have some kind of internal radar that detects infidelity, as well as her offensive claim that women have themselves to blame for choosing an untrustworthy partner. The public should expect more from an article in *Women's Health*.

Media's "Bimbo Tally"

Because women who had affairs with Tiger never stood upon any pedestal, media often reinforced the message that the height of their platform heels was as far up as they should ever get. Although hundreds of stories condemned Tiger, even more coverage disproportionately demonized the women. The media fixated on listing the women, even though the only thing that *all* of these women had in common was their affairs with Tiger Woods. Their relationships with a married man would understandably result in negative perceptions, but the media failed to portray them as individual human beings. Instead, these women became a group of mere dirty sluts, as parts of a "bimbo tally"—a phrase commonly appearing in coverage.

The Women's Physicality

First impressions matter, and the media's introduction of these women emphasized their physicality. Admittedly, some had posed for overtly provocative pictures, but many had not, and when the media place non-provocative photos in a collage with provocative ones, everyone is "guilty" by association. Robin Givhan of the *Washington Post* wrote a one-of-a-kind article, aptly entitled "Tiger Woods' Alleged Mistresses Are Facing a Sexist Double Standard," where she questions such portrayals. In fact, her unique coverage earned her a spot on NPR's *Talk of the Nation*. During this NPR appearance, she discussed how the media had photographed the women who had not already posed for provocative pictures: by catching them "when they were at a bar or in a club or at a party." She pointed out, "It's not as if they're catching them coming out of Sunday church service and putting those photos online."

Written descriptions, too, defined and grouped these women based on physical traits. For example, the gossip section of the immensely popular *NY Daily News* website states that "[t]wo more blondes and a brunette — Cori Rist, Jamie Jungers, and Mindy Lawton — were added to Tiger Woods' sultry scorecard Saturday, bringing the married father of two to six over par on his betrayed supermodel wife" (Goldsmith, Jaccarino, and Rush). Of course, physical attributes precede the women's names, and the authors portray them as mere "scores," making Tiger quite the impressive "player." On the same site, Corky Siemaszko writes, "Turns out Tiger has a cougar. A busty South Florida blond who's on the north side of 40 was outed yesterday as yet another Tiger Woods Mistress. Like [Elin] Nordegren, she's a curvy blond — the only difference being that Rogers is believed to be old enough to be her mother." Characterizing Teresa Rogers as provocatively as possible, Siemaszko labels her a "cougar," relaying the ageist and sexist message that this woman is even more disgusting due to her involvement with a younger man. Siemaszko also implies that *only* her age distinguishes her from Elin because they are both "curvy" and "blond" — as though physical characteristics alone comprise a woman's identity. While gossip pages like these were certainly guiltier than mainstream media of putting the women's physical traits center-stage with terms like "busty," many mainstream media outlets followed suit. For example, writing for the *ABC News* website, Russell Goldman mentions "Holly Sampson, 36, a busty blonde" and "[b]londe bombshell Cori Rist" ("At Least"). On the New York's *NBC News* website, Xana O'Neill introduces Jamie Jungers as a "buxom blonde" before providing her name in the second paragraph. These descriptions and others like them flooded the Internet, reinforcing the tendency to sexualize women based on their physicality.

The Women's Professions

Also reductive and sexist, many stories lumped the women together based on their professions. The small minority worked in the sex industry, making them easy targets, and the media certainly vilified them. Women who earn money by gratifying men do not deserve to be portrayed as *only* objects in every area of their lives, especially because the market, comprised almost exclusively of men, creates a demand for a sex industry in the first place. Nevertheless, the vast majority of the women linked with Tiger did not work in the sex industry. In her article "Rachel Uchitel Is Not a Madam," Caroline Graham continues the trend of lumping the women together based on their careers by writing that "the scandal ballooned out of control as a colourful procession of 15 women, including porn stars, strippers, waitresses and prostitutes, came forward to say that they had slept with Tiger." On the other hand, while describing her interview with Uchitel, Graham does note the media's reductive categorizing by writing that Uchitel's "career as a nightclub hostess" resulted in her being "reviled as little better than a prostitute." The media did revile, and examples abound.

Astutely decrying this tendency to sexualize and devalue these women, Givhan notes in her *Washington Post* article that the term "cougar" was useful to describe television broadcaster Teresa Rogers because "broadcaster" likely "didn't sound nearly tantalizing enough." In fact, "broadcaster" rarely made the media's list of the women's jobs. In his article for *Vanity Fair*, Mark Seals writes of the "array of women, including waitresses, nightclub hostesses, escorts, and porn stars" (161, 164). Russell Goldman identifies Jamie Jungers as "a lingerie model," and to up the salacious factor, he states later in the article that she "modeled for the lingerie line Trashy Girls" ("At Least"). The lingerie line Trashy, not Trashy *Girls*, is no more risqué than lines found at Victoria's Secret or Fredericks of Hollywood, but "Trashy Girls" certainly assures that the public made the "right" assumption that this modeling gig is just plain "wrong." Similarly, in her lengthy article for *New York* magazine, Lisa Taddeo writes, "Within the unblushing batch of Tiger Woods's alleged mistresses ... there exist both extremes: ladies of convenience, like Mindy Lawton, the waitress who served Woods and his wife breakfast at a diner near their home, and high-priced call girls like Loredana Jolie Ferriolo, who had to Google the player to find out who he was." Taddeo assumes that none of the women felt shame or remorse and, like so many other journalists and columnists, portrays them as a single "batch." She also indicates that Lawton's job at Perkins is somehow disgraceful, as "lady of convenience" would imply. Taddeo fails to differentiate this "batch" of women as individuals and sends the message that their careers equate to their lack of worth. Similarly, when the gossip section of the *New York Daily News* informs readers that a fourth woman had been linked to Tiger, writers Tracy Connor and Samuel Goldsmith state, "As the list of alleged mistresses grows a pattern begins to emerge: they are all cocktail waitresses." This report and so many others like it suggest that, if waitressing is what the women have in common, then waitressing must be indicative of their tendency toward reprehensible behavior.

Therefore, as the media took its swings at the women, all waitresses and models in America took a hit. Givhan shrewdly makes this very point in her article:

> The way in which jobs such as waitress and model have been tossed about
> in the Woods story, with a kind of wink and a nod, one would think there
> is something inherently tawdry about carting pancakes or martinis around
> on a tray. And while no small number of parents might hope that their
> daughters find a more intellectually stimulating profession than modeling

underwear or swimsuits, it's not as if posing in your skivvies ... is the equivalent of hanging upside down on a stripper pole with a wad of Benjamin Franklins stuffed in your G-string.

Givhan argues that adultery is indefensible, "but also indefensible in this ever-growing sex saga is how certain occupations seem to serve as generic evidence of the women's low moral standing as much as the actions they are accused of committing." Because those "certain occupations" included "model," Givhan insightfully notes how the media often described Elin as a "former model" before pointing out that she made the choice to pursue a career as an au pair and then as a psychologist. According to Givhan, notations on Elin's short-lived modeling career place her in the category of "Tiger Types," but such references also highlight the fact that Elin has reformed, that she is no longer one of *those* kinds of girls, especially now that she is a wife and mother. This allusion to Elin's reformation serves to reinforce the Madonna/whore binary — the whores being waitresses and models.

The media took swings at women who work in nightclubs as well. In her article, Lisa Taddeo overtly proliferates offensive perceptions: "Most of his mistresses lived in a nebulous in-between world. Not prostitutes, no, but just about halfway there. As surely as he has changed the game of golf, so too has Woods exposed the grazing ground of the halfway-hooker, and her natural habitat, the nightclub." Taddeo constructs a path to prostitution, complete with a halfway point, in an attempt to assure that women who offer VIP service equate to whores who service men. Interviewing people who work in big city nightclubs, including Rachel Uchitel, Taddeo argues that club employees are parallel to pimps, madams, and prostitutes — minus the *overt* exchange of money for sex. Her article begs a question: when no exchange of money and sex occurs, where exactly would she draw the line between appropriate and inappropriate servicing of patrons in the *service* industry? Furthermore, while she repeatedly characterizes these female nightclub employees as questionable characters, she makes less of the fact that wealthy and powerful men create the market for such services. It is a case of supply and demand, yet she, like so many others, portrays the demanders as significantly less culpable than the suppliers. At the end of her article, Taddeo does address the issue of consumerism when she comments on Jason Itzler, whom she describes as "the former founder of high-profile escort agency New York Confidential and inventor of the so-called girlfriend experience (GFE)." Taddeo summarizes Itzler's vision of "The Tiger Club" where waitresses would be "full hookers, but in a social environment, with less stigma attached." Taddeo ends her article with Itzler's dream, giving him the last word. She offers no commentary on the male role in such a venture. Although most clubs offer a great deal of sexual tension, they are hardly "the grazing ground of the halfway hooker."

The Women as Undifferentiated Group

In addition to stigmatizing the women based on their appearance and professions, the media presented them as a group — as simply "Tiger's mistresses" or "Woods' women." The *Examiner's* Liz Barrett simply describes them as "cheaper by the dozen." As a result, the public had no reason to view them as individual people. Givhan explains that Tiger was "portrayed as complicated and troubled" while the women involved with him were "merely types." She argues:

> The golfer has been called a dog, a liar, and worse. But he still gets the benefit of being perceived as an individual. He is still Tiger Woods.... Perhaps some of these women make a habit of sleeping with married men. But in the same way that the man in this tabloid drama gets the benefit of ad nauseam motivational dissection, so should the women. They are not as famous as Woods. They didn't change the nature of golf, or sports in general. But just like him, they are human and flawed.

Tiger had the privilege of remaining a subject rather than an object — criticized, yes, but at least more complex than a piece of meat. In fact, both Jamie Jungers and Cori Rist said in separate interviews on *Today* that they agreed to appear on the show because they felt compelled to publicly deny being prostitutes or escorts and to deny ever receiving money from Tiger or any media outlet. As Rist stated, "I'm not the party girl they're claiming that I am.... I'm not like most of these girls. And I'm not judging them, by any means." Rist clearly wanted to resist judging the other women, but she could not ignore the impact that stories of the scandal would have on her six-year-old son. Similarly, Rachel Uchitel told Caroline Graham, "I am not the same as the other girls and I never imagined in my wildest dreams that I would be caught up in a scandal like this." Based on these comments and others, Uchitel and Rist verbalized their perceptions that they had more value than the other mistresses, their comments possibly fueling the perception that the rest were indeed a worthless "batch."

Because the women, unlike Tiger, did not receive what Givhan called the "benefit" of "ad nauseam motivational dissection," one woman took the initiative to tell her own story. Rachel Uchitel presented *herself* when she appeared on *Celebrity Rehab with Dr. Drew* as a way of seeking help for her addictions, including a "love addiction." Viewers of the series watched week after week as Uchitel participated in therapy sessions and explored the roots of her unhealthy choices. After obtaining sobriety, Uchitel granted Caroline Graham an interview. Uchitel included no details about her relationship with Tiger, but she did say that she regretted sleeping with a married man and would "never, ever do that again." Graham wrote of Uchitel's loss of her fiancé as a result of the 9/11 attacks on the World Trade Center and of her father's death from a drug overdose when Rachel was young: "Given the sudden, premature losses of her father and fiancé, it is little wonder Rachel began to careen out of control, and that finding a replacement man became her leitmotif." Uchitel explained, "I'm only telling my story now so that people can discover what sort of girl I am and learn the truth about me." While some people dismissed Uchitel's appearance on *Celebrity Rehab* as a publicity stunt, she at least provided a more complete picture of an actual person.

As though objectifying and classifying the women were not bad enough, one columnist, Andrea Peyser, went so far as to blame these women for destroying feminism. In "These Boobs Set Women Back," appearing in the print and online version of the *New York Post,* she flatly asserts, "Feminism is dead." She then proceeds with sarcastic gusto:

> Long live the gold digger! It is with epic sadness that I inform serious ladies your day is over. The rat race has been done in by the drive-by boob job. The Ivy League, once the portal through which young things improved their minds, has been supplanted in cultural value by the red-velvet rope of the VIP cocktail lounge. As the ballad of Tiger Woods finishes its second week, the world has changed. Now, every housewife and diner waitress is intimately acquainted with the ascendant breed of woman who dominates our age, leading a life to which we all can aspire. Gold diggers. The type is as old as sex itself. But this new brand of digger has taken her calling to an art form, legitimizing what used to be called the world's oldest profession.

Here, Peyser *inaccurately* assumes that all the women involved with Tiger financially profited from their affairs, but her message exacts even more serious damage. First, why must this scandal threaten feminism rather than expose the underbelly of hyper-masculinity or serve as a warning to men about the consequences of infidelity and female objectification? Second, the day of the "serious lady" is only over if "bagging" Tiger Woods is her goal, and surely these "gold diggers" do not deserve to shoulder the blame for so many girls opting for the cocktail lounge instead of the college library. Third, as Peyser slams the "breed of woman" that "legitimizes" prostitution, then surely she should have taken at least one swing at the breed of man who legitimizes her. After all, she cannot do it alone. Of course, no parallel term for the wealthy man exists. Not "gold-dishers," for example. Why? Because a patriarchal culture assures that the women in such a situation shoulder the blame, despite the fact that a "gold-digger" only gets what someone else has the power and inclination to give. In fact, if these "gold-digging" women's professions are noteworthy at all, it is because their financial situations often place them in an economic power position far below the "gold-holder."

This socio-economic imbalance is perhaps most evident in Tiger's affair with Mindy Lawton, who reports how Tiger first called her while she was working as a hostess at the local Perkins to ask her out: "My mouth fell open and I was like, Wow! I was like, 'Sure!' I was trying to control my excitement." When describing their first sexual encounter, which she said occurred in Tiger's kitchen, she mentions the "fine porcelain tile and brushed-stainless-steel appliances" (Seals 158). Although she says that Tiger never gave her money and never bought her anything except a sub sandwich, she was clearly entranced by his wealth and fame. By exploiting his own position of socio-economic power, Tiger deserves at least as much criticism from the media as Lawton does, yet most media portrayed Lawton and the other women as temptresses rather than portraying Tiger as the tempter.

The Untold Story of Tiger the Tempter

The media neglected to point out the game Tiger might have played with these women. Some claimed to have fallen in love with Tiger and to have believed that the feelings were mutual. Due to all of the media's afore-mentioned classification, objectification, and reductive grouping, the public received message after message that the women were all trash, and because no one likes to rummage through trash, few people cared to examine why some of them made the choices they did and how Tiger might have manipulated them. Although the media did provide information about how the women perceived their relationships with Tiger, these details tended to serve merely as evidence of the affairs *themselves* rather than as evidence of *how* Tiger had manipulated them. As a result, much coverage portrayed Tiger Woods as a victim of easy women rather than as a predator stalking vulnerable prey. The media rightfully did not categorize the women as mere tragic victims, as they are adults who are responsible for their own choices. However, more journalists should have gone below the surface to explore — or at least leave room for the public to question — the role Tiger played in getting what he wanted. In her article for the website PopEater, Jo Piazza offers a relatively rare perspective: "We have no idea what Mr. Woods said to these women to get them into the sack, but we shouldn't discount his charm and ability to manipulate them. He did, after all, manipulate most of America into thinking he was a pretty straight-up guy." Too few writers made that point.

Six months after the scandal broke, Mark Seals came close to making that point in an article appearing in *Vanity Fair*. At the beginning of the article, he acknowledges that some women "were convinced that they were the only one with whom he had cheated." He then wrote, "These women are now having their say.... Through them we can get a clear look at the superstar at his most profligate, on the pedestal from which he would so dramatically fall" (163). Seals alludes to Tiger's deception and clearly blames him for duplicitous behavior. However, other aspects of Seals' article send all-too-familiar messages. The title, "The Temptation of Tiger Woods," reinforces images of Tiger as a victim of temptresses. A two-page photograph, serving as the background of the article's title page, displays the naked high-paid escort Loredona Jolie Ferriolo, whom Seals interviewed. When Seals describes his first impression of Ferriolo, he expresses his apparent attraction to her: "When Ferriolo arrives, her roller-coaster curves packed tightly into a cashmere sweater, spandex leggings, and knee-high boots, I have to admit that she's worth the wait" (209). The commentary hardly seems relevant, except to imply that no one should expect Tiger to resist such a "temptation." Like Ferriolo, all of the other women (Michelle Braun, Mindy Lawton, and Jamie Jungers) Seals interviewed pose provocatively for the *Vanity Fair* article. Lawton and Jungers, who do not work in the sex industry, did have lengthy affairs with Tiger and reported that he had manipulated them by convincing them that he loved them. They also offer salacious details that make it easy to dismiss them as mere bad, trashy girls. While Seals simply shares with his readers what the women shared with him, he includes no mention of women like Rachel Uchitel and Cori Rist, who remain unwilling to go on the record with intimate details about their relationships with Tiger. As a result, Seals paints a picture of "the temptation of Tiger Woods" without acknowledging that he offers only *part* of the picture, ultimately encouraging the public to view the women he interviewed as representative of a distasteful whole.

As Seals and others note, many women believed that they had more than a sexual connection with Tiger. Rather than highlighting how deftly he may have manipulated them and convinced them that he genuinely cared, most stories took the easy path. They plopped the women's talk of love next to descriptions that devalued them and/or buried expressions of real feelings inside the more interesting salacious details of the affairs. As a result, readers likely found it easy to dismiss *all* of the women as liars or stupid fools rather than to consider just how well this publicly adored, charming man might have played a very cruel game. Veronica Siwik-Daniels, adult film actress Joslyn James, said, "I was in love with Tiger, and because of what he said to me and the length of time we spent together and how long we were together, I believe he loved me too" (Allred and Siwik-Daniels). Tiger allegedly texted her, "Baby, I'm not going anywhere or doing anything. You please me like no other has or ever will. I am not losing that" ("Tiger Mistress"). While the media and the public wrote her off as a mere porn star, she is also a real woman who, like nearly all of the women, had far more than a one-night stand with Tiger. Similarly, Jamiee Grubbs texted Tiger, "u can be my boyfriend"; he replied, "then I am Jamiee" and continued to say, "quiet and secretively we will always be together" ("Jamiee's Texts"). Grubbs also describes one of their many nights together in an article for *US Weekly*: "We cuddled, watched 'Angels and Demons,' then had sex. It was very romantic" ("Tiger's 31-Month").

If this is, indeed, what occurred, then Tiger executed an effective strategy of weaving seemingly loving and sweet sentiments with sexual ones — a maneuver that the vast majority of the media neglected to acknowledge. Sharing intimate moments contributed to Jamie Jungers' belief that she and Tiger had more than a sexual relationship. She claimed to have been asleep with Tiger (after watching a movie) at his house when he got the news that his father had passed away. Jungers told Mark Seals, "I think he kind of tried to hide his emotion a little bit. You could just see it in his face. And I didn't know what to say. All I said was 'I'm sorry'" (208). According to Cori Rist in her *Today* interview, "He has a way to make you believe that he's a very honest and good man. And I'm not saying that he is not a good man. I don't think he's an honest man." Rist's observation begs a question that the media did not ask: what role might Tiger have played in manipulating these women? Rist stated, "I'm sure he did the same thing with everyone. I've been listening to the reports, and I see these girls talking. And it seems like there's a pattern." Rist comments on a pattern of seduction, yet the media remained intent upon only establishing a pattern of seductive "temptresses."

Another of Tiger's possible patterns did not get the media attention it deserved. Although the women knew, like the rest of the public, that Tiger was a married father, many of them claimed that Tiger led them to believe that theirs was the only extramarital relationship he was involved in and that they had a future together. For example, Graham notes that some of Rachel Uchitel's friends assert that "the golfer bombarded her with texts and emails promising to leave his wife and calling her his 'soul mate.'" Similarly, after Mark Seal's interview with Mindy Lawton, he writes, "Since her lover never discussed his marriage, Lawton became convinced that it would soon be over and that she was the only one he cared for" (158). Seals also writes, "She was falling in love, and she believed he cared about her, too. 'You're going to be the next Mrs. Tiger Woods!' a friend told her" (161). Remorseful Cori Rist said in her *Today* interview that Tiger "led her to believe" that they had a future together and then stated, "We all would like to think that we were special, even though we knew that what was happening was wrong. I had no idea that it was this intense, that the scale was this large." At first, many of these women denied being involved with Tiger. As the media exposed more and more of Tiger's mistresses, the women who did believe they were special experienced a rude awakening. They clearly felt Tiger had duped them, and *that* is when some of them began talking and revealing explicit text messages and voicemails, retaliating with the only ammunition they had.

Gold-Diggers Not Deserving Apology

The media failed to consider that perhaps some of these women eventually came forward as a result of their hurt and anger rather than, as the media so often suggested, for fifteen minutes of fame or financial gain. If they merely wanted notoriety, why deny the affair in the first place? And if they were only after money, why not blackmail Tiger long before the scandal broke instead of protecting him, sometimes for years, from potential scandal? The media seemed to ignore what may have been another part of Tiger's strategy: by winning the women's hearts, he better assured their discretion and loyalty. The media also failed to consider that he may have purposefully exploited emotionally vulnerable women or women of "low" socio-economic class. Rachel Uchitel recognized what the media did not: her wealth and education distinguishes her from the other women. Uchitel said, "I am not a whore, nor am I girl impressed by fame or money. I have a brain and I came from money" (Graham). Uchitel highlighted, intentionally or not, that the media painted the women with one broad stroke. Implying that they were nothing more than "low-class" girls, media coverage did not even hint that Tiger may have chosen women who would believe that they had, like poor Cinderella, found their Prince Charming.

But this was no fairy tale. In fact, the media was often quick to imply that these women were gold-diggers pursuing hush money received from Tiger and/or payments from the media. For example, Goldman describes "tightlipped" Veronica Siwik-Daniels as "a contrast from some of his other accused mistresses, a handful of whom have confided information to the media, many of them for pay" ("Tiger Woods Mistress List"). He then goes on to state that "for nearly every alleged mistress who will not talk to the media, there is another who is willing to tell all." Goldman assumes, without evidence, that many women received payment for their stories. Furthermore, with rhetorical savvy, he chooses not to write that for every woman who *is* willing to tell all, there is another one who is *not* because this angle is juicier. Furthermore, even if some women did receive "payoffs" from Tiger, which has never been verified as fact, the women may have seen financial payment as a way to make Tiger literally pay for emotional pain he caused them — to hit him where it hurts in a culture obsessed with wealth. The media tended not to mention that possibility.

The media also typically neglected to point out that many outlets would eagerly offer these women money to tell their salacious stories to feed hungry consumers. Consideration of the big capitalistic picture might have made it a bit more difficult for the public to dismiss the women as gold-digging whores. Most importantly, amidst the media's speculation about payoffs, Tiger received far less criticism for allegedly using his immense wealth to shut the women up than they received for allegedly accepting money that, for them, is not easy to come by. While journalists are certainly not obligated to portray anyone sympathetically, they should at least attempt fair play.

But fair play was not on the agenda — not for the media and not for Tiger Woods. When Tiger offered his lengthy apology at a press conference, he said, "I never thought about who I was hurting.... I hurt my wife, my kids, my mother, my wife's family, my friends, my foundations, and kids all around the world who admired me." The women he slept with — the ones who claim to have felt deceived and manipulated — did not make the list of people he hurt. Although some stories noted that a few mistresses believed Tiger owed them an apology, Jo Piazza was one of the few writers to agree with the women: "Woods apologized to pretty much everyone ... except his mistresses. Now, the other women he wronged are rising up en masse to ask for their own apology. And you know what? They deserve one."

Piazza's unique stance contrasts sharply with that of psychologist Cooper Lawrence, whom Piazza quotes: "When you want to save a marriage you have to disengage from your former lovers in every single way.... You do not apologize to mistresses if you want your wife back." Piazza also notes that Judge Jeanine Pirro had discounted Siwik-Daniels' desire for an apology "by holding up a list of the porn films" Tiger's former mistress had starred in. Piazza, with refreshing insight, argues, "To say these women don't deserve an apology because they work in an industry that some people look down upon is unfair. Would the women have deserved an apology if they had been kindergarten teachers and librarians instead of porn stars and lingerie models?" Piazza continues by noting that *media* devalued the women: "Now he should do what is right and make amends to everyone he hurt, not just the people that the media believe 'deserve' his apologies." When Tiger admitted during his press conference, "I need to make my behavior more respectful of the game," perhaps he should also have noted his need to be more respectful of women. Just as importantly, perhaps at least a few media outlets should have recognized that need.

Women as Literal Targets

Unfortunately, the media's most hurtful swings were reserved for the women — sometimes literally. An online game called "Whack a Ho," a variation of the game "Whack a Mole," appeared on several websites. Players, as Tiger, hit the women's heads with a golf club when they pop out of their holes, making them scream as they go back underground where they belong (outrageousapp). In another online game called "Tiger's Transgressions," the player's goal appears on the screen: "Tiger's mistresses are going to the press! Help Tiger knock them out with well-timed drives before they reach the news van" (Tocci). The creators of these online games offered them for free, feeding the public's hunger for entertainment at the women's expense. Does the media deserve all of the blame for such extreme disdain of the women with whom Tiger chose to have affairs? Certainly not. But the creators of these online games and the people who played them developed their perceptions as a result of media coverage. Furthermore, there is no commentary about the offensiveness of these games. More and more women should fear for their heads when the media ignores games that, at best, make light of violence against women and, at worst, encourage it.

When Givhan argues, "Adultery is indefensible .... But so is turning these women into interchangeable commodities," she had no idea then just how commoditized they would become. Mike Caldwell created a collection of golf balls called "The Mistress Collection: Tail of the Tiger." Each of the twelve balls features the face and first name of one of "Tiger's mistresses." After debuting the balls at a golf show in Orlando, Caldwell began selling the product online. He claimed shortly after their release to have made about $45,000. On the product's website, he explains that, because he wants this collection to be a true collectable, he is limiting the production to 65,000 sets: "I can think of no bigger rush than watching our Tail of the Tiger gift sets increase in value over the next few years." The site also advises consumers who might want to "put them in their bag and play a round or two" to buy two sets — "one for the course and one to display in your office" so that "you can then enjoy bragging rights both at work and at play." And, finally, the site's slogan: "He likes to play a round with them....now you can too." Although Mike Caldwell's misogynistic commentary does not represent the average American, it does reveal why the media should have been more circumspect about their characterizations of the women involved with Tiger Woods — if not to discourage the objectification of *those* women, then to discourage the objectification of *all* women.

Much of the media provided irresponsible coverage of the "Tail of the Tiger" golf balls. For example, Rob Hayes reports on the Entertainment page of KABC in Los Angeles, "It's not every day you wake up to find your face on a golf ball. But then again, you're probably not a porn star who had a year-long fling with Tiger Woods." By implying that Veronica Siwik-Daniels has less value than his more moral readers, Hayes discounts Siwik-Daniels and her attorney Gloria Allred, even when they held a press conference to explain that this product encourages violence against women. Even though Allred pointed out that the images of the women's faces would be covered with marks looking like bruises after they had been repeatedly hit with a club, Hayes was dismissive. As he asserts, the "angry porn star" and her "fired up attorney" were prepared to "tee-off in court." Hayes' patronizing descriptors call to mind cartoonish women swept up by terribly female emotions and irrationality. More outrageous is Scott Weber's description of the golf balls as a "gimmick" and *US Weekly*'s description of them as "quirky" ("Tiger Mistress")— both expressions failing to acknowledge that these products are grotesque. On a positive note, Weber does, unlike the other two authors, offer an extensive quote by Siwik-Daniels:

> I have come forward today because I feel that it is wrong for a golf ball to have my picture on it, because golfers hit their golf balls with a lot of force. As a victim of violence myself, it bothered me to think that someone would be standing with a dangerous club in their hands and hitting a ball with my face on it.... I don't think that Tiger would want a picture of me on a golf ball and I know that I don't.

Although Weber notes Siwik-Daniels' valid concern, he also includes Caldwell's rebuttal. Denying that the product promotes violence against women, Caldwell confirms that golf balls are hit and says, "I recommend people put them on the green and hit them gently." Weber ends with this quote, overtly minimizing violence against women and striking yet another blow aimed at the women in Tiger's life.

The public should not hold its breath for a pin the tail on the Tiger game — not when the women he chose to sleep with are much easier targets, not when women in general are so often held to higher standards than men when it comes to sexual behavior, not when women are more easily perceived as gross while the men who score a hole in one with them are somehow less gross, and not when the media fail to portray "mistresses" as actual human beings. And even if there were a "Pin the Tail on Tiger Woods" game, one would hope that the average American, male and female alike, would be too much of a "gentleman" to play.

Works Cited

Allred, Gloria, and Veronica Siwik-Daniels. Los Angeles. 3 Feb. 2010. Press Conference.

Barrett, Liz. "Cheaper by the Dozen: Tiger Woods List of Mistresses Could Expand to 12 or More." *Examiner.* 7 Dec. 2009. Web. 8 Sept. 2011.

Bernstein, Mark. "Tiger Woods Sex Scandal Takes Over the Web." *Independent.* 11 Dec. 2009. Web. 1 Sept. 2011.

Caldwell, Michael. *Tail of the Tiger Collectible Golf Balls*. 2010. Web. 5 Aug. 2010.

Chang, Juju. "What Makes Powerful Men Succumb to Temptation?" *Good Morning, America*. ABC. 3 Dec. 2009. Television. 15 Aug. 2010.

_____, and Sarah Netter. "Tiger Woods Sex Scandal: Why Powerful Men Can't Resist Temptation." *Good Morning, America*. ABC 3 Dec. 2009. Web. 15 Aug. 2010.

Childs, Dan. "Tiger Woods May Be Role Model for Battling Sex Addiction." *ABC News*. 25 Jan. 2010. Web. 25 Aug. 2011.

Connor, Tracy, and Samuel Goldsmith. "Jamie Jungers, Las Vegas Cocktail Waitress, Is Fourth Alleged Tiger Woods Mistress." *New York Daily News*. 5 Dec. 2009. Web. 5 Aug. 2010.

"Episode 1.11." *Queer as Folk: The Complete First Season*. Writ. Ron Cowan, Richard Kramer, and Daniel Lipman. Dir. John Greyson. Showtime, 2007. DVD.

Givhan, Robin. Interview with Neal Conan. *Talk of the Nation*. National Public Radio. 14 Dec. 2009. Web. 4 Sept. 2011.

_____. "Tiger Woods's Alleged Mistresses Are Facing a Sexist Double Standard." *Washington Post*. 13 Dec. 2009. Web. 10 Aug. 2010.

Goldman, Russell. "At Least 9 Women Linked to Tiger Woods in Alleged Affairs." *ABC News*. 7 Dec. 2009. Web. 1 Sept. 2011.

_____. "Tiger Woods a Sex Addict? Only if He's Lucky." *ABC News*. 10 Dec. 2009. Web. 25 Aug. 2011.

_____. "Tiger Woods Mistress List Rises to 11." *ABC News*. 9 Dec. 2009. Web. 18 Aug. 2011.

Goldsmith, Samuel, Mike Jaccarino, and George Rush. "Cori Rist, Jamie Jungers and Mindy Lawton Make It Six Alleged Tiger Woods Mistresses." *New York Daily News*. 6 Dec. 2009. Web. 1 Sept. 2011.

Graham, Caroline. "I Only Wanted to Be Loved: Rachel Uchitel Breaks Her Silence on Her Affair with Tiger Woods." *[UK] Daily Mail*. 13 Nov. 2010. Web. 5 Aug. 2011.

Hayes, Rob. "Golf Ball Line Bears Ladies Linked to Tiger." *ABC 7 KABC-Los Angeles*. 3 Feb. 2010. Web. 22 Aug. 2011.

Hong, Eleanor. "Tiger Woods' 'Transgressions' Go Volcanic." *ABC News*. 2 Dec. 2009. Web. 3 Aug. 2010.

"Jaimee's Texts from Tiger." *US Weekly*. 21 Dec. 2009: 68–69. *ProQuest*. Web. 17 Aug. 2011.

Jungers, Jamie. Personal Interview. *Today Show*. New York City. 12 Dec. 2009. Broadcast.

Nersesian, Elise. "Sex Addiction Real — or Excuse for Cheating?" *MSNBC*. 19 Feb. 2010. Web. 15 Aug. 2011.

O'Neill, Xana. "Alleged Tiger Mistress: He Broke My Heart." *NBC New York*. 30 June 2011. Web. 3 Sept. 2011.

outrageousapp. "Whack a Ho." *Newgrounds*. 26 Feb. 2010. Web. 10 Aug. 2010.

Piazza, Jo. "Tiger Woods' Mistresses Deserve an Apology, Too." *PopEater*. 22 Feb. 2010. Web. 4 Sept. 2011.

Peyser, Andrea. "Boobs Like These Set Women Back." *New York Post*. 10 Dec. 2009: 25. *ProQuest*. Web. 7 Aug. 2010.

Rist, Cori. Personal Interview. *Today Show*. New York City. 14 Dec. 2009. Broadcast.

Seals, Mark. "The Temptation of Tiger Woods." *Vanity Fair*. May 2010: 156–164, 205–209. Print.

Siemaszko, Corky. "Tiger Woods Mistress Update: Theresa Rogers, 40-Something from South Florida, Linked to Golfer." *New York Daily News*. 14 Dec. 2009. Web. 1 Sept. 2011.

Taddeo, Lisa. "Rachel Uchitel Is Not a Madam." *New York*. 12 Apr. 2010. *ProQuest*. Web. 10 Aug. 2010.

"Tiger Mistress: I'm 'Bothered' by Golf Balls with 'My Face' on Them." *US Weekly*. 3 Feb. 2010. Web. 1 Sept. 2011.

"Tiger's 31-Month Affair: Jamiee Grubbs." *US Weekly.* 14 Dec. 2009: 60–61. *ProQuest.*
   Web. 17 Aug. 2011.
Tocci, Dominic A. "Tiger's Transgressions." *Atom.* 16 Dec. 2009. Web. 5 Sept. 2011.
Weber, Scott. "Ex-Porn Star Slams Tiger Woods Golf Ball Gimmick." *NBC Los Angeles.*
   30 June 2011. Web. 22 Aug. 2011.
Woods, Tiger. Apology. Ponte Vedra Beach, FL. 19 Feb. 2010. Press Conference.
_____. "Tiger Comments on Current Events." *Tiger Woods.* 2 Dec. 2009. Web. 2 Aug.
   2011.

Tweet Your Troubles Away

Lynnette Porter and *Donna J. Barbie*

During the final round of the 2011 Masters, when Tiger Woods looked as if he might pull off a come-from-behind victory, other sports stars joined Tiger's fans to root for him via Twitter. Following those trending tweets, an ESPN reporter later posted a few made by the famous, such as Milwaukee Bucks guard Brandon Jennings, who announced "Tiger is about to win this," and Texans running back Arian Foster, who lamented that "I feel as if [I] missed that eagle putt with Tiger. What a Masters tourney this is!"[1] (Dorsey). Months later, after Woods' withdrawal from the 2011 U.S. Open — a decision fans first learned about through one of Tiger's tweets — loyal fans encouraged him through follow-up tweets, looking forward to the day when their ferocious Tiger would once again maul the competition. When Woods plays in a tournament or otherwise makes the news, the Twittering can be heard throughout the sports community.

Twitter has not been the only social media outlet that Woods and his supporters use, however. In late August 2011, more than a week after Woods failed to qualify for the PGA Championship, his Facebook page included a positive, family-oriented message very different from the summer's other posts that primarily touted Woods' sponsors or products. On August 22, for example, Woods posted a comment that was reused as the opening to a blog posted on his website ("Adjusting to a New Sight Line"): "Hello from Florida, where I'm just kind of relaxing and winding down. It's about to get busier with school getting ready to start for the kids soon."

More than 2800 fans Liked this Facebook post. Of the more than 900 replies, the vast majority indicated a desire to see him play in more tournaments or expressed support and encouragement. One of the more eloquent fans sums up the thoughts of many: "Just wanted to let you know how much

I miss you in the tournaments. Hope you get your game back on track and start playing again. Golf just isn't the same without you" (Berge). Such responses illustrate Tiger's enduring popularity with his fans, even if the rest of the world might doubt that he deserves fan adoration or remain skeptical about his ability to make a comeback. For those who wanted more news than the limitations imposed by a brief tweet or status update, the Facebook post was linked to TigerWoods.com, where fans could read more. Commenting on one of his poor showings, for example, he notes, "At the PGA Championship, when I trusted my game and my swing, it was there. When I didn't, I fell back into my old patterns. I just need more reps."

The pattern is clear: Woods announces news via Twitter. He later posts a Facebook message with further details or backs up tweets with a blog on his website. Thousands of fans respond, most with positive messages. Then Tiger's social media sites grow quiet until the next big announcement about a sponsored product, personal update (often regarding a philanthropic or fan event), or a tournament.

Since the popularity of the Internet has increased in the past decade, Woods seems to have acknowledged the usefulness of that tool to maintain his fanbase and even to rehabilitate his public image. In a November 2010 interview a year after his headline-making infidelity scandal and subsequent divorce, Woods states, "I think it's about time I made a connection to the fans, who have been absolutely incredible to me over the last year" (Paul). About the same time, another reporter's blog notes that Woods finally had begun sending tweets from a long-dormant account (Sobel). Social media has helped Woods send messages directly to his fans, as well as the rest of the watching world, even if tweets, updated Facebook status, and blogs provide a one-way line of communication from Tiger instead of offering true interaction with his fanbase.

Although TV entertainment news, jokes on late night talk shows, and skits that parody Tiger's troubles ended up providing bad publicity in recent years, Twitter has proven to be a positive way for Tiger to get information to his fans and to present his side of the story. Tweets are advantageous because they can be manipulated (i.e., written after careful consideration, edited to achieve the desired tone) before public consumption. Historically, Tiger Woods has been often uncomfortable during media interviews and press conferences, when he frequently responds with spontaneous, often negative answers to reporters' questions. As a result, carefully written, positive Twitter messages offer rich opportunities to present the golfer in the most personable light possible. Although his official Facebook page and website also help tell Tiger's tale, Twitter has become Woods' favorite social media outlet and the most likely way for him to announce decisions about his professional and sometimes even his personal life.

Unsociable Tiger's Public Persona

When Tiger's image is "managed" through television commercials or carefully scripted press conferences that limit spontaneous questions (Luscombe), he is less likely to leave a negative impression because those venues curb his tendencies to displays of peevishness and temper. To develop a kinder, gentler public persona, Tiger needs to come across not as the aggressive predator suggested by his name but as a reformed man or professional who is intent on rebuilding his life and game. Even when Tiger makes a mistake, such as the now infamous incident of spitting on foreign soil, his presence on social media, especially Twitter, can help him tweet those troubles away and retain a positive image in the eyes of his fans, if not the world. When Woods is confronted by the press and asked on camera for a spontaneous response, however, the result is more tenuous. Which Tiger will be seen live on television, and thus reported in the news — the humbled golfer striving to return to prominence or the angry man?

Woods' predilection for taking out his irritation on unlucky reporters illustrates why Tiger has limited his spontaneous comments to the press. A 2011 Masters post-round interview on CBS has been called "one of the 10 worst by a superstar in sports history" (Moran). In the past, a frustrated Woods did not suffer fools well. In that particular interview, he did not suffer one foolish reporter at all. On Masters' Sunday, Woods had just finished shooting a 67 and was one stroke out of the lead with a number of players still out on the course, agreed to the interview, and merely answered CBS' Bill Macatee's questions. In truth, the queries were not insightful or probing. The final questions ("Are you going to now go in to get something to eat, go to the range? What's your plan?") indeed left little room for Woods to offer a meaningful comment, but, as some critics suggest, Woods knew what Macatee was really asking and could have played along. He could have commented on his game plan or explained what he hoped to "take away" from his experience at this tournament. Instead, Woods simply answered, in his typically clipped, staccato style, that he was starving and ready to eat. Neither Tiger's words nor his manner impressed the press or viewers who did not already identify themselves as fans.

In essence, Woods underscored Macatee's weak questions and refused to help out the reporter. Canada's ScoreGolf analyst Bob Weeks was probably not alone in concluding that this was just another Tiger snub, an all-too-familiar occurrence. Although Woods' golf prowess seemed to be on the verge of returning, his less-than-pleasant or compliant attitude during the interview became the more publicized topic of the day. Spontaneous, on-camera Woods typically does no favors for his publicist or their combined efforts to improve his public image.

Almost as soon as articles critical of Tiger's behaviors hit the Internet, his fans complained on social media sites. Posts compared critics' treatment of Tiger to cyber-bullying and questioned why he was subjected to the same muckraking treatment given to actors like Charlie Sheen or rock stars like Lady Gaga, who also made headlines for their controversial public behavior. Fans argued that Woods' personality should be off limits; they bitterly noted that the media today are all about tearing down public figures instead of focusing on their achievements. Tiger and his fans must have known that his behavior during interviews would invariably make headlines, many of them negative. Despite the pattern of media attention, his fans have been surprisingly loyal and vocal in their defense of their idol whenever he has been the subject of controversy.

Of course, some people writing letters to *USA Today* or posting comments to Weeks' blog agreed with Tiger's critics. In one letter to the editor, the writer, admittedly never a Tiger fan, describes Woods' interview behavior as rude and disrespectful. Worse, however, was the fact that Woods "blatantly ignored his adoring fans" (Steckel). Nevertheless, for every anti–Tiger comment there were at least three positive posts or a counterbalancing letter. The other letter published online that day in *USA Today* praises Woods because he "brought us a lot of hope, thrills and excitement ... and the crowds and cheers for him back this up." This fan reminds readers that Tiger will always face opposition "from the ones who never liked him anyway, so it is up to his loyal supporters to sing his praises" (Henley).

Responses to Tiger Woods' behavior after the 2011 Masters follow another now long-established trend. Woods' talent as a golfer is often overshadowed by media reports or spectator revelations about the man behind all the titles and awards. Whereas some fans post online commentaries remarking that they forgive him his sins (a highly Christian response to Tiger's well-publicized marital infidelity) or give him seemingly limitless opportunities to prove he is "worthy" of their adoration, others note that they are simply tired of the way Woods has tried to mask who he really is. For these fans, the issue is not whether Tiger swears or snubs reporters or whether he has a string of women awaiting him when he leaves the club. Instead, they want Tiger to be himself instead of a contrite puppet trying to curry favor with the public. The person posting a video clip of Woods' April 10, 2011, interview on Black Sports Online.com explains that he "couldn't stand the fake, apologizing, sex rehab, whining, sniveling, crying, and non-brohoing Tiger. The reason being that wasn't the real him" (Littal). For some fans, honesty is apparently the most believable policy, and at the 2011 Masters, Tiger Woods was returning to his true form, as a golfer and a controversial media celebrity.

As these patterns indicate, Tiger's continuing difficulty to remain cordial with the press makes any spontaneous interviews or unscripted comments risky, if the goal is to improve the public's perception of him. Social media, on the other hand, provide Tiger a way to control the message being sent to his fans (but also picked up by the public) and to create a very different image, one that ostensibly is still "real" but much more palatable.

Tiger and the Social Network

With the rise of the Internet and the constant availability of information, both through formal channels such as 24/7/365 network news (e.g., ESPN) as well as informally shared information (e.g., YouTube videos, tweets, blogs), sports celebrity has become similar to that of television or film stars, charismatic politicians, or royalty. Celebrities' every move makes headlines, and that has certainly been true of Tiger Woods, whose every word or deed, related to golf or not, promotes commentary.

No matter what the general public thinks, Woods' fans are surprisingly loyal, as underscored by the many Twitter or Facebook examples provided throughout this chapter. Woods' fandom, as evidenced in the online press and social media sites like Facebook or Twitter, perceives the golfer in one of three ways: a sports legend, media personality, or global representative of the United States. Some fans undoubtedly see Woods in all three roles simultaneously, even if they choose to post messages online commenting on only one of these three roles. Although golf lovers initially comprised Woods' fanbase and still make up the majority of his public supporters, Woods long ago became more than a golf legend to the American public, and much of his fandom — or lack thereof— is based on public perception of the man behind the legend. To analyze Tiger Woods' fandom requires a broader lens than one focused solely on sport. Like actors or politicians whose media persona has taken on a separate life outside their original claim to fame, Woods is a bona fide celebrity who enjoys all the perks of fame but has been poisoned by it as well.

Tiger Woods' status as celebrity is clearly evidenced through social media, where both Woods and his fans post comments. Despite the controversy arising from Woods' behavior after the 2011 Masters, the golfer's upbeat tweets sound gracious and even a bit humble. On March 31, for example, the official Tiger Woods Twitter account posted this message: "Logging so many hours heading into Augusta this week. Nervous, excited, hoping the hard work pays off." On April 11, the same day as the now-infamous CBS interview, Tiger tweeted a starkly different message: "It was a great Masters, fun to get it going like that on the front. Congrats to Charl, heck of a way to win. Birdied last four holes." Unlike the self-absorbed, petulant child that was revealed in the interview, this Tiger actually acknowledges the winner and cheerfully congratulates him on the win. Here is a player who can be gracious even in defeat.

Whereas the information posted about Woods often spans the extremes of negative or positive comments, Tiger's posts to his fans via Twitter come across as sincere. Through his tweets, Tiger seems to be a man who truly loves playing golf, works hard to return to top form, and apologizes when necessary. In April 2011, Tiger Woods had more than 770,000 followers on Twitter; in June the number had swelled to more than 990,000; by August (perhaps a pivotal time in Tiger's career) 1.25 million followed him, making this account (and its retweets) a viable way for Woods immediately to reach his fans and media followers when controversy arises and to control the information sent directly from him. Although the Tiger Woods official Facebook page lists more than 2 million people (in August 2011) who "Like" his page, Twitter provides an immediacy that even Facebook lacks. Apparently Woods is doing something right, or the number of people flocking to his social media sites would not continue to grow exponentially in a year when his performance on the golf course was exceptionally poor.

Not surprisingly, because of his vast following, Woods first turned to Twitter to present his side of the story after he was fined by the European Tour for spitting on a green, seemingly in disgust, after missing a putt during the Dubai Desert Classic in February 2011. He also tweeted a formal apology. A February 14 tweet from Woods agrees that "The Euro Tour is right — it was inconsiderate to spit like that and I know better. Just wasn't thinking and want to say I'm sorry." A follow-up tweet that day adds, "Everyone was terrific all week, fans especially. Dubai is always a fantastic host. Just wish the week could have ended better."

Tweets responding to Woods' apology at first acknowledged the golfer's gaffe and commented that everyone makes mistakes. Fans sending these tweets were very forgiving and seemed to indicate an understanding that Tiger had done something wrong but had apologized — end of story. As the controversy gained momentum in the media, however, fans became protective of Tiger. The real-time tweets seemed dismissive of the spitting incident or ignored it completely in favor of bolstering Woods' spirit after a defeat. Some positive comments immediately after the spitting incident and Tiger's Twitter apology, gathered through a search using #TigerWoods, include the following:

> "In due time Tiger. You have been my golf idol for years and will remain there as long as you are around."
> "The next one is yours, Tiger."
> "Everything happens for a reason, be it good or bad, happy or sad. That's why when your on top again it will be that bit sweeter."

"Don't be so hard on yourself. Forgiven. The first 3 days you killed it. Happy Valentine's Day."

Fewer tweets were critical, such as "Suggest you listen to Sky sports commentary on your spitting. Ewan Murray says it all for pro's and armchair fans like me." As the criticism mounted in the press, more Twitter fans grew agitated, posting comments like "Criticism he's getting 4 spitting on green is ridiculous. Didn't anyone see him wipe it away w/ his putter?" and "Should footie players now be fined for spitting on the pitch?" One fan summarizes the attitude of many: "Quit apologizing and play golf! ... Us fans just want to c u play."

The rest of the non-fan world was not as forgiving. *The Huffington Post* article ("Tiger Woods Spits on Green") quoted Britain's Sky Sports commentator Ewen Murray calling the act "disgusting" and "one of the ugliest things you will ever see on a golf course." Australia's *Perth Now* feature displayed a photo of Woods tossing a putter ("Tiger Woods Fined for Spitting"). Although the press also covered the results of the tournament and Woods' upbeat comments about his improved performance on the course, the newspaper reported that "on the 12th green, after missing a par putt, Woods made his mark — spitting just a few centimeters from the hole." Incidents like the one in Dubai are likely a large part of the reason that, again in 2011, Woods was Number 4 in E-Poll's survey of most disliked people in sports; 52 percent of the 1000 adults polled disapproved of Tiger Woods (Van Riper).

Woods not only uses social media to offset negative publicity from other sources but to promote public appearances, contests, charitable events and activities, and new products. "Check out the cool custom Masters gear Nike sent me," the spokesman posted on Facebook on April 5, 2011; close-ups of Nike shoes and a jacket showcased the products, something sure to please both sponsor and Woods' fans. As might be expected, more than 3700 "Liked" this post.

When a new iPhone app became available shortly before the 2011 Masters, Woods' official Facebook page provided a link to an article at his website and a promotional comment about the app: "After a lot of work, I'm happy to announce my new iPhone app Tiger Woods: My Swing. It's a swing analysis app based on the methods I use at home and on the road, and it includes instruction and tips from me. Profits from the app benefit my Foundation. Enjoy!" The March 24 post garnered more than 2000 Likes and generated more than 525 comments, evidence that Tiger's most devoted fans (i.e., those who frequent his Facebook page or follow him on Twitter) quickly become aware of the latest news, products, and promotional comments from Woods himself. Social media seem to be an effective way for the golf legend to keep his core fanbase happy and to let them know his thoughts on everything. He communicates about videogames and phone applications bearing his likeness or name and comments on/counters/corrects news reported about him. Tweets and Facebook updates also help sell products being introduced through social media. Even if Woods is not as familiar a face on television commercials as he once was, he can effectively make fans aware of new products online.

Throughout spring 2011, upbeat updates communicated Tiger's progress toward the next tournament or personal comments about endorsed products. Then the next golfing bombshell hit in early June. At that time, an injured Woods decided to withdraw from the U.S. Open. As had become his habit, Tiger first tweeted the news: "Not playing in US Open. Very disappointed. Short-term frustration for long-term gain."

Predictably, fans soon rallied support behind their favorite player, especially on his website. Critics, however, twittered about Tiger's injury, the real reason behind the announcement, and likely fallout. Within two hours of Tiger's Twitter announcement, the following responses had been tweeted and retweeted: "Breaking News. Tiger Woods pulls out of the US Open. Additional Breaking News: US Open loses 85 percent of its expected viewers" (Talbot); "Tiger Woods is out of the US Open due to an injury sustained at the Masters. A few players will be glad, but bookies will be gutted" (fbfreetips); and "Tiger Woods decides to miss US Open — 'listening to his doctor' or facing reality? Time to hang up the clubs?" (aaR4). In addition to the expected range of tweets concerning Tiger's professional life, a few had to get in digs about the golfer's "pro" reputation, such as "No need for chastity belts and divorce lawyers at the US Open this year. Tiger Woods out injured" (Anderson-Ogle).

The fact that Tiger prefers to tweet news to reach his fans is well known to sports writers, who also monitor the account. Soon after Tiger's tweet, Josh Wolford's article acknowledged the Twitter announcement in his opening sentences on WebProNews.com: "It's always a bad day for golf when Tiger Woods has to miss a big tournament, so I guess you can call it a pretty terrible one for fans." Wolford then listed the Twitter announcement and several follow-up tweets. Fan responses to announcements such as this are becoming an important part of sports news, and Twitter is becoming increasingly recognized as the place for insider information straight from the source.

Surprisingly, Woods' Facebook page was not immediately updated, so fans had nothing new to which they could post their responses. However, a lengthier discussion of the reasons for Tiger's decision to withdraw from the U.S. Open was provided almost immediately on his website. That became the place where fans posted more "permanent" messages than the rapid-fire but soon-gone tweets.

After the June 7 Twitter announcement, a much longer statement explaining the rationale for Tiger's decision garnered many more supportive comments from fans. The website describes the injury and explains Tiger's worry over its severity if he were not to take the required time to heal ("Injuries to Keep Tiger Out of U.S. Open"). The news-style article on his website ends with Tiger's statement that "It's been a frustrating and difficult year, but I'm committed to my long-term health.... I want to thank the fans for their encouragement and support. I am truly grateful and will be back playing when I can."

In response, fans immediately posted notices such as these:

> "Tiger, me and all your true fans will miss you at the US Open. but only you know your body best. we all wish you a speedy recovery. I know you will fight to the end. and the end is not even close. Get well soon and get back to the game you Love" [This comment was made by a true fan, evidenced by the name Tigerslam18holes].

> "Tiger, We really really miss you, Get well soon and take good care of yourself. You will always have 100% support from your Fans. We love you Tiger, take care" [Tatum].

Although Twitter and Facebook provide fans instant messages, the website not only highlights Tiger's achievements but presents a permanent archive of Woods' fan-friendly statements and insights into the tournaments in which he plays.

In addition to Facebook and Twitter, Woods uses his website to promote the positive aspects of his career and personality. Woods' blog includes a smiling photo beside each entry. Although the blogs are posted sporadically, they present a highly professional view of the golfer's latest achievements. A November 2010 blog entitled "A Busy Stretch of Golf Ahead," begins with the homey sentiment, "It's nice to be home for the holidays after two weeks on the road." In this blog detailing Woods' international travels and tournaments, he specifically comments on fans at the Ryder Cup in Newport, Wales: "I have to say the people of Wales were extremely nice and very accommodating. The fans were incredible. They were partisan, obviously, but they were so respectful of both sides and great crowds to play in front of."

The blogs most often do not deal with contentious topics but provide fans with a genial view of the golfer's professional life. The mixture of Internet-based fan posts may not be regularly read, however, by the majority of the public, who primarily know about Tiger Woods from televised golf tournaments or online or print newspaper articles chronicling his controversial career and personal life. Social and online media nonetheless provide a personalized forum for Tiger Woods to send messages straight to his most loyal supporters, who then propagate the message and post contrasting views in response to critics' blogs or articles.

Tiger Woods Fan Survey

Because of Woods' ostensibly loyal fanbase, as well as his recent forays into social media, the authors of this essay designed and administered a brief online survey directed at golf lovers, especially Tiger fans.[2] The project aimed to ascertain if respondents perceive themselves as Woods fans and, if they do, the intensity of that support. The project also sought to determine the extent of participation Tiger fans have with social media to bolster their fan identities. Invited to participate in the project primarily through Facebook and Twitter, 322 people responded to the five-question survey during summer 2011.

The design of the survey was informed by work completed by sports psychologists Daniel Wann and Nyla Branscombe. In conjunction with their investigations of how and why people become emotionally invested in sporting teams, Wann and Branscombe developed the Sport Spectator Identification Scale (SSIS), an instrument designed to discover the amount of anxiety and arousal highly-identified fans experience during sporting events, as well as the underlying reasons for their attachments (Wann, Melnick, Russell, and Pease 3–4).

As part of his comprehensive work on fandom psychology, Wann also defines and describes several tactics that highly-identified fans typically employ in response to their favorite team's or player's successes and failures. Fans celebrate victories by basking in reflected glory (BIRGing) (169). Responding to and coping with disappointing performances are much more psychologically strenuous, however, and ardent fans may attempt to avoid the sometimes severe depression of a loss by cutting off reflected failure (CORFing). Because highly-identified fans strive to maintain their allegiances in the face of failure, even seemingly endless failures, successful CORFing insulates fans from negative emotions by identifying external or internal causes for those failures (172). Using a different tactic, disheartened fans sometimes engage in Blasting (derogating enemies) in order to regain their own esteem by restoring their team's or player's dignity (169).

Although the Tiger fan survey did not use Wann's terminology or follow the structure of the ISIS, the findings indicate whether golf fans perceive themselves as Tiger fans, as well as pointing to the intensity of their connection. In addition, the results invite some interesting speculation about the effectiveness of Woods' use of social media to connect with his fanbase. The tables appearing at the end of this chapter provide the following information about each survey question: the response options, the number of people choosing each response, and the percentage of people choosing each response. The response that appears in bold was most frequently selected for that particular question.

As can be seen in the tables, each question offers four options: the first option (no highlighting) indicates antipathy or lack of interest in/support of Tiger; the second option (no highlighting) indicates little/very moderate interest in/support of Tiger; the third option (light grey highlighting) indicates considerable interest in/support of Tiger; the fourth option (darker grey highlighting) indicates high levels of interest in/support of Tiger. As these categories would imply, data from options one and two, combined, indicate the number/percentage of respondents who would not self-identify as Tiger fans. In addition, data from options three and four, combined, highlight the number/percentage of respondents who would likely self-identify as Tiger fans. Subtotals of non–Tiger fans and Tiger fans are provided for each question in the tables.

Analysis of Survey Results

Although the relatively small sample size of the survey would necessitate caution in interpreting the results, some significant trends are worthy of note. The percentage of respondents signaling little connection to and even antipathy toward Tiger is quite consistent. As can be seen, approximately 30 percent of the entire cohort selected option one or two for the following questions: one (lack of identification as a Tiger Woods fan), two (lack of emotional investment in how well Tiger plays), and four (denial that they follow Tiger). These data would imply that a sizable portion of golf fans do not at the current time and possibly never did perceive themselves as Tiger fans. This finding is somewhat surprising because the survey title clearly indicated the focus of the project. In addition, notifications requesting participation not only signaled the focus, but also the placement of announcements and reminders would seem to have attracted Tiger fans nearly exclusively. Another reality could have countered the expectation that most participants would consider themselves to be Tiger fans, however. Because Tiger has been such a controversial figure, some golf aficionados may have completed the survey not because they are Tiger fans, but to take advantage of a chance to express negative perceptions.

In addition, the percentage of survey-takers who selected options one and two, the non-fan responses, for two questions stands out. In question five, a higher percentage (47.2 percent) than the 30 percent "baseline" of non-fan responses indicated that they do not follow Tiger on social media. Those data would seem logical, however, because people who claim no connection to Tiger would likely expend little, if any, effort to follow him through non-traditional means.

The most interesting findings from the non-fan data set arise from question three (feelings concerning Tiger's rivals). Only 4 percent signaled that they actively root against Tiger. This small percentage of Tiger-baiters would seem unusual, especially in light of how many respondents indicated that they are not Tiger fans, how polemical Tiger has been during his career, and how voluble his detractors have been since the scandal broke. Matt Sheehan, contributor to the online Bleacher Report, offers a possible explanation for the paucity of respondents selecting the most contemptuous option for question three. As Sheehan asserts, "niceness" is one of the hallmarks of golf, an essential element of the decorum expected of players and fans. All observers, regardless of which player they favor, are precluded from displays of unattractive partisanship during play. Sheehan notes that "it's a 'Leave No Man Behind' deal every single shot of the ball. Everyone claps, everyone wants the chip shot to go in, and nobody in the gallery wants to see a player tank." Although survey respondents are clearly outside the jurisdiction of such rules, true golf lovers embrace the ethos of the game. Respondents who do not necessarily perceive themselves as Tiger fans would nevertheless appear to have taken the concept of fan "niceness" to heart by refraining from rooting against him.

Data submitted from respondents who would likely self-identify as Tiger fans illustrate a similar pattern as noted above. A fairly consistent percentage of respondents (69.3 percent, 69.9 percent, and 73 percent) selected either option three or four for questions one, two, and four, respectively. These findings suggest that Tiger has sustained a fairly substantial fanbase. Although higher percentages might have been anticipated for these questions, the previous discussion concerning survey participants likely adheres.

The degree of respondent connectedness, revealed by teasing out data from options three and four, is also worthy of analysis, especially for questions one and two. As can be seen, 28 percent of the cohort reported that they will "always" be Tiger fans, and more than 20 percent indicated that they feel "elated" when he plays well or wins a tournament. These data would seem to verify that a considerable number of Tiger's followers remain hardcore, highly-identified fans.

Data arising from fan-responses to question three are also pertinent. More than 35 percent of respondents indicated that they do not prefer a rival of Tiger's to play well or win, and nearly 13 percent confirmed that they actively root against a rival. Although Sheehan's remarks about golf fan "niceness" would seem to apply to Tiger's fans, his followers are apparently less constrained, at least in their survey responses, about adhering to the unwritten rule of decorum. Such an apparently cut-throat approach might seem reasonable since Tiger has been playing quite poorly for nearly two years. Not only have they had very little to celebrate, but these fans could also be attempting to cope with potential depression and loss of esteem by "Blasting" Tiger's "enemies."

Findings from question five indicate that 52 percent of respondents follow Tiger through social media with some frequency. Although that reality may be perceived as signaling strong support via the Internet, 52 percent is considerably lower than the nearly 70 percent who identify themselves as Tiger fans and the 73 percent who follow him through television, radio, and on-course observations. This lower reporting rate would appear particularly anomalous because all respondents learned of the project through social media. Several factors may help to explain why fewer Tiger fans follow him through less traditional venues. In general, "typical" Twitter or Facebook users are frequently online and often tweet or update their status more than once a day. Fans, particularly highly-identified fans, probably follow, friend, or Like the objects of their adulation. Therefore, each time they log into a social media site, they should automatically see recent messages. If they check Woods' sites more often, they can easily go to his Facebook or Twitter accounts and see if something new has been posted. Because social media is asynchronous, ardent fans might be expected to "follow" Woods via the Internet more closely than they would through television, radio, or attendance at tournaments.

Although Woods' use of Internet "connectivity" has increased recently, he would likely benefit by tweeting or updating his status more frequently because "connected" fans would then be consistently reminded of his online presence. When regularly prompted, Internet-savvy fans would be more likely to check Tiger's Facebook page or search for additional tweets and to respond more often. In essence, social media users' attention and subsequent responses tend to be proportional to the number of and intervals between posts, tweets, and updates that are aimed at them. Because Tiger can control the content he posts on Twitter, Facebook, or his website, the public image he shapes through those vehicles is likely to be more appealing than spontaneous comments made during interviews or press conferences. Tiger's tweet success with social media offers him a significant opportunity to build a better public image and reach millions of people who follow him online. After the 2011 Masters, a sports critic blogged that "Woods is going to be with us for years to come. Maybe he'll win another major ... maybe he'll never win again.... But no matter what, we'll be watching. We may have different reasons, but we're all in this together" (Busbee). No doubt Tiger's millions of Facebook friends and Twitter followers agree — and will happily tweet their support for whatever Tiger does next.

APPENDIX: TIGER WOODS FAN SURVEY

Question 1: Do you see yourself as a Tiger Woods fan?

Not a fan	36	11.2%
Occasionally a fan (for example, when he's in contention)	63	19.6%
Subtotal: Non-Tiger Fans	99	30.8%

Usually a fan	**133**	**41.3%**
Always a fan	90	28.0%
Subtotal: Tiger Fans	223	69.3%

Question 2: How important to you is it that Tiger Woods plays well or wins?

Prefer that he does not play well or win	14	4.3%
Have no preference concerning his playing well or winning	84	26.1%
Subtotal: Non-Tiger Fans	98	30.4%
Prefer that he plays well or wins	**158**	**49.4%**
Feel elated if he plays well or wins	66	20.5%
Subtotal: Tiger Fans	224	69.9%

Question 3: How do you feel about Tiger Woods' rivals?

Actively root for rivals; prefer rivals play well or win	13	4.0%
Prefer an exciting tournament, no matter who is in contention	**155**	**48.1%**
Subtotal: Non-Tiger Fans	168	52.2%
Prefer rivals do not win or play well	113	35.1%
Actively root against rivals	41	12.7%
Subtotal: Tiger Fans	154	47.8%

Question 4: How closely do you pay attention to Tiger Woods (in person at a tournament, on television or radio, or in the news)?

Do not follow Tiger Woods	23	7.1%
Seldom follow Tiger Woods	64	19.9%
Subtotal: Non-Tiger Fans	87	27%
Closely follow Tiger Woods, especially when he is playing in a tournament	**169**	**52.5%**
Very closely follow Tiger Woods, even when he is not playing in a tournament	66	20.5%
Subtotal: Tiger Fans	235	73%

Question 5: How closely do you follow Tiger Woods via his website or on Facebook or Twitter?

Do not follow Tiger Woods	68	21.1%
Seldom follow Tiger Woods	84	26.1%
Subtotal: Non-Tiger Fans	152	47.2%
Closely follow Tiger Woods, especially when he is playing in a tournament	**112**	**34.8%**
Very closely follow Tiger Woods, even when he is not playing in a tournament	58	18.0%
Subtotal: Tiger Fans	170	52.8%

Notes

1. Because messages sent via social media are spontaneous, they often are posted without being edited. The wording and punctuation used in the quoted messages have

not been corrected and thus include any grammatical errors posted in the original message.

2. Social media, especially Facebook and Twitter, served as the primary means of advertising the survey and encouraging participation. Facebook announcements were placed within comments on Tiger Woods' page, and Wall posts were left on fan sites identified by "Tiger Woods" or "golf" somewhere in the Facebook username. The Tiger Woods Fan Survey page was established in August, and frequent reminders became part of Lynnette Porter's status updates. Participation spurts followed the initial announcement and updates. The hashtags #TigerWoods, #golf, #golffans, #TigerWoodsfans, and similarly themed keywords were used in tweets providing the survey's URL. Direct tweets to @TigerWoods also were used frequently to remind fans that the survey was still available.

Works Cited

aaR4. Twitter. Web. 7 June 2011.

Anderson-Ogle, Murray. MurrayAogle. Twitter. Web. 7 June 2011.

Berge, Timi. *Official Tiger Woods*. Facebook. 24 Aug. 2011.

Busbee, Jay. "Tiger Woods Makes Both His Fans and Haters Smile." *Devil Ball Golf.* Yahoo! Sports. Web. 10 Apr. 2011.

Dorsey, Patrick. "Tiger Woods Has Rooting Section on Twitter." *ESPN*. Web. 11 Apr. 2011.

fbfreetips. FreeBetsFreeTips.com. Twitter. Web. 7 June 2011.

Henley, Jean. "Tiger Woods Still Has Fans Cheering." Letter to the editor. *USA Today.* Web. 14 Apr. 2011.

Littal, Robert. "Video: Tiger Woods' 'I'm Going to Eat' Interview with CBS' Bill Macatee." *Black Sports Online.* Web. 11 Apr. 2011.

Luscombe, Belinda. "Was Tiger Woods' Apology a Game Changer?" *The New York Times.* Web. 19 Feb. 2010.

Moran, Bill. "Our Phil of Tiger: Golf Needs Respect." Letter to the editor. *The New York Post.* Web. 15 Apr. 2011.

Paul, John. "What Do We Want from Tiger?" *The Wall Street Journal.* Web. 20 Nov. 2010.

Sheehan, Matt. "No Peanuts in This Gallery: Why PGA Fans Are the Most Welcoming in All of Sports." *Bleacher Report.* 10 Apr. 2011. Web. 24 Apr. 2011.

Sobel, Jason. "Can Tiger Woods Restore His Image?" *ESPN*. Web. 17 Nov. 2010.

Steckel, James F. "Fed Up with Rude Behavior." Letter to the editor. *USA Today.* Web. 14 Apr. 2011.

Talbot, Bob. Talbot Talks. Twitter. Web. 7 June 2011.

Tatum, Carolyn. *TigerWoods.com*. Web. 7 June 2011.

"Tiger Woods Fined for Spitting, Disgusts Fans and Commentators." *Perth Now.* Web. 15 Feb. 2011.

"Tiger Woods Spits on Green, Criticized by Announcers at Dubai Desert Classic." *The Huffington Post.* Web. 14 Feb. 2011.

Tigerslam18holes. *TigerWoods.com*. Web. 7 June 2011.

Van Riper, Tom. "The Most Disliked People in Sports." *Forbes*. Web. 31 Jan. 2011.

Wann, Daniel, Merrill Melnick, Gordon Russell, and Dale Pease. *Sports Fans: The Psychology and Social Impact of Spectators*. New York: Routledge, 2001. Print.

Weeks, Bob. "Tiger and That Interview." *ScoreGolf*. Web. 12 Apr. 2011.

Wolford, Josh. "Tiger Woods Out of U.S. Open, Announces Via Twitter." *WebProNews.com*. Web. 7 June 2011.

Woods, Tiger. "Adjusting to a New Sight Line." *TigerWoods.com*. Web. 22 Aug. 2011.

_____. "Injuries to Keep Tiger Out of U.S. Open." *TigerWoods.com*. Web. 7 June 2011.

_____. *Official Tiger Woods.* Facebook. Web. 23 Mar. 2011.

_____. *Official Tiger Woods.* Facebook. Web. 5 Apr. 2011.

_____. *Official Tiger Woods.* Facebook. Web. 8 Aug. 2011.

_____. *Official Tiger Woods.* Facebook. Web. 22 Aug. 2011.

_____. "Tiger's Blog. A Busy Stretch of Golf Ahead." *TigerWoods.com.* Web. 23 Nov. 2010.

_____. Twitter. Web. 14 Feb. 2011.

_____. Twitter. Web. 31 Mar. 2011.

_____. Twitter. Web. 11 Apr. 2011.

_____. Twitter. Web. 7 June 2011.

About the Contributors

Donna J. Barbie is the chair of the Humanities and Social Sciences Department and professor of humanities at Embry-Riddle Aeronautical University in Daytona Beach, Florida. She received her Ph.D. in American Studies from Emory University. Long interested in playing, observing, and researching golf, she contributed a chapter on Tiger Woods to *Horsehide, Pigskin, Oval Tracks, and Apple Pie: Essays on Sports and American Culture*, edited by Jim Vlasich and published by McFarland in 2006.

Sarah D. Fogle, professor of communication and humanities at Embry-Riddle Aeronautical University in Daytona Beach, Florida, received her M.A. in English at the University of Florida. She is past president of the Popular Culture Association in the South. She has published articles on detective and crime fiction, is the contributing co-editor of *Minette Walters and the Meaning of Justice: Essays on the Crime Novels* (with Mary Hadley, McFarland, 2008) and editor of *Martha Grimes Walks into a Pub: Essays on a Writer with a Load of Mischief* (McFarland, 2011). She has taught courses in the genre and has a special research interest in Florida crime fiction.

Jonathan French, professor of human factors at Embry-Riddle Aeronautical University, in Daytona Beach, Florida, holds a Ph.D. in physiological psychology from Colorado State University. He teaches aerospace physiology, sensation and perception and the neuroscience of cognition, among other classes. He has published more than sixty articles in biological science journals, dealing primarily with human performance, medications, and the intersection of human performance and stress.

Joe Gisondi, associate professor of journalism at Eastern Illinois University in Charleston, Illinois, earned a master of fine arts degree in creative nonfiction at Spalding University. He is the author of *The Field Guide To Covering Sports* (CQ Press, 2010). He is also a contributor to the National Sports Journalism Institute's website and blogs about sports journalism at SportsFieldGuide.com, and he was recently president of the Illinois College Press Association. At EIU, he teaches courses in advanced reporting, sportswriting, sports media, and editing.

John Lamothe is an instructor in the Humanities and Social Sciences Department at Embry-Riddle Aeronautical University in Daytona Beach, Florida. He received his M.A. in English from the Pennsylvania State University, specializing in rhetoric and composition. He is completing a Ph.D. in text and technology at the University of Central Florida; his research centers on the social implications of performance-enhancement technologies in sports.

Steve Master is an assistant professor of communication and humanities at Embry-Riddle Aeronautical University in Daytona Beach, Florida, and the coordinator of the University's communication degree program. He earned his M.S. from Northwestern University's Medill School of Journalism. Prior to his teaching career, he worked for twenty years as a sports writer for the *Daytona Beach News-Journal*, where he still contributes as a correspondent. His 2006 story commemorating the 40th anniversary of Jackie Robinson breaking baseball's color barrier earned a national award from the Associated Press Sports Writers.

Michael V. Perez is an instructor of humanities and composition at Embry-Riddle Aeronautical University in Daytona Beach, Florida. He earned an M.A. in English from Florida State University and a Masters of Fine Arts in creative writing from the University of Houston. His poems have appeared in *Crab Orchard Review* and *BLOOM Magazine*, and he was a finalist for the 2004 War Poetry Prize from WinningWriters.com. He also co-wrote a chapter with Margaret Mishoe for *Florida in the Popular Imagination* (Steve Glassman, ed., McFarland, 2009). He specializes in the Southern grotesque, as well as ecological literature and sustainability themes.

Lynnette Porter is a professor in the Humanities and Social Sciences Department at Embry-Riddle Aeronautical University in Daytona Beach, Florida. She received her Ph.D. in English, with specializations in rhetoric, composition, and technical communication, from Bowling Green State University. She has written six books, including *Tarnished Heroes, Charming Villains and Modern Monsters* (McFarland, 2010), and co-authored seven others. She is a contributing editor for the online popular culture magazine PopMatters and writes a monthly film and television column. She also is a member of the editorial board of the journal *Studies in Popular Culture*.

Libbie Searcy is the director of the Writing Program and assistant professor in the Humanities and Social Sciences Department at Embry-Riddle Aeronautical University in Daytona Beach, Florida. She received her Masters of Fine Arts in Creative Writing from Bowling Green State University and her Ph.D. in English from Western Michigan University. Her areas of interest include creative writing, feminist and queer theory, and popular culture.

James G. Shoopman, assistant professor in the Humanities and Social Sciences Department at Embry-Riddle Aeronautical University in Daytona Beach, Florida, received his Ph.D. in interdisciplinary humanities, with an emphasis in religious studies, at Florida State University. He is also an ordained Protestant minister with a Master of Divinity degree from New Orleans Seminary and has published articles in *Christian Ethics Today*. He teaches courses at Embry-Riddle in ethics, speech, and comparative religions and has a special research interest in the intersection of ethics and religious life.

Linda H. Straubel is an associate professor of humanities at Embry-Riddle Aeronautical University in Daytona Beach, Florida, where she teaches a variety of composition and humanities classes. She received her M.A. and Ph.D. in creative writing from the University of Wisconsin–Milwaukee. She has also written and delivered papers focused on Margaret Atwood, Stephen King, TV's *The West Wing*, and the heuristic use of concept mapping in composition and creative writing. She is at work on a textbook on concept mapping and *Mystic Fruit*, a novel set in the late '60s.

Index